The Food Lover's Handbook

The Food Lover's Handbook

Everything you need to know
about your favourite foods

*How history, geography and production
affect quality and price*

Mark Price

EBURY
PRESS

1 3 5 7 9 10 8 6 4 2

Ebury Press, an imprint of Ebury Publishing,
20 Vauxhall Bridge Road,
London SW1V 2SA

Ebury Press is part of the Penguin Random House group of companies
whose addresses can be found at global.penguinrandomhouse.com

Text copyright © Mark Price 2016
Design copyright © Ebury Press 2016

Published by Ebury Press in 2016

www.eburypublishing.co.uk

A CIP catalogue record for this book is available from the British Library

ISBN 9781785031984

Printed and bound in China by Toppan Leefung

Illustrations by Tim Hopgood
Edited by Howard Watson
Project management by Lydia Good
Design concept by David Fordham
Typesetting by Hugh Adams

Penguin Random House is committed to a sustainable future for our business, our readers and our
planet. This book is made from Forest Stewardship Council® certified paper.

Contents

Foreword

One of my earliest memories of growing up in the 1960s is of the huge Christmas hamper my father received every year.

We lived in Crewe and Dad, who at one time had owned a small grocery store in the town, now ran a wholesale business delivering biscuits and snacks to shops, schools and leisure centres across Cheshire. The hamper was an annual thank you from one of his suppliers.

I can still vividly recall the excitement I felt when this seemingly vast wicker basket arrived and we would open the lid to find it filled to the brim with a treasure trove of biscuits, confectionery, pickles, preserves, cooked meats and all manner of exotic delicacies.

In my adult life, I've been fortunate enough to have a career that has provided me with that exact same thrill over food on so many occasions. As marketing director, retail director and – for the last nine years – managing director of Waitrose, considered by many to be the best food retailer in the United Kingdom, I have enjoyed some extraordinary experiences.

I have stood on a river bank in Iceland and eaten wafer-thin melt-in-the-mouth pieces of delicately flavoured raw salmon sliced from a fish I'd caught just minutes earlier. I've driven in the rain along red-brown dirt roads to reach a coffee plantation high in the Blue Mountains of Jamaica and, when the rain cleared, been staggered by the jaw-dropping views across that beautiful island.

I've feasted on a steak bigger than my plate, and barbecued over the glowing embers of old vines in an Argentinian vineyard, while drinking the amazing Malbec made on the estate.

I have visited suppliers and growers across the 60 countries that Waitrose imports from and exports to, and I have spent time with the world's top chefs and food writers. Whenever I visit a restaurant for the first time, I ask, 'What are you famous for?' and then order that.

I sample as many different types of food as I can, and pride myself on having always tried each new line that comes into Waitrose. In fact, of all the foods I have ever tried from all over the world, I can think of only one that I actively dislike – the durian. This soft, fleshy fruit, unaccountably popular in south-east Asia, smells of rotten meat and doesn't taste any better. However, my point is that over the years I have learned a great deal about food and drink.

I first got the idea for this book in Christmas 2014, after a discount food chain announced it would be selling caviar at £9.99 for 20g. The press lapped up the news. Huge banner headlines declared how remarkable this was, comparing the price to caviar being sold in a top London food emporium at £150. It was a repeat of a story that had played out over a range of foodstuffs from beef and salmon to lobster tails, wine and champagne. In every case the somewhat breathless message from the media was that the discount chain was performing the equivalent of a retailing miracle by selling identical goods to those found in the finest shops but at a fraction of the price.

What they didn't acknowledge, or were perhaps reluctant to say, is the fact that the discounter's caviar came from a type of hybrid-cross sturgeon in China. These sturgeon are prolific and so the caviar is abundant and costs just £500 per kilogram. The much-derided top London fine-food emporium, on the other hand, sold Beluga caviar. Beluga is farmed for maximum taste on dedicated farms in far more limited amounts and as a result costs £5,000 per kilogram. The resulting products are so different they could be two entirely different foodstuffs, and to compare the two is meaningless.

The treatment of this food story got me thinking. Why are people so prepared to turn a blind eye to the facts when it comes to groceries? Most people can explain very clearly why one broadband provider is better, and therefore costs more, than another. It is similarly straightforward to explain why a fashionable, designer coat is considerably more expensive than a mass-produced one from a high-street chain. No one would have much trouble listing a fair few reasons why a Ford car costs less than a Bentley. Yet, sadly, these same people are less able to articulate why fish, meat, tea or coffee have wildly different price points. There appears to be a tacit acceptance that one type of produce is all the same, regardless of variable factors such as quality. Food, it seems, has become a commodity judged almost exclusively on price, and consumers may well confuse price with value.

Perhaps it is time to redress the balance and take a more thoughtful approach to the food and drink we buy.

This book sets out to explain why foods cost what they do, from the cheapest fare to top-of-the range goodies. It is a distillation of the knowledge I have acquired over almost two decades at Waitrose and a lifetime of being interested in food.

I have been careful not to use subjective judgements over taste. All our taste buds are wired differently and in some cases an individual may well prefer the taste of something less expensive. My aim is to explain objectively why price variants exist, so when shopping for everyday use or for a special occasion, you can do so knowing exactly what you are getting for your money. I also hope, once you have read the incredible stories of the foods in this book, it prompts you to create a 'bucket list' of items you now just have to find and try.

Organic:
A General Note

Throughout this book I refer to different farming methods and the impact they have on the cost of producing food. To avoid repetition in every chapter it may be useful to begin with a note clarifying the status of organic.

Organic food is not always more expensive, but organic farmers generally charge more for their produce because many organic farming practices take longer and produce lower yields. It is more labour-intensive than conventional agriculture and fields have to be taken out of food production while they go through three years of organic conversion, or fertility building, which is a slower process than using artificial fertiliser.

Organic produce is grown using a system of crop rotation, without the use of most artificial pesticides and fertilisers. Organically farmed animals are kept in ways that minimise the need for medicines and other chemical treatments, such as growth hormones. They cannot routinely be fed antibiotics but conventional medicines can be used if an animal is acutely ill. They should also be fed an organic diet.

All food labelled as organic must be certified by a government-approved certification body such as the Soil Association or Organic Farmers & Growers. The producer must also hold a licence issued by one of these bodies. The certification bodies follow regulations set down by the European Union (EU), which are implemented in the UK by Defra (Department for Environment, Food and Rural Affairs).

Tea

I have visited tea plantations in Africa, China and India, and there is no more beautiful landscape than immaculately manicured tea bushes set in sweeping valleys, bathed in sunshine. Pickers with large sacks on their backs wander back and forth amid the rows collecting the newest shoots.

To appreciate fully what goes into making our tea, and why some tea costs more than others, let's begin by understanding tea's history.

A BRIEF HISTORY

TEA, THE WORLD'S MOST POPULAR DRINK, has its origin in ancient China. The legend goes that some 4,500 years ago the Emperor Shen Nung was sitting beneath a tree while his servant boiled drinking water. Some leaves from the tree, a *Camellia sinensis*, fluttered down and accidentally landed in the pot and the resulting pleasant brew was what we now know as tea.

By the Tang dynasty (AD 618–906), tea had become firmly established as the national drink of China.

The Dutch first imported tea to Europe, bringing it to Holland in 1606, through a trading post on Java that they had established six years earlier. In tea grading, the top grade is still called 'Orange Pekoe', the orange deriving from the historic Dutch House of Orange royal family.

Tea arrived in Britain in 1664, via the East India Company, and its popularity was sealed by the marriage of Charles II to his tea-addicted bride, Catherine of Braganza.

It didn't take long for the authorities to attempt to exploit the popularity of the drink and the first British tax on tea, in 1698, was so high it nearly stopped sales altogether. It certainly led to a considerable amount of smuggling and adulteration. It's hard to believe now, but a favourite way of eking out more product was to add sheep's dung to black tea. Leaves from numerous other plants also made their way into the mix. If that was not potentially perilous enough, green teas were dyed with highly toxic additives like copper carbonate and lead chromate. It took nearly a hundred years for the British government to put a stop to this odious behaviour, perhaps after finally cottoning on to the fact it had played a part in the problem. Tea tax was slashed from 119 per cent to 12.5 per cent, instantly rendering the drink affordable and reducing smuggling incentives.

Tea truly became the drink of the masses following the end of the East India Company's monopoly on trade with China. The company began to grow their own tea in India and, by 1888, British imports of tea from the region were greater than those from China.

Our relationship with tea changed irrevocably during the Second World War. Prior to 1939, people would chose tea from their grocer in a similar way to how we now pick wine. Tea-buyers would prioritise quality and flavour from the vast array of teas available from across the globe and bought the best they could afford. Rationing changed all that. People bought the cheapest they could, which was invariably industrial grade, black tea. This switch, I am afraid to say, coupled with the Americans giving us the tea bag some years before, resulted in subsequent generations knowing and appreciating tea far less well.

GEOGRAPHY

ALL TEA COMES from the plant *Camellia sinensis*, an indigenous mountain plant. It is usually grown between the Tropic of Cancer and the Tropic of Capricorn but can be grown in any area with the right climate and conditions. There is even tea grown in the UK, in Cornwall.

The tea industry is a significant employer in many of the 35 countries where it is grown. China has 80 million tea growers, India has an estimated one million permanent tea workers, while in Kenya tea supports the livelihood of an estimated three million people.

China still produces some of the finest examples of green and white teas. However, India, Sri Lanka and East Africa, most notably Malawi and Kenya, are now producing some of the world's finest black teas.

HOW TEA IS PRODUCED

THE WAY TEA is picked and processed determines whether it is white, green, yellow, black oolong or pu-erh tea. Each involves different leaves being selected at different times and being treated in a different way. 'Speciality' teas are blends of teas that take their name from a growing area, time of day or person's name, such as Earl Grey and Darjeeling. English Breakfast, incidentally, was a name coined by Americans to describe the black tea English people drank for breakfast. Speciality teas contain fewer types of tea than cheaper, more popular blends. For the purist, it's worth saying that herbal teas, such as camomile, mint, rooibos or ginger, are not teas at all. They are herbal infusions.

The production of black tea has four stages: withering, rolling, oxidation (fermentation) and drying. There are two methods of production: traditional (Orthodox) or 'cut, tear, curl' (CTC), which has a large bearing on price as explained below.

Teas are then blended to make a consistent-tasting tea. Typically, tea reaches the supermarket shelf 20–30 weeks after it has been plucked from the bush.

WHY THE PRICE VARIES

THE CHEAPEST tea bags in the UK cost just 2p, the most expensive many, many times that. Here's why ...

LOCATION

Many of the things you might know about wine are also true of tea. The *terroir* – the natural environment – massively affects the flavour: the pH of the soil; the gradient; the altitude; when the sun first hits the plants in the morning and how long it stays through the day; the climate; the rainfall. The varietal used (of which there are many thousands) also plays a role. If you grew the same varietal in China, India and Malawi, you would get different flavours from the leaf, just as you would with Riesling grapes grown in Austria, France or New Zealand.

Flavour can also differ from field to field and producer to producer. Not all champagne grown in the region tastes the same. Similarly, not all tea in Darjeeling is the same quality.

THE LEAF

Tea-estate owners have to choose between making large volumes of basic tea or a smaller amount of top-quality produce. If they go for the top-quality option, they pick only from the freshest shoots at the top of the bush when the best leaves are produced in the spring.

Tea bushes grow faster at lower altitudes, producing many flushes of new leaves. They give greater volume, but lower quality tea. These are the leaves used to make cheap tea. A study by the University of Derby found that supermarket economy tea blends contained from 75 per cent to 120 per cent of the recommended daily intake of fluoride; almost double the amount found in more expensive brands. This is because tea plants accumulate fluoride in their leaves and therefore mature leaves contain more.

The cheapest teas are also harvested mechanically, so often have a higher ratio of stalk to leaf. The leaf is the only bit that carries flavour, so you are paying for dead wood, literally.

All leaves are graded for quality and condition. Fannings are the small pieces of leaf left over after the higher quality leaves have been sold. Very small bits of leaf are called dust. These are what go into lower grade economy tea bags as they are cheap and produce a quick, strong brew. One thing to watch out for, though: these terms do mean different things in different places. For instance, Pekoe dust is highly sought after in Kenya and, in Darjeeling, 'fannings' is the collective term for tea-bag-grade tea.

PRODUCTION METHOD

Here you find the greatest difference between cheap and high-quality tea.

The traditional, Orthodox, method is used for loose-leaf teas. Hand picked leaves are allowed to wither until they are soft enough to roll without the leaf splitting. Then they are either rolled by hand or with machines that lightly crush the leaf. As a rule of thumb this leaf tea is made up of higher quality leaves; the best teas don't go into bags. The gentle processing means the leaf retains a greater depth of flavour.

It is possible to make more than one cup of tea from a small amount of these leaves. Leaf teas have a greater surface area and each piece of leaf retains more amino acids and polyphenols, which produce really interesting, complex flavours. In China it is said that the second or third infusion is more delicious than the first as the water penetrates further into the leaf to reveal new flavours.

While leaf tea is more expensive than bags, you can get a great deal more from a small amount. Cup by cup it works out just a few pence more than bags; an affordable luxury.

By contrast tea bags are produced using the cut, tear, curl (CTC) method. Leaves are fed through a machine that rolls them up tightly. Other methods for processing tea for tea bags exist and sometimes involve threshing leaves to break them up. The process is harsh so tougher leaves need to be used, resulting in a lower quality of flavour in the tea bag.

Flavouring, flowers and pieces of fruit and citrus peel can be added to improve the taste of really cheap tea. Cochineal, made from shells of crushed beetles, is often used to give a ruby redness. One American iced tea has even been found to use castoreum, a secretion from glands under a beaver's tail, to introduce a vanilla flavour!

Earl Grey has always had something added: originally this was bergamot, an essential oil from a rare citrus fruit from southern Italy. Bergamot is expensive, however, so most modern Earl Greys are made with flavourings. If you are not sure whether you are using a brand of tea bags made with flavourings, rather than oil, then open one up and smell. If flavourings have been used, you will recognise a synthetic lemon smell similar to that used in bathroom cleaners. Real bergamot is bright, fresh and unmistakable in comparison. It is there to enhance the tea, not disguise poor quality with an overpowering lemon flavour.

PACKAGING

Cheap teas are often packaged less well than expensive teas, perhaps just in a cardboard box. As time passes, the quality of the goods inside deteriorates since the tea bags are open to the air. More expensive teas are hermetically sealed, perhaps inside a foil wrapper to ensure the tea is fresh and doesn't pick up aromas and flavours from external sources like the cardboard and glue of the box. You can clearly smell the difference when opened.

ETHICS

Pesticides, herbicides and fertiliser are used in the production of most crops, but can be heavily and irresponsibly used to maximise yields in cheaper teas, with very little concern for sustainability. The same is true for the wages paid to tea pickers in the developing world, which can be very low, as highlighted by recent media coverage of working conditions on tea plantations in India.

Some tea producers choose to pay a premium to estate workers. Fairtrade, for example, guarantees an extra 50 US cents per kilo.

THE MOST EXPENSIVE TEAS

Yellow Gold tea buds: this tea comes from only one mountain in the world, in Singapore, and is steeped in mythology. I've been told by several people in the tea industry that it is harvested on just one day of the year in spring, using gold scissors. The buds are then painted with 24-carat gold flakes and the finished product costs around $105 US for 50 grams (enough to make around 25 cups). It does sound a little unlikely to me, but I have heard the same story again and again.

Panda dung tea: this tea has reportedly been sold for around $200 per cup. Pandas only eat wild bamboo and only absorb around 30 per cent of its nutrients. That leaves 70 per cent in their dung, which is then used to fertilise tea plants. The leaves from those plants are apparently said to have a special flavour!

Da Hong Pao: the leaves are said to come from just three fabled bushes in Fujian province in China. The story goes that these bushes produced the tea that cured the illness of a Ming-dynasty emperor's mother. The leaves are wiped with goat's milk to give them shine as they grow and are baked in small batches over charcoal.

In 1998 the Chinese government sold some of this tea, reputedly from the eighteenth century, for around $1,250,000 per kilogram, more than the cost of gold. Currently, the leaves retail for $650,000 a kilo, which equates to $180 for a pot giving four small cups.

TRY BEFORE YOU DIE!

–

JASMINE SILVER TIP
££££

This is a completely pure tea that has been laid out with jasmine flowers to take on their scent. It is the very highest grade jasmine tea and was originally created as an exclusive tribute to the Chinese emperor and forbidden outside the imperial household. Jasmine tea can be made using any tea as a base and flavoured with oils and synthetic flavouring to mask low-grade leaves. This tea, however, is the highest grade white silver tip, scented with fresh flowers. White silver tips are also known as silver needles, or Bai Hao Yinzhen, and are the delicate leaf bud plucked at the point of unfurling.

The Rare Tea Company have a silver-tip tea sourced from a farm high in the Fujian mountains near the village of Fuding. This is the 'champagne' of white-tea regions. The processes are completed by hand using traditional methods to retain the delicate flavour.

The finest silver tips can be plucked for a few weeks in late March/early April and only on days when there is no rain or cloud so the leaves can be carefully dried in the high-mountain sunshine.

The leaves are then taken to a jasmine farm for scenting, using jasmine blossoms that have been picked at night when the flowers give off their heady perfume. The silver tips are laid out on bamboo frames with the fresh flowers to spend the night together. The room is set at an exact temperature and humidity for the tender silver tips to absorb the jasmine's scent. Each morning the jasmine flowers are removed and replaced that night with fresh flowers. This is repeated six times, over six consecutive nights, to add a unique depth and flavour.

. . . .

How to make the perfect cup of tea

I'm mindful that making a simple cup of tea need not be complicated but I think that after taking the trouble to search out a high-quality, lovingly produced tea, it's worth taking the time to prepare it properly.

Tea loves oxygen; it allows the flavours to open up. Re-boiled water has less oxygen in it than freshly run cold water, so always use the latter.

Make sure your teapot is clean and warm it with boiling water before making your tea.

Different teas benefit from water heated to varying temperatures. For instance, good leaf tea should be brewed with water below boiling point. This is because the amino acids (which produce the flavour) dissolve at a lower temperature than tannins. Tea made with water at 100°C (boiling point) will be more astringent and less sweet.

For good teas stop the kettle before it reaches the rolling boil when bubbles are rising up the kettle's side. Or, if you have a kettle with a thermometer and can be precise, the following is a guide to the ideal temperature for most teas:

- Green and white teas: 70°C
- Black and oolong teas: 85°C
- Herbal infusions: 100°C and 90°C for camomile
- Industrial tea bags: 100°C

The brewing, or steeping, time depends on the type of tea and how strong you like it. The British Standards Institute (BSI) recommends an ideal brewing time of six minutes for long-leaf tea. Popular tea-makers suggest two to three minutes for tea bags. The makers of rare, high-quality tea suggest up to three minutes for white tea, two minutes for green, a minute for black and 30 seconds for oolong.

A good rule of thumb for the ratio of tea to water is a teaspoon of tea and a cup of water per person. Add one for the pot if you like your tea stronger.

Historically, if milk was added to your tea, it went in first to protect the bone-china cup. Now, with less delicate china, it's up to you whether it is added before or after your brewed tea.

Store opened cartons of tea in a sealed container to prevent the leaves from collecting kitchen smells and moisture.

. . . .

Coffee

At home in Crewe, we were very much a tea-drinking family. We'd have the occasional cup of instant coffee but we didn't have the paraphernalia to make the proper stuff. However, I quickly developed a love for coffee, especially as it felt far more exciting to go out to a coffee bar than to visit a tearoom. When I went to university I decided I was going to get into coffee more seriously, and my first purchases as a student were a coffee grinder and percolator. Since then, my love of good, black coffee has never diminished. It was only when I visited coffee growers in Rwanda that, for the first time, I truly appreciated the time and trouble that goes into making the packaged product. My visit to that beautiful country – they call it the Land of a Thousand Hills – was humbling. I met coffee growers who have perhaps just 100 coffee bushes, which they tend lovingly. All their hopes and aspirations for their families are intrinsically bound up with their modest output.

The process of producing coffee begins with the care for the plant as the beans are grown and then harvested. Next it is on to the wash station. On my trip, wash-station number seven was revered for the best beans because the best growing land lay around it. Samples from all the farms were extensively tasted to access quality and flavour before the beans were exported for roasting. Then, having arrived by sea in London, I saw them being roasted, packaged and sent on for sale. After witnessing the whole journey, from bush to supermarket shelf, I marvel at how little it costs for a cup of coffee.

A BRIEF HISTORY

WE DO NOT KNOW EXACTLY when coffee first appeared, but the place was somewhere around modern-day Ethiopia. Its appeal spread to the Arab world and, by the sixteenth century, it had reached all parts of the Middle East, Persia, Turkey and northern Africa. From there coffee moved on to world domination, being enjoyed in Italy, then the rest of Europe, and on to Indonesia and to the Americas.

Coffee became more widely accepted after being given the nod of approval from Pope Clement VIII, who declared it to be a Christian beverage in 1600. The first European coffee house opened in Italy in 1645.

The explosion of coffee drinking in America can be traced back to heavy taxation on tea by the British. Americans switched from drinking mainly tea to coffee as an expression of freedom. The unrest peaked with the 'Boston Tea Party' when protesters destroyed an entire shipment of East India Company tea by throwing it in Boston Harbor. Tea drinking never returned to favour, even after independence, and today Americans consume on average three to four coffees a day.

Britain's first coffee shop opened in Oxford in 1650, followed by the first in London two years later. Coffee shops soon became the fashionable place to do business. Unlike pubs, they were peaceful and the coffee kept customers alert.

The espresso was born in 1822 when Frenchman Louis Bernard Rabaut invented a machine that forced hot water through the coffee grounds instead of leaving it to drip through. Achille Gaggia perfected the technique in Italy in 1946 and brought the espresso machine to London in the 1950s. You might like to know that it usually takes 42 coffee beans to make an espresso.

The first instant coffee was the work of a Japanese-American chemist called Satori Kato. Brits may take pride in the fact that the first mass-produced instant coffee was the invention of George Constant Washington, an English chemist living in Guatemala. Instant coffee accounts for 13 per cent of all coffee drunk today.

Some more coffee trivia with which to enthral your coffee-loving friends:

- Cappuccino is said to have been named after the drink's peak of foam, which resembles the cowl of a Capuchin friar's habit.

- The US Navy used to serve alcoholic beverages on board ships. However, in 1914, shortly after Josephus 'Joe' Daniels became Secretary of the Navy, he outlawed alcohol on board, except for very special occasions. Coffee then became the drink of choice and some believe this was the origin of the term 'Cup of Joe'.

- Italians do not drink espresso during meals. Drinking espresso is considered to be a separate event and is given its own time.

- In Greece and Turkey, the oldest person is traditionally served their coffee first.

- In the ancient Arab world, coffee became such a staple part of family life that one of the causes allowed by law for marital separation was a husband's refusal to produce coffee for his wife.

- Scandinavia has the world's highest per capita annual coffee consumption at 26.4 pounds.

HOW COFFEE IS PRODUCED

COFFEE GROWS in more than 50 countries around the equator between the Tropics of Cancer and Capricorn and is the second largest export in the world after oil.

All coffee beans come from plants in the genus *Coffea*. The coffee tree can grow at sea level up to an altitude of approximately 6,000 feet. It produces its first full crop at about five years old. Thereafter, it produces consistently for 15 to 20 years and sometimes much longer. A mature coffee tree will produce one pound of coffee per growing season.

Coffee beans are the seeds of the coffee 'cherry'; two seeds normally grow within each cherry. To make a roasted pound of coffee it takes around 2,000 handpicked coffee cherries.

Although there are thousands of species of coffee plants, only two are of commercial importance: *Coffea arabica* and *Coffea canephora*, more commonly called *robusta*. Robusta coffee beans grow best at lower altitudes, whereas arabica is better suited to higher altitudes. Arabica accounts for about 70 per cent of worldwide coffee production.

Robusta tends to be a hardier, more disease-resistant bean than arabica. It is also less costly to maintain and produces a higher yield. Consequently robustas are used for the less expensive canned and instant coffees.

Arabica coffee grows best at high altitudes (from 1,500 metres to 2,500 metres) while robusta coffee does well in lowlands and rainforests. Before roasting, the colour of robusta beans are yellow to light brown in appearance whereas arabica beans are green with silver/blueish shades.

When ready to be harvested, the fruit on the coffee tree turns a dark cherry colour. This usually occurs about eight to nine months after flowering has taken place. North of the equator, the harvest takes place between September and March. South of the equator, the harvest usually takes place in April and May. In some countries, such as Kenya and Colombia where the division between the wet and dry seasons is not as distinct, there may be two flowerings a year, in which case a main and secondary crop often occurs. Countries on the equator are able to harvest fruit all year round.

Where the terrain allows, automatic machines have been designed to harvest, completing the work of 100 men and gathering 95 per cent of the fruit in one go. Although using a machine is cheaper, it does mean ripe cherries are not picked out from the others. If any green cherries get mixed in with the others, the resulting coffee will taste especially bitter. If overripe cherries get lumped in to the mix, then the final product is likely to have an unpleasant, acrid taste.

The majority of coffee is still handpicked by either selective or strip picking. In strip picking, the entire crop is picked in just one pass. Selective picking involves pickers making several passes among the coffee trees at intervals of around ten days to ensure only fully ripe beans are taken. Selective picking is more expensive and generally used for arabica, rather than robusta, beans. It does, however, produce the best results.

In both cases, processing begins immediately to prevent the pulp from fermenting and deteriorating. Coffee beans can be prepared for roasting in one of two ways.

The oldest, simplest and cheapest is the dry method. Firstly, harvested cherries are sorted and cleaned to separate the unripe, overripe and damaged cherries and remove dirt, soil, twigs and leaves. This is commonly done by hand, using a large sieve. Alternatively, ripe cherries can also be separated by flotation in washing channels.

When the ripe cherries have been washed they are spread out on large patios or on waist-height trestles to dry in the sun. They are raked to avoid fermentation and to dry evenly. If it rains or the temperature falls considerably, the cherries have to be covered for protection. Alternatively, after two or three days, coffee can be put in drying rooms, where burners are used. It can take up to four weeks for the moisture content of each cherry to fall to the optimum amount, when the outer shell becomes dark brown and brittle. The cherries are then stored in large silos where they continue to lose moisture.

The drying operation is the most crucial stage of the process, since it affects the final quality of the green coffee. Overdried coffee will become brittle and produce too many broken beans during hulling when the outer shell is broken away. Coffee that's not sufficiently dried will be too moist and prone to rapid deterioration caused by the attack of fungi and bacteria.

The other technique to prepare cherries is the wet method and is mainly used in Central America, Mexico, Colombia, Kenya and Tanzania. Here, more money and care is needed to produce the bean but the quality is thought to be better. The main difference is that the wet method removes the pulp and shell from the bean within

12–24 hours of harvesting instead of allowing the cherries to air dry. It's all done by machines and once separated the beans are washed and dried.

Some coffee beans may be polished. While polished beans are considered superior to unpolished ones, in reality there is little difference between the two.

Although coffee beans are of fairly uniform size and proportion they are graded first by size and then by density. The top export-grade of bean is referred to as SHB (strictly hard bean) or strictly high grown, which means that the coffee beans are produced at a minimum altitude of 4,000 feet above sea level.

On arrival in the destination country, the shipments are sent to warehouses or direct to the roaster. When green, coffee keeps for a long time, provided it is protected from damp; keeping it, in fact, improves it. It is entirely devoid of smell at this stage. To release the aroma, coffee has to be roasted.

Coffee is usually blended using beans from various origins to achieve a constant quality. A single coffee bean will generally not possess the complexity necessary for great espresso. Many espresso blends contain three to seven different types of beans.

In the development of flavours, roasting is key. It is during the roasting that the sugars and other carbohydrates within the bean become caramelised.

Well-roasted coffee should be brown, but never black. If it is not sufficiently roasted, it produces a colourless infusion, which is rough and astringent. If overroasted it produces a black drink that is bitter and unpleasant.

During the industrial roasting process, a small quantity of sugar molasses or various other products is sometimes added to 'coat' the berries. Unfortunately this process can also make it easier to mask the use of inferior quality or damaged beans.

Speciality coffees, on the other hand, are generally roasted in small batches. The two most common roasting methods are drum and hot-air roasting. Drum-type roasting machines roast the coffee beans as they tumble in a rotating drum typically heated by gas or wood. When the desired roast is achieved, beans are poured into a cooling hopper to prevent overcooking. Hot-air roasters roast the coffee beans as they tumble on a current of hot air.

In both processes, most green coffee is roasted at approximately 200°C. During this time coffee beans swell and increase in size by over 50 per cent, while at the same time greatly reducing their weight.

A lightly roasted bean would not generally be used for espresso since it produces a sharper, more acidic taste than do darker roasts.

Darker roasts, in contrast, have a fuller flavour, approaching a bittersweet tang. As the roast darkens, caffeine and acidity decrease proportionately. The darker the roast, the more you taste the char, rather than the flavour of the bean. As a result, extremely dark roasts tend to have a smoky flavour and are better suited for brewed coffee rather than espresso.

WHY THE PRICE VARIES

CONSISTENCY

Consistency is a key driver of price. The best producers demand a consistent specification throughout the year, which requires beans to be from particular sources. Others might get a much cheaper price by buying beans on the open market throughout the year as and when there is a glut and prices are low.

PACKAGING

The quality of packaging is significant because the freshness of roasted beans has the greatest impact on taste and aroma. Premium packaging has a one-way air filter, which aids freshness by allowing carbon dioxide, emitted after roasting, to escape. Foil-wrapped, vacuum-packed containers don't allow this to happen and beans will go stale.

Once opened and exposed to the air, roasted coffee beans begin to oxidise and become stale so they are best stored in an airtight container in a cool, dry place and not on your kitchen counter in direct sunlight. Some coffee aficionados advocate keeping it in the freezer, but there are arguments for and against this practice. The smallest amount of condensation at the defrosting stage could undo all your hard work by dissolving coffee oils.

Where possible buy packets with the roasting date printed on the packaging, the newer the better. Pre-ground coffees will be less fresh than buying beans and grinding them at home.

VARIETY OF BEAN

Robusta beans are generally harsher and cheaper than arabica. Premium robustas are essentially reserved for espresso blends, and are primarily used to improve the crema (the creamy froth on top of the coffee) and add bite to the shot.

It can be very difficult to find an exceptional robusta; growers and processors are not often willing to dedicate as much effort to robusta as to arabica. Robusta-only coffee is rarely sold. Instead, poor-quality robustas may be added to freeze-dried coffees or to coffee-flavoured frozen drinks where sugar and cream overwhelm the off-notes.

Robusta has notably more caffeine than arabica. In the interest of greater profit, some retailers blend in more robusta beans than arabica, resulting in a brew that can upset the stomach.

GEOGRAPHY

Taste differs between bean varieties and growing regions. A variety grown in one part of the world will taste different from the same one grown elsewhere. Flavours detected can be as varied as berries (blueberry is often particularly noted in Ethiopian Harrar), earthy (a characteristic associated with Indian and Indonesian coffees) or citrus (common with Central American beans).

Coffees from higher altitudes are generally considered to be better quality, mainly due to the fact that arabica, which is the only bean used in gourmet coffees, will not grow at lower altitudes.

Processing methods

Wet processing is more capital-intensive than dry processing. The care and attention taken throughout the process makes a difference to quality and to price. The same goes for mechanical or strip picking versus selective picking.

Ethics

Around 90 per cent of coffee production is from the developing world and around 25 million people worldwide depend on coffee for their livelihoods, but many of them fail to earn a reliable living. In Rwanda, for example, the lack of good roads in rural areas means the crops can go to waste.

Price volatility has significant consequences for those who depend on coffee for their livelihood, making it difficult for growers to predict their income for the coming season and budget for their household and farming needs.

If you want to know that farmers have been paid a fair price for the coffee you buy, check for the Fairtrade label or check with the retailer.

Sustainability

The coffee industry is playing a growing role in deforestation, which has been blamed for species extinction, changes to climatic conditions, desertification and displacement of populations. Coffee producers are clearing forests to plant new, hybrid varieties of coffee, bred to withstand the sun and be farmed more intensively without tree cover.

Coffee that is marked as 'shade-grown' means it was produced within the forest itself and is less likely to have caused deforestation. Also look out for Rainforest Alliance certification, with the little green frog logo. Rainforest Alliance works closely with coffee farmers, educating them on the most environmentally friendly ways to grow coffee crops. Beware, though – Rainforest Alliance certification doesn't necessarily mean that 100 per cent of the product is certified. The quantity certified can be anywhere from 30 to 100 per cent. There should be a statement on the label near the logo, that states how much.

TRY BEFORE YOU DIE

–

JAMAICAN BLUE MOUNTAIN
££££

My honeymoon was spent in Jamaica and this is where I first tried, and became converted to, Blue Mountain coffee. The young man who looked after us at The Plantation Inn brought us a sachet of coffee one day and said: 'This is the best coffee in Jamaica, have a try.' We made some in the cafetière in our room and it was wonderful so we arranged a visit to the Blue Mountain region, which is the highest point on Jamaica. Only coffee grown on certain estates may be called 'Blue Mountain'. These include Wallenford, Mavis Bank, Silver Hill, Moy Hall and more recently Old Tavern Estate. The region's high altitude, over 7,000 feet at its peak, and its excellent climate create dense beans with a rich flavour. Jamaican Blue Mountain (or JBM) is therefore expensive, often selling for $30 a pound or more at the time of writing.

The sale, roasting and export of Blue Mountain coffee is strictly controlled by the Jamaican government and the Coffee Industry Board. Sadly, however, I am told there is a considerable quantity of counterfeit JBM being marketed. Not all of it is outright counterfeit; some is simply misleading. You may see 'Jamaica Blue Mountain style' coffee or 'Jamaica Blue Mountain Blend'. The former probably doesn't contain any JBM, and the latter needs to contain as little as 5 per cent authentic JBM to be called a JBM Blend. There is also Jamaica High Mountain, which refers to coffee grown by estates in the area that cannot use the JBM label. These may well be high-quality coffees, but you should not pay nearly as much for them as true, and limited, Jamaican Blue Mountain.

KONA
££££

A visit to Kona was high on my to-do list on a visit to Hawaii with my family a few years ago. The Kona region is on the western side of the island and only coffee grown there can earn the label Kona. A rainy growing season and a cool, dry harvesting season, means the region is particularly well-suited to coffee production. Coffee was first planted there in 1829 and many of the coffee trees are over a hundred years old. Thanks to the island's isolation and the state's strict import restrictions on agricultural products, minimal pest control is required and, as a result, no pesticides are used.

In the same manner as Jamaican Blue Mountain blends, 'Kona blend' may by law contain as little as 10 per cent real Kona coffee. Pure Kona comes with a '100 per cent Kona' certificate or a 'Kona Coffee Council 100% Kona' seal.

KOPI LUWAK/CIVET COFFEE
£££££

I haven't yet tried this, but kopi luwak, also commonly referred to as civet coffee, has the number-one spot on the list of the top-ten most expensive coffees in the world. It's extremely expensive at currently $160 per pound because of its uncommon means of production. This particular Southeast Asian coffee is produced after coffee beans have been consumed and passed through a civet, a mongoose-like animal.

BLACK IVORY COFFEE
£££££

If you are intrigued by civet coffee, then you might be interested in the rare variety of Black Ivory, or elephant dung, coffee. Arabica coffee beans grown on an estate in northern Thailand are fed to elephants and then collected from their dung. The elephants' stomach acids break down coffee proteins and impart a unique, smooth flavour to the coffee, or so it is claimed. This coffee is manufactured in north Thailand only and available in exclusive high-end resorts in the country for $50 per cup, or $500 a pound. Let me know what you think if you try some.

· ·

How to make the perfect cup of cafetière coffee for those in doubt!

- Fill your kettle with freshly drawn water and bring to the boil. Once boiled, warm your cafetière with the boiled water, rinse and discard. Leave the remaining boiled water to cool for around 30 seconds to allow the temperature to drop to 96°C.

- Measure 7g of freshly ground coffee per serving into your cafetière. That's about one rounded dessert spoonful per cup for a normal strength coffee. An eight-cup cafetière will take 55–60g for a full, rounded brew. You can easily adjust to your taste preference and add more coffee to increase the strength, rather than leaving the coffee to brew for longer.

- Pour just enough water over the coffee to saturate the grounds. Swirl the bottom of the cafetière to wet the grounds thoroughly, allowing them to absorb the water and create a bloom. Leave for just a few seconds.

- Pour the rest of the water over the grounds. Use 250ml per cup, or fill to just below the rim or 'max level' measure and gently stir.

- Place the lid with the plunger resting on top of the grounds and leave for another 3–4 minutes before plunging.

· ·

Wine

Everyone knows a wine buff. They are the sort of person who is preoccupied with Pinot Noir or can't get enough Crozes-Hermitage. They'll describe their wine in terms of top notes, acidity, mineral, with undertones of this, that and the other. That wine buff may even be you.

For those who don't fall into this category, wine can seem a bit of an intimidating minefield. One difficulty is the fact that particular types of wine go in and out of fashion. For example, the prevailing view seems to be that sauvignon blanc is somehow superior to chardonnay but, personally, I prefer chardonnay. You like what you like.

And, yes, there are thousands of books dedicated to the output of countries, regions and even single chateaux, plus piles of information on grape varieties, topography and vintages. At university I used to buy and read Hugh Johnson's *Pocket Wine Book* every year. But what does it all really mean? Even if you don't particularly care about impressing your wine-loving friends, how can you be sure to choose a good-value, pleasant plonk?

I have been incredibly fortunate to spend time in some of the great vineyards in France, Italy, Spain, Greece, Turkey, North America, Argentina, South Africa, Australia and New Zealand. I have even attended a ceremony in an ancient church in the Left Bank of Bordeaux for which I wore an ermine-lined cloak, and was made a Chevalier of the region.

In this section I have used what I have learned through those journeys to help you understand what you are getting for your money.

A BRIEF HISTORY

MAN **PROBABLY** discovered alcohol completely by accident after eating fermented fruit. Archaeological evidence has established that the earliest known production of wine was during the Late Neolithic period, around 7,000 years ago, in what we now know as the Caucasus region (Georgia and Azerbaijan, between the Black and Caspian seas). Wine played an important role in ancient Egyptian society, but it is thought that the Etruscans and ancient Greeks truly made it their own, also introducing it into what is now the Italian peninsula. The ancient Romans spread viticulture among their conquests and winemaking became commonplace across modern-day Iberia, central Europe, France and Great Britain. It is said that Britain had some of the finest wine in the empire after the Roman conquest.

By the Middle Ages, wine was enjoyed by all classes in southern Europe, but in central and northern Europe it was the preserve of the merchant class and nobility. Since wine was required to celebrate mass in churches, Benedictine monks became the largest producers in modern-day France and Germany, closely followed by other monastic orders, including the Cistercians, Templars and Carmelites. For the same religious reasons, it was the Spanish conquistadors who introduced viticulture to Central and South America in the fifteenth century. The rest, as they say, is history.

GEOGRAPHY

GRAPEVINES **NEED** a period of winter dormancy and are unable to stand very high summer temperatures; hence grapevines are predominantly grown between the 30th and 50th parallels in both northern and southern hemispheres. With some notable exceptions, the regions acknowledged for producing the best-quality wines lie between 35° and 45° north and 35° and 45° south. Altitude, climate and the soil, or *terroir*, all have a noticeable impact on the taste and quality of wine.

Each variety of vine thrives in slightly different conditions. A whole range of factors, including the length of the ripening season, annual weather conditions, soil type and fertility, drainage, topography, sun exposure and pest problems, play their part in the quality of the grapes produced. The one factor that all grapevines have in common is the need for good drainage. All vines need water, but the fruit will ripen better if there is only just enough.

Despite all the care and attention that goes into selecting and growing vines, the greatest influence is the weather in any given year. The ideal season will comprise a cool, wet winter with plenty of water, a warm, frost-free spring, a mild summer with no rain or heat waves, and warm, dry days in the run-up to harvest.

HOW WINE IS PRODUCED

THE JUICE of all grape varieties is clear. The colour of a wine is determined by the length of contact the grape juice has with the crushed skins that contain the pigment. The difference between white and red winemaking is therefore that, for whites, the juice is fermented after the skins have been discarded, while for reds the juice is fermented on the skins to extract colour. Rosé wine is created by allowing a few hours of skin contact; the longer the contact, the deeper the pink colour of the wine.

The basic process for making wine is the same: vines are planted, grapes are grown, picked and crushed, their juices are allowed to ferment and the resulting liquid is bottled. However, the decisions winemakers take about exactly how each stage is carried out will have a big impact on the wine produced.

GROWING THE GRAPES

Over 10,000 varieties of grapevine exist. About 3,500 of them are cultivated but only about 230 are significant in the world of wine. Just a dozen are commercially popular.

Left to their own devices, vines would grow wildly across the ground, putting their energy into shoots and tendrils that could cover up to an acre. Since ancient times, vine growers have propped up the vines to prevent fruit lying on the ground where it could be eaten by rodents, or attract other pests or diseases. The Romans planted elm trees in their vineyards for the vines to grow against. Gradually it was recognised that training the vines along canes leads to better, more evenly ripening fruit and eventually that developed into the beautiful rows we see in vineyards today.

During winter, vines are pruned right back to the main stem. It is a highly skilled job to ensure the right amount of pruning results in the right amount of crop (too many grapes will result in lower quality, and too few will be uneconomical). As the weather warms into spring, the vines begin to grow back and flower. Early flowering is thought to be a sign of a good vintage. Any harsh weather at this stage can be disastrous. After flowering, tiny, hard green berries appear and over the next 100 to 120 days they develop into grapes.

HARVEST

In the northern hemisphere harvest takes place from August to October (sometimes even deeper into the autumn for late-harvest styles), depending on the climate. Choosing when to harvest is very important and the decision is made on the basis of the sugar levels, colour and taste of the grapes. Many vineyards harvest by hand while others do so mechanically. Handpicking is the method preferred by fine-wine makers as it results in less bruising of the fruit. Mechanical harvesting is more cost-effective and means grapes can be harvested in the cool of the night to allow for better retention of fruit characters and improved control of the subsequent fermentation.

Once harvested, fruit destined for the best wines is checked on a conveyor belt and poor-quality grapes are removed. Grapes for red wine have their stems removed by a machine and grapes for white wine will go straight into a crusher.

FERMENTATION

Grapes are then put into large fermentation vats where the process of turning the sugars into alcohol begins. Grapes naturally have wild yeasts on their skins so this process may go ahead unaided, but many winemakers now add cultured yeasts to give more consistent results. Some also add sugar to increase potential alcohol. Stainless steel vats or oak barrels are typically used for white and the best red wines. The type of vessel used, and for how long, is one of the key decisions winemakers will take to determine the particular flavour and character of their product. The size of the barrel, source of the oak and whether it has been used before will all affect the taste.

Fermentation times vary according to variety and time of harvest; perhaps less than a week for champagne and 10–15 days for full-bodied reds. Fermentation can take several weeks for dessert wines because the grapes are usually picked late into the autumn when the low ambient temperature may impede natural fermentation. They may even have to be warmed by the winemaker to kick-start the fermentation. Extreme examples, such as Tokaji Eszencia from Hungarian vineyards, may continue to ferment slowly for several years.

POST-FERMENTATION OPERATIONS

Once fermentation is complete, the new wine is removed from the fermentation vats, leaving behind the used yeast. The wine is then clarified and filtered to remove any remaining particles.

It is often thought that sulphites in wine give a worse hangover but this isn't true. Sulphur dioxide (SO^2) is a natural by-product of alcohol fermentation, so all wines contain a little SO^2. Indeed, within the winemaking process SO^2 is added in small quantities to freshly picked grapes, grape juice, fermenting must and final wine just prior to bottling in order to help protect against oxidation and to clarify the wine. The greatest amount of sulphites are found in sweet wine, then white, then red, and organic wine has even lower permitted levels.

A small proportion of adults are intolerant to sulphites. However, since they are also widely used in food preservation they are very likely to be consumed whether wine is part of the diet or not.

AGEING

Wine is then aged from as little as a few hours – as in the case of Asti DOCG where the point of the exercise is to capture the pure grapey character of the moscato fruit – to decades. Tawny port, for example, is blended from wines that are at least 40 years old. Ageing can occur either in barrels or bottles, or a combination of both.

Non-fortified wines, such as Gran Reserva Rioja, must be aged for at least five years before release, with at least three in oak and two in the bottle. Major producers invariably exceed these timescales. Most vintage champagnes are aged for at least eight years (all in-bottle) although the legal minimum is three years.

WHY THE PRICE VARIES

QUALITY WINES cost more to make than lower quality wines because the methods used are more expensive. Like any other commodity, though, rarity and prestige also significantly determine final price.

GEOGRAPHY

Just because a wine's label says it is from a particular prestigious chateau doesn't necessarily mean it is good wine. The importance of *terroir* and microclimate cannot be overstated when it comes to quality. These elements can vary hugely across even very small distances, so not all locations in a good wine-growing area are equal. Indeed, different areas of a vineyard on an individual estate can produce wildly different characteristics. Some grapes will be unique and therefore able to command a higher price. Other areas on the same estate will produce grapes of a far inferior quality. Of course, this also means that vineyard land prices vary hugely.

WEATHER

The quality of the grapes produced is hugely dependent on the weather in any one year. 'Enemies' of the vine can strike throughout the growing season. To see how this can affect the fortunes of one particular grape, look at how the climate has affected the quality of Bordeaux:

- **Frost:** often experienced early in the season when the vine may have been fooled into early budburst. If these delicate buds are 'burned' by the frost, no fruit will set and potential yield plummets. While economically disastrous, the twist here is that the fruit that survives can be exceptional. Bordeaux 1961 is a coveted (and costly) vintage.

- **Hail:** can strike at any time but is especially dangerous in the summer when vines are full of fruit. Bordeaux was hit in the years 1999, 2003, 2008, 2009, 2011 and 2013, which affected yields.

- **Mildew:** powdery or downy mildew is due to damp conditions. Bordeaux was affected in 1969, leading to one of its worst ever vintages.

- **Rot:** black rot (caused by a fungus), sour rot (spread by fruit flies) and white rot (common after hailstorms) are all disastrous. The 2013 Bordeaux vintage was affected by all three. NB: Not to be confused with noble rot (*Botrytis cinerea*), which creates the raisin berries used to make the great dessert wines of Sauternes and Barsac.

The year the grapes are harvested dictates the wine's vintage and this therefore has a significant bearing on price, with vintages known for better quality commanding a higher premium. Of course, the season is different in each wine-growing area, so a bad vintage in one may be a good vintage in another. Non-vintage wines sell at a lower price because producers combine grapes from several years to control the flavour of the end product.

GRAPES

The quality of grapes is critical. The yield, the age of the vines and how carefully the grapes are selected at harvest all impact price. A larger yield usually produces lower quality grapes, but a larger volume of wine. Yield is measured in hectolitres per hectare (hl/ha). Yields from the very best vineyards can be as low as 30hl/ha, compared to over 100hl/ha for poor-quality wines. Older vines produce more intensely flavoured grapes, but fewer of them. Tricks used to mask inferior quality, excessive oxidation or off-characters include adding residual sugar, acidity or other ingredients. Off-characters occur when grapes are not selected carefully enough and include a percentage of rotten ones.

PRODUCTION METHOD

The way grapes are grown (viticulture) and how they are made into wine (vinification) are the two main factors that affect wine quality. Winemakers can choose to produce their wines cheaply or expensively.

Harvesting by hand is more expensive than by machine but enables more selective grape picking, thus ensuring only the ripest grapes are harvested. Wine can be fermented in concrete vats rather than in expensive oak barrels, whether new or used. The longer it is aged, the higher the cost.

'Estate-bottled' wines are grown, produced and bottled on the estate, as opposed to wines that are a mix of grapes and wines from different places. Estate-bottled wines tend to be better quality and more expensive. You can spot them by looking out for phrases such as *Mis en bouteille à la propriété*, *Mis en bouteille au domaine* (both France), *Embotellado en la propiedad* (Spain) or *Imbottigliato all'origine* (Italy). The expertise and attention to detail cost time and money at each stage and all impact on a wine's cost.

SCARCITY

Supply and demand play a key role in determining price. The very best wines are generally made on a smaller scale because winemakers have to choose whether to focus on quality or quantity, and this also means the best wines are scarcer. Fine wines are often bought and sold several times before they are drunk, with the price increasing in line with their rarity.

TAX

Tax is a major factor affecting the price of wine, particularly in the UK where the duty is higher than on the Continent. The table below shows the impact of taxation on wine in the UK. Note how much more actual wine the consumer is able to buy as the retail price rises to mitigate the impact of fixed excise duty. More expensive wines are therefore arguably better value.

UK WINE PRICING (2015)				
RRP (Selling Price)	£5.00	£7.50	£10.00	£20.00
Retailer Margin	£1.09	£2.03	£2.85	£6.89
Excise Duty	£2.05	£2.05	£2.05	£2.05
VAT	£0.83	£1.25	£1.67	£3.33
Packaging	£0.36	£0.36	£0.36	£0.36
Logistics	£0.20	£0.20	£0.20	£0.20
Money for Wine	£0.47	£1.61	£2.87	£7.17

HOW DO YOU KNOW WHAT YOU ARE BUYING?

THERE ARE TWO methods of classifying wines: by region, such as Bordeaux, or by grape, such as Chardonnay. In 'old world' wine-producing countries (primarily Europe), wines are generally classified by region, whereas 'new world' wines (from places such as Australia, New Zealand and South Africa) tend to be classified predominantly by grape type.

Wines classified by region don't usually list the grape variety on the label, expecting you to know the variety common to the area. Each country has different classifications of wine quality with strict rules about grape types, crop yield, alcohol percentage and other quality standards.

Generally, quality increases from a 'table wine' (*Vin de table* in French, *Vin da tavola* in Italian and so on) to a wine with typical regional characteristics (*Vin de pays* in French, *Vino de la tierra* in Spanish and *Indicazione geografica tipica* in Italy). The next step is on to a strictly controlled standard, such as an *Appellation d'origine contrôlée* (AOC) in France, *Denominazione di origine controllata* (DOC) in Italy and *Denominacion de origen* (DO or DOCa) in Spain. There are other terms used but these are the most common.

The production of the top tier of wine, such as Chianti or Brunello in Italy, Rioja in Spain or Chablis in France, is very strictly controlled by law. Within each of those categories there are further terms differentiating superior wines from their counterparts, which is where it starts to get very complicated!

Take Bordeaux, for example, which is AOC-classified in more detail than any other wine region in the world, with 57 different appellations under six classifications. There are 10,000 wine producers in the Bordeaux region, farming 120,000 hectares of vineyards. Red wine, with a minimal amount of rosé, accounts for 88 per cent of production. The vineyards lie around the confluence of the Dordogne and Garonne rivers and the Gironde estuary. Those vineyards lying to the west of the Garonne and Gironde are deemed to be wines of the Left Bank, those to the east, the Right Bank. The various sediments deposited by these rivers produce different soil types in each sub-region, resulting in a range of alternative characteristics in wine.

Each chateau in Bordeaux is certified to produce wine to a particular standard, indicated by the terms *Premier cru*, *Grand cru*, *Grand vin* and *Vin de château* in increasing order of quality. However, each AOC region of France has different terminology so it is worth researching the terms for your favourite types of wine so you know what quality you are buying.

Wines produced outside Europe are not generally governed so strictly, which makes it harder for consumers to identify the quality from the label. The price and the reputation of the producer are often the only guides. Another indicator is how the region is described. Generally, a more specific location suggests better quality wine. Thus 'Napa Valley' may indicate a better buy than 'California'. There are no rules about the precise meaning of *Reserve* wine, but many producers use the term to indicate their best wines. Conversely, the terms *Riserva* (Italy) and *Reserva* (Spain) do have specific ageing requirements, which may vary according in those appellations where the term is permitted.

TRY BEFORE YOU DIE!

–

Taste is very subjective but, if I could choose any, my final four bottles with dinner would be ...

CHAMPAGNE:
HOUSE: POL ROGER, CUVÉE: SIR WINSTON CHURCHILL
££££

Pol Roger was Churchill's favourite champagne and the estate placed a black border around the label of all Brut NV bottles shipped to the UK after his death in 1965. The great man is quoted as saying of this tipple: 'In victory, deserve it. In defeat, need it!' In 1984, Pol Roger launched the Pinot Noir-dominant cuvée in his name, which is bottled in both 75cl. bottles and magnums (1.5 litres). It is generally aged for at least ten years before release and only the following 15 vintages have been made: 1975, 1979, 1982, 1985, 1986, 1988, 1990, 1993, 1995, 1996, 1998, 1999, 2000, 2002 and 2004. The current vintage sells for £150 for the bottle but you will pay more than twice that for the more sought-after magnum. The few remaining bottles of the first 1975 vintage can fetch over £1,000 each at auction.

WHITE BURGUNDY:
ESTATE: DOMAINE LEFLAIVE, WINE: BIENVENUES BÂTARD-MONTRACHET GRAND CRU
£££££

The most sought-after vintages – 1976, 1978, 1985, 1986, 1989, 1990, 1992, 1994, 1995, 1997, 1999 – sell for between £45,000 to £89,000 per dozen at auction. As an alternative, I would choose Domaine de la Romanée-Conti Montrachet Grand Cru.

RED BORDEAUX:
ESTATE: CHÂTEAU HAUT BRION, WINE: LE GRAND VIN
££££

Château Haut Brion dates back to 1525 and has caught the eye, or palates, of the English since 1649. King Charles II kept the wine in his cellars and Samuel Pepys noted it in his famous diaries in 1663. Le Grand Vin is the estate's main cuvée, which attracts the best grapes and most expensive oak treatment. The most sought-after vintages are 1961, 1982, 1986, 1989, 1990, 2000, 2005, 2009 and 2010. The wine sells from £4,000 per dozen bottles of the 1986 at auction to over £17,000 for the few remaining cases of the fabled 1961 vintage.

DESSERT:
ESTATE: CHÂTEAU D'YQUEM, WINE: LE GRAND VIN
££££

Château d'Yquem is made in exceptional years only and these do not always coincide with the great Bordeaux vintages because of the very specific climatic conditions that 'noble rot' requires. The most sought-after vintages are 1962, 1967, 1971, 1976, 2001 and 2009. Auction prices range from £4,200 per dozen for the 1971, to over £8,000 for the few remaining cases of the 1967 vintage.

Whisky

Whisky, or 'whiskey', has been dubbed by some 'the nectar of life', when in actual fact the name in Scottish Gaelic reads '*uisge beatha*', which translates as 'water of life'. The sentiment is pretty close anyhow and, either way, people who love this tipple often do so with an almost religious fervour.

A wonderfully roguish colleague first introduced me to its pleasures when I went to work in Scotland for several years in the late 1980s. We would head off for a weekend of whisky tasting in the Highlands or islands until my companion was thoroughly satisfied I had completed my whisky education. This is what I learned.

A BRIEF HISTORY

THERE IS MUCH debate over the origin of this drink. What we do know is that Italians first distilled wine to produce a rudimentary brandy in the thirteenth century. Distillation of alcohol then spread throughout monasteries in the Middle Ages, leading to drinks that were used mainly for medicinal purposes and the preservation of herbs – effectively the first unsweetened liqueurs. The first historic mention of whisky appears in Ireland in 1405, when the death of a chieftain is attributed to 'taking a surfeit of aqua vitae' over the Christmas celebrations. The world's oldest distillery is Old Bushmills in Ireland, which can claim continuous production all the way back to 1608.

Although whisky is traditionally associated with Scotland, it is today produced in many countries around the world, including Australia, Canada, Denmark, England, Finland, Germany, India, Ireland, Japan, Sweden, Taiwan, Wales and the USA.

Two spellings are used, but it is accepted that 'whiskey' applies to Irish and North American spirits, while 'whisky' is used in every other country where the spirit is produced. I am not indicating favouritism by using the spelling without the 'e' in general terms here, but have done so for consistency.

Scotland is considered to be the finest producer of whisky thanks to many centuries of continuous production, the abundant availability of good-quality barley, the purity of fresh water and a cool climate, which allows for a long, slow ageing process. In the interest of balance, I should say that Japan's whisky industry is highly respected and has a long tradition of high-quality production. Japanese whiskies have fared very favourably against Scottish malts in blind tastings. I certainly found that to be the case on a visit to Tokyo!

The most 'whisky' in the world is consumed in India, but 90 per cent of what is imbibed there is a cheaper product made from neutral spirits or spirit distilled from molasses, with limited, if any, maturing time and extensive use of flavourings. Technically there are doubts whether it is really whisky at all. Certainly, the Scotch Whisky Association have taken legal action to try to call a halt to bulk imports of cheap Indian 'whisky' into the European Union, where it is blended with genuine whisky and sold as 'blended whisky' in supermarkets.

HOW WHISKY IS PRODUCED

DISTILLATION

Whisky is a distillate made from fermented grain mash. Various grains are used for different types of whisky. Barley is traditionally used in the manufacture of Scotch whisky, while corn (maize), rye and wheat are more usually favoured for North American whiskies. The finished spirit is then usually aged in oak barrels. Bourbon is made in the USA from at least 51 per cent corn mash and has no minimum ageing requirement. 'Straight bourbon' is, however, aged for at least two years.

Grain for Scotch is malted by tricking it into germinating, by wetting it and kicking off a succession of chemical reactions to change the starch contained in the barley into sugar. The real skill in the malting process is finding the right moment to stop germination. Malting takes between 8 and 21 days, depending on the season. The barley needs to be turned over regularly to maintain a consistent moisture and temperature, and when ready it is dried over fire in a kiln. The kiln is typically heated using a local, or traditional, fuel source, such as peat, and the smoke produced often determines the unique initial flavour profile of the whisky.

When the malt is dry, it is ground to make a coarse flour known as grist. The grist is then mixed with hot water in a mash tun with large rotating blades. At its base are small perforations to let the water and grist liquid flow out, while retaining the larger particles (known as draff), which are sold off as cattle food.

The mix of water and grist looks like porridge and after about an hour its starch changes into fermenting sugars. This sugared juice is called wort and is transferred into 'wash backs'. These are large, flat cylindrical fermentation vessels traditionally made from Scottish larch or Oregon pine, although stainless steel wash backs are becoming more common because they are easier to maintain. Yeast is added to the wort to start fermentation and produce alcohol and carbon dioxide. Up to this point in the operation, there are no substantial differences between the process of making whisky and that for making beer.

From here the difference between the two processes becomes more apparent as beer is aromatised with hops and whisky is distilled without further additions. The distillation process separates alcohol from water and other substances contained in the newly formed 'wash'. Distillation takes place in stills where the liquid is heated. The principle is simple: water evaporates at 100°C while alcohol does so from 80°C. The alcohol turns into a vapour before the water does, rising in the still before being siphoned, cooled and collected.

There are two main methods of distillation, using either traditional pot stills or a column still. A pot still takes batches of wash one-at-a-time and is said to produce the best and most characterful spirits, while the column-still method is a continuous process and so more efficient.

The pot still is a simple piece of equipment consisting of a single heated chamber and a vessel to collect purified alcohol. Elements such as the shape and height of the stills are considered very important in creating a specific house style. Indeed, when distilleries come to add or replace a still they always try to commission a still with the same capacity and shape to guarantee consistency.

The pot-still distillation process usually occurs in at least two stages in separate stills with different capacities and shapes. The first distillation occurs in the wash still and transforms the wash into 'low wines', at about 21 per cent alcohol. Waste from the first distillation is called 'pot ale' or 'burnt ale', and is transformed to feed cattle, too. The second distillation occurs in a spirit still, which is generally smaller than the wash still, since there is less liquid to process.

During the second distillation, only the 'distillation heart' (between 63 per cent and 72 per cent alcohol) is retained for ageing. The 'heads' (above 72 per cent) and 'tails' (below 63 per cent), also called 'feints', are reused and mixed with the next distillation batch.

Column stills are most commonly used in the production of bourbon and other American whiskeys. These stills behave like a series of single pot stills, formed in a long vertical tube, and can achieve a vapour alcohol content of nearly twice as much as a single pot still.

Stills were commonly made of copper, since this element removes sulphur-based compounds from the alcohol that could taint the final spirit and make it unpleasant to drink. Modern stills are usually made of stainless steel with copper innards. In days gone by, stills were heated with coal or peat, depending on the region and possible fuel sources. Currently, nearly all of them are heated with steam (usually gas-heated) as this method allows better control of the process.

Scotch whisky is double distilled whereas Irish and some North American whiskies are triple distilled.

AGEING

Ageing is one of the key factors that distinguish whiskies from different distilleries. The casks used and the nature of the warehouse and location all play a part. Whisky aged in casks stored in seaside warehouses can have a distinct salty note, for instance.

Oak barrels are used to mature alcohol because they are porous. Oxygen softens, homogenises and harmonises the spirit within. The barrels also allow some of the spirit to evaporate and this 1 or 2 per cent loss of alcohol per annum is known as the 'angel's share'. The proportion lost is also partly based upon the atmospheric conditions within the warehouse. A dry cellar will accentuate water evaporation, creating a drier whisky with a higher alcoholic percentage, while a damp cellar will produce a rounder, smoother whisky with a lower alcohol percentage. Given the proportion of alcohol likely to evaporate each year, it is very rare for whiskies to be aged in barrel for more than 30 years since 40 per cent alcohol is the minimum allowed for an aged spirit to be legally called whisky.

Only bourbons are traditionally aged in new oak casks, although Tennessee bourbon (Jack Daniels) has to go through a slightly different process, which includes it being filtered through charcoal.

Scotch whisky is usually aged for several years in ex-bourbon casks, finishing its maturation in barrels that impart distinct new flavours. These might include ex-rum barrels or barrels previously used in ageing fortified wines such as sherry, port or Madeira.

After ageing, whisky is then bottled and the cask strength (alcohol content) is reduced to the required level using distilled water. An increasing number of premium single malts are bottled at cask strength once ageing is complete. High demand for aged single malts has led several distilleries to release whiskies under a new 'no age statement' category using sub-brands such as Talisker Storm, Caol Ila Moch and the Macallan colour series (Gold, Amber, Sienna and Ruby) to enable them to manage maturing stocks more flexibly.

DESIGNATIONS

ALL WHISKY MADE in Scotland must be aged for at least three years to earn the 'Scotch Whisky' designation. The following are the various types of Scotch whisky, with branded examples:

- **Single malt whisky:** the pot-still production of a single distillery, e.g. Laphroaig. An age statement such as '12-year-old', is normally displayed, indicating the minimum age of the youngest component in the blend of barrels used. Single malt whiskies are best suited to ageing and have the most complex and regionally specific flavour profiles. It therefore follows that many of the world's greatest whiskies have either a high proportion of, or are 100 per cent, single malts. In Scotland, the only grain allowed to be used in a single malt whisky is barley.

- **Blended malt whisky:** a blend of more than one single malt, e.g. Cutty Sark.

- **Deluxe blended Scotch whisky:** a combination of malts and blended whiskies but with a high proportion of the former, e.g. Chivas Regal.

- **Blended whisky:** produced by the continuous distillation method, e.g. Bell's. Some branded blended whiskies may contain a proportion of malt to achieve a house style. Johnnie Walker's distinctive smoky notes are due to a proportion of Islay malts within the blend.

Spirits from each whisky-producing country have distinct characters. However, the greatest regional distinctions are found in Scotland. The whiskies produced on each island of the Inner and Outer Hebrides have unique and prized characteristics, for example. In general, four main regions are recognised in Scotland with the following key characteristics.

- Islay & Skye – peaty and maritime

- Highlands – smooth and floral

- Speyside – fruity and delicate

- Lowlands – light and fresh

WHY THE PRICE VARIES

LABELLING

Many countries make excellent-quality whiskies but cheaper whisky can be produced by avoiding the 'Scotch Whisky' designation. Whisky (rather than specifically Scotch whisky) has no minimum ageing requirement and can be made with less costly neutral spirits, but it will be harsher on the palette. In the US, blended whiskey can also contain neutral spirits (95 per cent alcohol produced from repeated distilling) and flavourings.

INGREDIENTS

The proportion of malt whisky in a bottle, together with the quality of barley and purity of water used, will affect price.

AGE

The longer a producer has to keep the whisky maturing in a barrel, the more expensive it will be, not least as volume is lost to the angels.

PRODUCTION METHOD

The part of the distillate used has a significant bearing on price. The heart of the distillation yields the finest spirit; using more of the 'feints' (the heads and tails of the distillation) gives a far lower cost, poorer flavoured spirit. There is also a price differential between whisky made in smaller quantities using pot stills or in larger volumes in a column still. The type of cask used also affects cost.

Lower quality spirits have been blamed for giving worse hangovers because they contain more 'congeners', which is the term for impurities and other types of alcohol created through the fermentation and distilling process. It is believed that lower quality ingredients and a shorter distilling process lead to the resulting whisky containing a higher proportion of congeners, which act as toxins for the body and cause problems on the morning-after-the-night-before.

TRY BEFORE YOU DIE!

—

When I left university, I wanted to be either a pro golfer or a marine archaeologist. My dear old dad gently suggested that perhaps I should consider getting 'a proper job'. He was right of course. If I'm honest, I've never had the physique to be a diver and I just wasn't good enough to be a professional golfer. I do still love the game, though. And not just the game itself but everything that goes with it.

I'm thinking in particular of Gleneagles' whisky room adjacent to the famous golf course in Perthshire. Owned by the company that makes Johnnie Walker, the Blue Bar is the showcase for Johnnie Walker Blue Label whisky. With heated leather sofas, luxurious throws and a large circular firepit, it's the perfect place to relax, particularly after you have played 18 holes.

The bar, which is outdoor but undercover, is invitation only and, for those who partake, has a wonderful range of Cuban cigars, too.

For home drinking I would recommend:

SPEYSIDE:
GLENFIDDICH SNOW PHOENIX
£££££

In January 2010, unprecedented snowfall covered the remote warehouse roofs of the Glenfiddich Speyside Distillery, which subsequently collapsed. The precious casks were under heavy snow and exposed to the elements for several days. Fearing the worst, the Malt Master was taken aback when he tasted the spirit and was inspired to bottle these few barrels as a limited release. The final blend was bottled at 47.6 per cent as a combination from the oloroso sherry and bourbon casks affected by the snow, and shows an unusually vibrant nose, with honey and chocolate on the palate, followed by sherry notes through the long, mellow finish. The few bottles that remain can fetch anything up to £400 at auction.

ISLAY:
LAPHROAIG QUARTER CASK
££

This whisky harks to an old tradition of maturation in smaller casks, which has the double advantage of imparting greater richness of flavour and allowing the smugglers of old to move casks more easily via donkey or mule. Laphroaig malts are famous for their overt peaty character and these classic notes are married with toffee and caramel on the nose with a full palate of fruitcake and spice followed by a long, smoky, rich finish.

LOWLAND:
AUCHENTOSHAN 21 YEAR OLD
££££

Auchentoshan is unusual in triple-distilling its spirits to produce sweeter, more delicate flavours than many Scotch whiskies. This 21-year-old single malt has been aged in second-fill sherry casks, creating soft fruity notes on the nose with a citrus twist, followed by a very floral palate with honey notes and a hint of nuttiness. It has a full, long finish with apricot conserve flavours and dry citrus notes.

Beer

Beer has been a big part of our lives throughout history. Egyptian pyramid workers were paid in the stuff, at the rate of 1 gallon per day. In the Middle Ages it was more widely drunk than water, since it was viewed as safer than water, which usually came from filthy sources. President George Washington had his own brewery in the grounds of Mount Vernon. There is even a medical term for fear of an empty beer glass – cenosillicaphobia, since you ask. But how much do we really know about this most ubiquitous of drinks?

A BRIEF HISTORY

BEER IS ONE of the world's oldest drinks, possibly dating back to the early Neolithic period, or 9500 BC, when cereals were first farmed. References certainly exist in the written histories of ancient Iraq and ancient Egypt. Early Sumerian writings contain references to beer, including a prayer that served as a method of remembering its recipe in a culture with few literate people. A fermented drink made with rice and fruit was made in China as early as 7000 BC.

Beer-making most probably didn't spread via human migration; most cultures developed beer independently. One by one it was recognised that a sweet liquid could be obtained from a starch and that almost any substance containing sugar can naturally undergo alcoholic fermentation.

Consumption of beer spread through Europe via tribes in Gaul and Germania as far back as 3000 BC, although their version of beer might not be recognised by modern standards. These early European beers contained fruits, honey, spices and herbs. Hops were not mentioned in Europe until around AD 822.

In 1516, William IV, Duke of Bavaria, adopted the *Reinheitsgebot* (purity law) for beer, which is perhaps the oldest food-quality regulation still in use in the twenty-first century. According to this law, only water, hops and barley-malt are permitted for beer production.

During the Industrial Revolution, beer moved to being produced on an industrialised scale. The advent of accurate hydrometers and thermometers allowed more control of the process and greater certainty of the results. Quality and consistency went up.

Today, beer is manufactured and consumed in nearly every country in the world. Roughly 130 billion litres of beer are produced and sold each year. China is the biggest consumer, with a market roughly twice that of the next in line, the USA.

GEOGRAPHY

Although beer is produced around the world, several countries and specific areas have a particularly rich tradition in brewing and have also concentrated on some iconic styles of beer, including:

- **Czech Republic and Germany** – pilsner style

- **Belgium and Germany** – wheat beers

- **Belgium** – lambic beers, using naturally occurring yeasts

- **England** – India pale ale (IPA), a style created to survive the long voyage to colonial India

- **London** – classic dark porter and stout

- **Dublin** – Guinness

- **USA** – modern craft beers (many based upon Belgian beers or India pale ale)

HOW BEER IS PRODUCED

BASIC INGREDIENTS ARE water, a starch source (usually malted barley), yeast and a flavouring (usually hops).

Like whisky, the malting process is achieved by soaking grain in water and 'fooling it' into partially germinating. It is then dried in a kiln and this process produces enzymes, which convert the starches in the grains into sugars that can be fermented. Different malting times and temperatures are used to produce different colours of malt from the same grain. Darker malts produce darker beers.

The starch source is converted into the wort (a sugary liquid) by the addition of hot water, known as liquor by brewers. This process of converting the starch into sugar (called mashing) lasts up to two hours and is carried out in a mash tun. The sweet wort is then drained off and the grains washed to extract as much fermentable liquid as possible. This is known as sparging and in large-scale breweries is a continuous process, collecting progressively weaker wort, which will, in turn, produce weaker beer.

The sugary wort is now transferred into a kettle (usually made of copper) and boiled for roughly one hour, which allows some water to evaporate and concentrates the sugars. Hops are usually added at this stage to impart both flavour and bitterness to balance the sweetness of the wort. The longer the boiling process, the more bitterness is extracted from the hops and the less aroma and flavour remains in the final beer.

The hopped wort is now cooled in preparation for the addition of yeast. The subsequent fermentation transforms wort into beer and this process can last from a week to months, depending on the yeast strain and alcoholic strength of the beer. The by-products of fermentation are ethanol and the particulate matter from the spent yeast, which settles, leaving the beer clear.

Once fermentation is complete, the beer is ready for packaging in casks, kegs, glass bottles or aluminium cans. A small proportion of beers are aged before being packaged, either in stainless steel tanks or oak casks where some oak character and complexity may be part of the beer's style.

The beer's taste will be influenced by:

WATER
As the main constituent of beer, regional differences in water mineral content mean there are geographic differences that suit certain styles and therefore give a regional character to the end product. Dublin has hard water, which suits stout production. The waters of Burton upon Trent contain high quantities of gypsum, and so lend themselves to pale ale production. Plzeň in the Czech Republic has soft water, which is well-suited to making the pilsner (lager) style.

STARCH SOURCE
Starch contributes to the ultimate alcoholic strength and flavour of beer. Malted grain is the most common starch source and barley is the most common cereal used. However, there are many regions in the world where alternatives are used, such as wheat, rice, oats and rye. Sorghum, which is widely grown in Africa, as well as cassava root are other sources, as is potato in Brazil and agave in Mexico and the Pacific. Agave has proved an interesting source for brewers seeking to produce gluten-free beers.

The amount of each starch source in a beer recipe is termed 'the grain bill'.

FLAVOURING

The only real commercial use for the flower of the hop vine is to flavour beer. Other than the orchard or forest fruits used to produce fruit beers, hops are the main flavouring used in beer production, imparting a bitterness that balances the sweetness from the malt. Different varieties are grown all over the world and can result in widely varying flavours in the final beer. Hops also act as a preservative.

YEAST

Individual yeast strains have a unique influence upon the brewing process and therefore impart very specific flavour characteristics to the final beer. Yeast occurs throughout the natural environment, so most brewers are particularly concerned with maintaining a specific strain and consider this part of the heritage of each of their individual brews. Indeed, UK brewers guarantee the purity and sustainability of each strain by maintaining a core sample at the National Collection of Yeast Cultures in Norwich.

WHY THE PRICE VARIES

INGREDIENTS

Cheap or low-quality ingredients: water, malt and particularly hops have the greatest bearing on price. Secondary starch sources, such as maize, rice or sugar, as a lower-cost substitute for malted barley can produce cheaper beers.

FERMENTATION

Slow and careful fermentation produces a beer with more depth of flavour and texture; a quick fermentation produces a less-flavoured brew. Many premium producers also allow their beers to age for a period of time (some brewers, such as Fuller's and Innis & Gunn, have oak-aged styles) to impart particular flavours and textures as well as to allow better homogenisation. The cost and extra time involved preclude cheaper beers from undergoing this process.

REGIONAL VARIATION

The best beers can claim as much provenance as good wines. No matter what the style, seek out beers tied to a region and country of origin, rather than those brewed 'under licence' to a recipe. For me, the best Guinness is served in Dublin.

TRY BEFORE YOU DIE!

—

I suspect any recommendations I make will be hotly contested and so I picked four expensive and extravagant beers and my favourite three in the UK.

My personal favourites first:

FULLER'S LONDON PRIDE
££

To sink one in a London pub at the end of a busy day is a joy. Brewed by Fuller's since the 1950s on the banks of the Thames in Chiswick, this delicious beer was named after a small flower dubbed 'London Pride' when it grew up through the rubble after the Blitz.

BODDINGTONS
£

Boddingtons was my beer of choice when I was a student. Back then, in the late 1970s, Boddington & Co was an independent Manchester brewery and it produced the creamiest, loveliest pint. It is now produced by global drinks giant AB Inbev, but still from its Lancashire home.

TANGLEFOOT BADGER BEER
£

Brewed by Hall and Woodhouse in Blandford, Dorset, this is a golden ale with hints of melon and pear. It got its unusual name when the head brewer tasted it with his team, stood up to go and realised his dog had wrapped its lead all around his feet.

And the more extravagant:

THE END OF HISTORY
£££££

Scottish brewery BrewDog released its 55 per cent alcohol End of History beer, which came encased in the skin of a dead squirrel or stoat, in 2010. Only 11 bottles of this blond Belgian ale, named after a book by political economist Francis Fukuyama, were produced. It was made using nettles from the Scottish Highlands and fresh juniper berries and was said at the time to be BrewDog's last high alcohol by volume (abv) beer.

ANTARCTIC NAIL ALE
£££££

Antarctic Nail Ale is a 4.6 per cent, limited-edition, Australian pale ale made from water melted from a block of Antarctic ice. It was released in 2010 by Jarrah Jacks brewery in Pemberton. The ice was collected by the crew of a Sea Shepherd ship, by helicopter, from an iceberg in the Southern Ocean. The ice was then flown to Tasmania, melted and transported to Western Australia. Only 30 bottles were produced.

JACOBSEN VINTAGE
£££££

Danish brewers Carlsberg released its three vintages in 2008, producing fewer than 1,000 bottles of each variety. Vintage No.1 was aged in Swedish and French oak barrels, and filled just 600 bottles. Jens Eiken, head brewer at Jacobsen, said the project began as a wild idea and a wish to create a new type of beer that had never been tasted before.

He said, 'During the ageing process in new barrels, lots of chemical processes take place. Not all reactions are known but they taste wonderful.'

Each bottle is labelled with an original, hand-stilled lithographic print by Danish artist Frans Kannik. The beer is mainly sold to collectors and through three upscale restaurants in Copenhagen, Denmark.

SINK THE BISMARCK
£££££

Sink the Bismarck was an attempt by Scotland's BrewDog – yes, them again – to take the title of world's strongest beer from Schorschbräu. Sink the Bismarck did hold the title briefly before it was lost to its German rival. BrewDog describes it as a 'quadruple IPA' that contains four times the hops, four times the bitterness and is freeze distilled four times to produce a 41 per cent abv.

Cider

My family home is in Dorset and my wife is a huge fan of Thomas Hardy, the author who wrote so extensively and evocatively about this wonderful county. In Hardy's Dorset there would have been an apple orchard and cider press on almost every farm. Cider even formed part of a farmworker's wages. Sadly, for a long while cider fell out of favour and many of the orchards were grubbed out. In recent years, though, it has seen somewhat of a revival, not just in Dorset, but elsewhere too, although nothing like the scale of the glory years. There is a growing network of commercial producers not only making cider, but in some cases rediscovering old apple varieties with wonderful, resonating names such as Buttery Door, Dabinet and Yarlington.

A BRIEF HISTORY

PEOPLE HAVE known how to make cider for thousands of years. Archaeological evidence shows that in ancient Europe and Asia a crude version of cider was made as early as 6500 BC. During the sixth century, the profession of brewing was established in Europe to make beer and cider.

It is believed that apples were first introduced into Britain during the Roman invasion. Army veterans were given settlements on which to grow fruits as an inducement to stay. However, not until the Norman Conquest of 1066 is there any significant mention of cider-making. The Normans had a strong tradition of apple-growing and cider-making and introduced many types of apple to Britain.

By the sixteenth century, Normandy had become one of the largest cider-making areas in the world. Cider was also produced in America during this time and the drink became an important part of each culture where the practice thrived. Through the passing of time, experimentation with apple varieties and improvements in technology have led to the consistent high quality we enjoy today.

GEOGRAPHY

THE **UK HAS** the highest per capita consumption of cider in the world and therefore, not surprisingly, the largest cider-producing companies. The drink is also popular in other European countries including Ireland, France (in particular Brittany and Normandy), and northern Spain and the Basque country. Central Europe has its own types of cider, and Germans in Rhineland-Palatinate and Hesse drink a particularly tart version known as *apfelwein*.

HOW CIDER IS PRODUCED

A **FULL-BODIED** cider requires the use of several different types of apples to give it a balanced flavour. There are four different types of apple juices: aromatic, astringent, acid-tart and neutral tasting. Generally, sweet and tart apples are blended together to make cider and a typical blend might therefore include 50 per cent neutral base, 20 per cent tart, 20 per cent aromatic and 10 per cent astringent. Some cider producers may also improve flavour by adding tannic, malic and other natural acids. Tannins add a slightly bitter taste and astringency while malic, citric and tartaric acids give a zesty tingle. They also help to inhibit microbial contamination.

To produce 100 litres of cider requires roughly 120kg of apples. The skin of the apples contains many of the compounds that contribute to the taste so apples are not peeled before being used. The seeds are not removed either; however, in typical milling machines, they are not broken open and do not significantly contribute to taste. Once the apples have been juiced, fermentation begins naturally, or yeast is added to achieve a house style. This converts the apple sugars into ethyl alcohol and carbon dioxide in two steps. First, yeast converts the sugar to alcohol and then lactic acid bacteria convert the natural malic acid into carbon dioxide. The resulting cider contains 2–3 per cent solids and 2–8 per cent alcohol. Sulphur dioxide is usually added to the freshly pressed juice before fermentation to kill most of the bacteria.

To help yeasts grow and speed-up fermentation, yeast nutrients, such as ammonium sulphate and thiamine, may be added. For similar reasons, extra sugar, honey or other sweeteners may also be added to improve fermentation and increase the alcohol content if needed.

Individual varieties of each type of apple used to be common and have much regional significance in the UK, but many of these have sadly declined in popularity and very few examples now exist. Cider apples that currently have significant plantings in the UK are:

Flavour	Variety
Bittersweet	Harry Masters Jersey, Foxwhelp, Black Dabinett, Yarlington Mill, Tremlett's Bitter
Sharp	Frederick, Fair Maid of Devon, Crimson King, Brown's Apple
Bittersharp	Stoke Red, Ashton Brown Jersey
Sweet	Dunkertons Late, Sweet Coppin, Court Royal

WHY THE PRICE VARIES

APPLES

Nearly all of the characteristics of the final cider depend on the quality of the apples. To produce the best cider, these apples must be juicy, sweet, well ripened and have adequate levels of natural acids and tannins.

CONCENTRATE OR FRESH JUICE

Mass-produced cider brands invariably use apple-juice concentrate, either in part or in totality. It is rehydrated but makes for a poorer base material than fresh juice. The obvious comparative here is the clear difference in flavour and texture between freshly squeezed orange juice and orange juice from concentrate.

FERMENTATION

Slow, careful fermentation at a lower temperature will produce a more aromatic cider with more depth of flavour and texture than quick fermentation, which will produce a lesser quality cider. Many premium producers also allow their ciders to age for a period of time (traditionally in oak casks) in order to encourage better flavour and texture homogenisation, but the cost and cash-flow implications preclude cheaper ciders from undergoing this process.

REGIONALITY

Like wine, the best ciders can claim a particular provenance around the quality of their ingredients or the skill of the artisan cider-maker and therefore command a higher price. I always try to look for ciders that are produced in the same region or country where their key ingredients, fresh apples, are grown.

TRY BEFORE YOU DIE!

—

MASHINO WINERY APPLE WINE
££££

This producer in the Nagano Prefecture, Japan, crafts 'wine' from both grapes and apples. Mashino's apple wine is one of the most expensive in the world due to the cost of the primary fruit in a country where agricultural land is very expensive. Like all Japanese ciders, this has a sake-like hint and a clean, refreshing palate despite being 10 per cent alcohol.

ASHRIDGE SPARKLING VINTAGE BRUT CIDER
£££££

Made like a traditional-method sparkling wine from several varieties of bittersweet and sharp apples grown in Devon, this is really a cross between a cider and a sparkling wine. The 7.5 per cent alcohol is balanced and bottle-conditioning gives this cider a lovely texture with fine bubbles and a clean, crisp finish.

ASPALL IMPERIAL VINTAGE CYDER
££

The Chevallier family started making cyder (their spelling) at Aspall Hall in Suffolk in 1728 and their brand is one of the most respected in the world of cider. Their Imperial Vintage has muscovado sugar added as part of the recipe, which adds hints of smoke, peat, malt and molasses to the ripe apple notes. The taste is particularly amazing when matched with the best British blue cheese. The year 2013 marked the 285th vintage and this format is commemorated on each consecutive vintage label.

CRISPIN 'THE SAINT' ARTISANAL RESERVE CIDER
£££

The craft cider movement is gaining momentum in the United States and this is one of the best examples, which comes from Minneapolis, Minnesota. It is fermented using Belgian Trappist beer yeasts to create a yeasty, herbal complexity. A small amount of organic maple syrup is added for mouth feel. It is full-bodied at 6.9 per cent alcohol, yet clean and refreshing.

Olive Oil

When I was a child, my food world was, I think, relatively wide. My father was from south Wales so we were familiar with laverbread and cockles and other traditional Welsh foods. My mother was from Cumbria and she had distant relatives in farming; and, living in the heart of rural Cheshire, we always had fresh cheeses and eggs, not to mention a cracking turkey every Christmas, and of course the annual hamper. One thing we never ever had, however, was olive oil. Olive oil was then sold in chemists for some reason. The only Olives I knew were a friend of my mother's, and Popeye's wife.

I didn't go abroad until I was 19. I was reading archaeology and ancient history at Lancaster University, an interest fostered by childhood visits to Chester – an area of great importance during the Roman occupation of Britain. After my first year of studying, I travelled to Rome to spend the summer. I was working on archaeological finds but my trip was as educational about Italian cuisine as it was about ancient history. Rome was a mind-blowing revelation. The pasta, the sauces, the amazing variety of vegetables, the ice cream, the coffee, the grappa – all the things the Italians do so well. I was determined to try everything and over the course of that summer, and successive summers in Assisi and Gravina, I had a pretty good go at it. It was during these long, glorious Italian trips that I finally embraced olive oil. It was a visit to a picturesque olive grove in the north of the country, to see at first hand the skill of the artisan producer and then taste various oils, that made me a convert. A little like wine, there is a degree of complexity to understanding what you are buying when shopping for olive oil.

There are so many olive-oil labels it can be baffling. Are 'extra virgin', 'virgin' or 'olive oil' in descending order of quality? What's the difference between 'commercial' or 'estate-bottled'? Which is best for cooking with and which ones make the best vinaigrettes when you blend in mustard and vinegar?

It's helpful to begin with a little history to understand the origins of the best.

A BRIEF HISTORY

THE OLIVE IS commonly thought to have spread from Iran, Syria and Palestine to the rest of the Mediterranean basin around 6,000 years ago. Shrub-like 'feral' olives still exist in the Middle East and represent the original stock from which it is believed all other olives are descended.

The olive is among the oldest known cultivated trees in the world. Records show olives were grown on Crete by 3000 BC and were the source of the wealth of the Minoan kingdom. Athens is named after the goddess Athena who, legend says, brought the olive to the Greeks as a gift. Zeus had promised to give Attica to the god or goddess who made the most useful invention. Athena's gift of the olive, useful for light, heat, food, medicine and perfume, was picked. Athena then planted the original olive tree on a rocky hill that we know today as the Acropolis. The olive tree that grows there today is said to have come from the roots of the original tree.

From Greece the olive spread to southern Europe and North Africa. Olives have been found in Egyptian tombs from 2000 BC and the olive trees on the Mount of Olives in Jerusalem are reputed to be over 2,000 years old. Olives were later taken to central and northern Europe by the Romans.

In the past several hundred years, olive growing has spread to North and South America, Japan, New Zealand and Australia.

GEOGRAPHY

LIKE VINES, olive trees grow best when they are subjected to some stress. They like a little cold over the winter to kill bugs and a little heat in the summer to make their fruit ripen. They do not like too much of either, though. Therefore the ideal climate for growing olives is found around the Mediterranean.

Different varieties of olives are grown in different countries and, just as different grapes produce various styles of wine, so olives make a range of oils. The soil and climate also contribute to the final taste and aromas, as do harvesting and pressing.

HOW OLIVE OIL IS PRODUCED

DEPENDING ON variety, olive trees start fruiting about four years after planting and reach full production after about ten years. Trees can live for over a thousand years.

For the best-quality virgin olive oils, olives are harvested at exactly the right stage of ripeness (overripe olives can produce oil that is rancid) and then washed.

Next, they are ground into paste. The traditional method uses large millstones, but steel drums are now used, too. Judging the right amount of time for grinding is key; too short a time and the oil will have a less ripe taste, too long and flavour is lost because of increased oxidation.

After grinding, the olive paste is spread on fibre disks, which are stacked on top of each other in a column, then placed into the press. Pressure is applied to the column to separate the oil from the paste. When a steel drum is being used, in more modern production, the paste is slowly stirred and microscopic oil drops unite into bigger drops before mechanical extraction. In both cases, this liquid still contains significant amounts of water.

Olive oil should not contain significant traces of water as this speeds up the degeneration of the oil. Traditionally, oil was separated from residual water by gravity, since oil is less dense. This very slow separation process has been replaced by centrifugation, which is not just faster but more thorough, too. The centrifuges have one exit for the (heavier) watery part of the liquid and one for the oil. The separation in smaller oil mills that don't do this is not always perfect, and sometimes a small watery deposit containing organic particles can be found at the bottom of oil bottles.

Only oil produced by this physical method can be called virgin oil. Oils that do not reach the legal standards to be classified as 'Virgin' go through a refining process, which gives a clear tasteless product. To get technical for a moment, 'Virgin olive oils' have to have a free acidity (oleic acid content) of less than 2g per 100g. 'Extra virgin olive oils' have a free acidity of less than 0.8g per 100g. Additionally, to be extra virgin olive oils, they have to be tasted by a panel and be clear of any taste defects.

Sometimes you might see a label that says 'filtered olive oil', which is typically done to remove any remaining bits that can reduce shelf life. Unfiltered fresh olive oil has a slightly cloudy appearance and is called 'cloudy olive oil'.

The remaining paste (pomace) still contains a small quantity of oil, which cannot be extracted by further pressing, so chemical solvents are used. This is done in specialised chemical plants, not in oil mills. The resulting oil is not 'virgin' but 'pomace oil'.

The term 'first press', sometimes found on bottle labels, is pretty meaningless today as there is no 'second' press. It is a throwback to ancient times of stone presses, when virgin oil was produced by battering the olives.

When the label of extra virgin olive oils says 'cold-extraction', it means that the olive grinding and stirring was done at a maximum temperature of 25°C. Processing at higher temperatures risks decreasing the olive oil's quality, texture, taste and aroma.

Given that northern hemisphere olives are harvested and pressed in October and January, they will in all likelihood need to be warmed to extract the oil effectively. Olives being pressed in warmer climates won't need to be heated, but they are still considered cold pressed as they are pressed at less than 25°C.

Extra virgin olive oils are either 'commercial' or 'estate-bottled'. Commercial oils are blended to a standard and price. Estate-bottled oils come from specific farms and from specific varieties of olives.

Pure, classic, light and extra-light are terms introduced by marketeers to help customers understand the varying strength of taste. They are nothing to do with calorific content.

TASTING

OLIVE OIL IS a little like wine; you should taste to find what you like. Pour some oil into a dark, stemless tasting glass. (Dark glass is used so you are not influenced by the colour. There is a general misconception that dark-green oils are the best.) Warm the glass in one hand while covering the top with your other hand, to trap the aromas. Release the aromas and take a good sniff. Then take a good slug of it. Suck in some air to dissipate the oil around your mouth. Finally, swallow the oil to get the final taste sensations at the back of the mouth.

WHY THE PRICE VARIES

DESIGNATION

If it is commercial, it is likely your olive oil is a blend of oils from more than one country; even if the label indicates 'Extra Virgin' and says that the oil was bottled or packed in a stated country, it does not necessarily mean that the oil was produced there.

If the oil is expensive, has a smart bottle and displays the name of the producer, it is likely to be 'estate-bottled' from a particular country, specific region and farm, made with often specified varieties of olive. These oils are good for finishing dishes as a condiment over hot food or for mixing with lemon juice, or good wine vinegar, for a salad dressing.

INGREDIENTS

Aside from being a blend from different regions, it has been alleged that not all extra virgin olive oils are 100 per cent the juice of the olive. A book published in 2013, *Extra Virginity* by Tom Mueller, gives the full details of these alleged malpractices, which include adding chlorophyll to sunflower and soybean oil, or labelling non-virgin oil as extra virgin.

AGE

Look at the best before date: estate-bottled oils should really be used within 18 months or so of harvest, and you can often work out when the trees were harvested from this date. In the northern hemisphere, this will be from October to January; in the southern hemisphere, from April to June. Older oils will not harm you, but they will have lost some of their zing.

Buy from retailers that have quite a good turnover in oil. Most good oils are stored in dark bottles now, as light detracts from the flavours of oil, but even so, if an oil has been on the shelf or under a spotlight for ages, it will not be at its best.

PRODUCTION METHOD

The care with which olives are harvested and transported is critical to the fruit's quality. Ground fruit is second-class and should be separated from tree fruit for the best oils. Fruit should be processed soon after harvest as oxidation and fermentation begin once the olives are picked. Left too long and you will get off flavours in the oil. Processing at the right time and temperature and good storage after processing permit proper ageing and conserve the flavour.

TRY BEFORE YOU DIE!

—

Here are four estate-bottled oils that should prove useful to have up and running in your kitchen at any one time:

FRESCOBALDI LAUDEMIO
££££

From Tuscany try Frescobaldi Laudemio, made by a famous wine-producing family. It is made from three varieties of olive, Frantoio, Leccino and Moraiolo, which produce an intense oil with sweet meadow grass flavours at first, going on to a walnut-skin bitterness, and then to a green-peppercorn finish. Beautifully balanced, it is produced under the auspices of the Laudemio consorzio, which guarantees provenance and quality. This is a powerful oil, perfect to pour over slices of barbecued steak or to dress a Tuscan bean soup.

MORGENSTER ESTATE MONTE MARCELLO
££

For more delicate dishes you need a lighter oil than the Frescobaldi. In a good year, I love oils from Liguria made with the Taggiasca olive, but they can be quite variable in quality. So, why not see if you can find a 'new-world' version, for example Morgenster Estate's Monte Marcello. This is made by Giulio Bertrand, an Italian with a passion for Italian varieties of olive trees, which he planted on his estate near Cape Town, South Africa. His 'everyday' oil is delicious, and so too is his Monte Marcello. If you can't find it, try Alziari from Nice, which has all the characteristics of an oil from that region; it is light and delicate, with aromas of ripe avocado and ripe bananas, with a touch of creamy almond at the finish.

CASTELAS, FRUITÉ NOIR
££££

From the Vallée des Baux in Provence I have selected a slightly eccentric oil made by Jean-Benoît Hugues. It is made in the style traditional to that area. After harvesting, the producer leaves the olives to ferment under controlled conditions for a few days, which results in a sweet, richly flavoured oil with the aroma of black olives and flavour of mushrooms. Technically, this aroma is a 'fault', so it is not allowed to be called extra virgin, only virgin, but it is delicious. Try it on a goat's cheese and beetroot salad or stirred into potatoes lightly crushed with green olives.

COLONNA GRANVERDE LEMON OIL
££££

Colonna Granverde's lemon-flavoured olive oil is an essential addition to any store cupboard. On his farm in the Molise, central Italy, the late Prince Francesco Colonna used to throw some lemons from the tree growing outside his front door into the press as the last of the year's harvest of olives was being processed. This had two purposes: to start the cleaning process of the machinery and to produce a wonderful lemon-scented olive oil. He used it to dress a piece of grilled fish, to anoint steamed green vegetables or to mix with balsamic vinegar as a dressing. Now this wonderful oil is produced by his daughter, Marina Colonna, who has taken over the farm.

Crisps

You may think it a little odd for crisps to have a chapter in this book. They do so for two reasons: I have eaten a lot of them and I suspect you have too! Several years ago I had a 'road to Damascus' crisp moment, having eaten the same well-known brand with my lunch for more years than I can remember. I was at a charity event and was offered some crisps during pre-dinner drinks. They were artisan, hand-cooked crisps and everything about them was a revelation: taste, texture and quality. The humble crisp took on a new status in my mind. All crisps are definitely not the same.

The discovery took me on a journey to understand what made the perfect crisp and why some cost more than others.

A BRIEF HISTORY

THE **VERY FIRST** potato chips were created in Saratoga Springs, New York, by Moon Lake House chef George Crum in 1853. Frustrated by a customer rejecting his fries for being 'too thick', the chef reacted by frying paper-thin slices of potato to make them impossible to eat with a fork. To Crum's surprise, the customer was delighted with his accidental invention and word of this delicious new discovery soon spread.

During the twentieth century the development of mass-produced crisps proceded apace with several manufacturers establishing themselves around 1910. Initially, crisps were sold from markets, scooped out of glass bins into wax-paper bags. The introduction of cellophane really allowed the market to take off, enabling crisps to be well preserved and not crushed.

Smith's in London were the first company to try adding a pinch of salt as seasoning but it wasn't perfected until the 1950s when Joe 'Spud' Murphy, owner of Irish company Tayto, found a way to add seasoning in the production process.

The Pringle-style potato chip was launched in 1967, but caused controversy by containing only 42 per cent potato, the remainder being made up from a variety of other types of flour (wheat, maize, rice).

HOW CRISPS ARE PRODUCED

THERE ARE SEVERAL thousand varieties of potato in the world, all with different characteristics suiting them to different uses. Potato variety is critical to making a top-quality tasty crisp. Crisping potato varieties are generally selected for high dry-matter content, which enables them to fry well. Lady Claire and Lady Rosetta are most commonly used in crisp production but there are many others, including 'chipping' potatoes for chunkier crisps, which some producers believe cook better.

The perfect potato has a high starch content and a low 'reducing sugar' content. It is the 'reducing sugars' (glucose and fructose) that give darker brown colours during frying and a better taste.

The skill of the growers is to stop crop growth and prepare for harvest at just the right moment. In the northern hemisphere, potatoes are picked from July to October. The grower then grades the potatoes. The intention is to remove potatoes that are too small or too big. Removal of small potatoes is important because they are generally immature, discolour easily, cook unevenly and produce a mass of small bits when sliced. Large potatoes have the opposite problem and they may well be too big to pass down into packing machines.

The next job is to store potatoes correctly in high-tech, temperature-controlled warehouses where CO_2 levels and humidity are regulated to monitor sugar and starch levels so the crop can be kept for up to ten months.

Slicing is the crucial step in producing a fantastic crisp; the more starch in the potato, the thinner it can be sliced. But, if the crisp is sliced too thinly, it will fold over once fried. Even slicing ensures the crisps are evenly cooked, breakages are reduced and taste is consistent.

Potato slices are then put in a fryer where oil is heated to around 150 to 180°C. This reduces the moisture from more than 70 per cent down to around 1.6 per cent. The oil replaces the water in the potato to produce a crisp. Hand-cooked crisps will be fried in batches, while mass-produced crisps will be on a continuous flow through the fryer.

If the frying temperature is too high, the slices may become overcooked and brittle. If too low, the slices will be soft and unpleasant to eat. For such a simple product, making crisps is an exact science!

WHY THE PRICE VARIES

INGREDIENTS

Less expensive and poorer quality crisps are made from a wide range of potato varieties, many of which are not necessarily perfect for crisp production. Quality crisps tend to be cooked in sunflower oil, which has higher oleate levels than other oils. This helps to manage the cooking consistency. Lower quality crisps may be cooked in standard vegetable oil, or a blend of different oils, which makes it hard to know how old the oil is and so to manage the lifespan of the crisps. Inferior (lower cost) crisps often have artificial flavours and additives, such as monosodium glutamate (MSG), which are cheaper than real food ingredients but deliver strong flavours.

PRODUCTION METHOD

Hand-cooked crisps are cooked in small batches with experts moving the crisps in the fryer to ensure even coverage of oil. Mass-produced crisps are made in a continuous frying process that requires little human intervention.

PACKAGING

Packaging is cheaper and less robust in less expensive versions. This means the crisps are less well protected from crushing and won't stay fresh for as long. More expensive, metallised, laminated packaging helps protect crisps during transportation, provides a barrier to oxygenation and sunlight, and stops crisps going rancid.

CONSISTENCY

To ensure consistency, some manufacturers use dedicated potato growers, whereas others will buy on the open market. Committing to the former is more costly.

TRY BEFORE YOU DIE!

–

SAN NICASIO POTATO CRISPS
£££

My absolute favourites are San Nicasio potato crisps, produced in the Andalusian olive-growing area of Spain. A premium variety of Spanish potato is used, the 'Agria', which is a natural, not genetically modified variety that gives a unique taste. The chips are cooked in 100 per cent extra virgin olive oil. They are flavoured with Himalayan pink salt, low in sodium and exceptionally pure, which does not saturate or diminish the taste of San Nicasio chips. The bag has been designed to ensure the crisps are never crushed. They say you can put a 100kg weight on it and your crisps will still be fine, but that's an experiment I wouldn't want to try. They sell for around three times the price of an everyday bag of crisps.

TORRES BLACK TRUFFLE CHIPS
£££££

This is a relatively new variety from a company started by a Spanish couple in 1969 in the small Catalonian seaside town of Premià de Mar. Their crisps were so good that demand grew and their children expanded the business. They now export internationally but have the same dedication to artisanal production, using the best ingredients.

The crisps are made from the highest calibre potatoes, grown in some of the best gardens on the Iberian peninsula. The altitude and climatic and geological conditions make a high-quality potato, which helps make excellent crisps.

TYRRELLS
££

Established by a Herefordshire farmer in 2002, Tyrrells uses only English potatoes grown in Herefordshire. The crisps are hand-cooked with their skins on, to give extra flavour, and are 'spun' to get rid of excess oil.

KETTLE CHIPS
££

Lastly, Kettle Chips were inspired by some hand-fried potato chips the founder, Cameron Healy, tasted on a beach in Hawaii. Once home, he recreated the simple process and launched Kettle Chips in 1982. The crisps are hand-cooked in sunflower oil, with thicker slices than other crisps, and seasonings made with authentic ingredients.

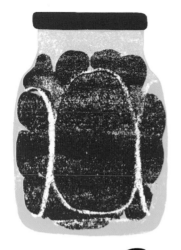

Conserves and Marmalades

From my earliest days I can remember my mother making jams and marmalade; fruit and sugar would simmer in a large pan for what seemed like hours on end, releasing the most extraordinarily tempting sweet smells into the kitchen. Then, after much testing and tutting, the bubbling, brightly coloured contents were ladled into second-hand jars of all shapes and sizes. Lids were screwed tight and labels attached.

I particularly loved the sight of the jars lined up in neat rows on the kitchen table, bursting with big, chunky roughly cut berries, mainly collected from along country lanes, or marmalade made from oranges that had been sold off cheaply.

Sadly, fewer people make their own jam today, so here's my guide to why prices vary so much and the best ones to try.

A BRIEF HISTORY

THE EARLIEST surviving cookbook, *De re coquinaria* (*Of Culinary Matters*), dates back to first-century Rome and contained recipes for making jam. The preserve was also eaten in the Middle East where there was an abundance of sugar thanks to the introduction of cane from its natural habitat in India. In the Middle Ages, its popularity spread to Britain after Crusaders returning from the Middle East brought jams and recipes back with them. Later still, the Spanish took jam-making to the West Indies and the Americas.

Although the immigrants to America brought their own recipes with them, the first book on making jam appeared there in the seventeenth century. Early settlers in New England used molasses, honey and maple sugar to give their jams a sweet taste and pectin from boiling apple peel to thicken the mixture.

One of the main reasons for jam's rapid spread in popularity was that people who rarely saw fruit and veg in the winter months could now benefit from the vitamins in fruit all year round. Once it became known that vitamin C prevented scurvy, jam became a staple on ships. Fresh fruit did not last long, whereas jam lasted for the length of the trip.

Legend links the origin of marmalade to Mary, Queen of Scots. Supposedly, her physician mixed orange and sugar to help with her seasickness. Her attendants summoned the doctor saying: 'Marie est malade.' However, it seems more likely that the term marmalade came from the Portuguese '*marmelo*' meaning 'quince jam'. Marmalade was a firm favourite with some royals, though. Louis XIV of France had a variety of marmalades at his feasts, made from fruits grown in the palace gardens, which included pineapples and other exotic fruits.

HOW JAMS AND CONSERVES ARE PRODUCED

CONSERVES ARE straightforward to produce. Fruit, sugar, a large boiling pan and a few jars are all that is required to get started. Artisanal jams are still made this way today, while more commercial jams use the same principles, simply on a much larger scale.

To make jams to a consistently high standard, ingredients must be added in carefully measured amounts: 1 per cent pectin, 65 per cent sugar and an acid concentration of pH 3.1. Too much pectin will make the spread too hard, too much sugar will make it too sticky. That is really all you need to know! Clearly, large-scale production will reduce the price but this is not the main reason prices vary.

WHY THE PRICE VARIES

INGREDIENTS

The proportion, quality and freshness of the fruit that goes into jam make all the difference. Minimum fruit content in jams and marmalades is governed by international legislation and varies depending on the particular variety of fruit. Higher levels of fruit content do tend to give a better product. Traditionally, strawberry jam might be prepared with around 50g of fruit per 100g of jam, while pineapple jam might use as much as 85g of fruit per 100g of jam.

It's an obvious point to make, but top-quality conserves really do begin with top-quality fruit. Home-grown and nurtured as close to the factory as possible is best. Likewise, respected sources are better, such as Seville for marmalade oranges and Australia for ginger.

If you are after a top-quality product, look out for a simple ingredients list with fruit, sugar and perhaps a little natural pectin to help the set. There's no need for anything artificial in a conserve. A nice set with pieces of fruit visible is ideal in a jam, while a smooth, glossy finish is required in a jelly.

At the lower end of the spectrum, the ingredients list will include cheaper fruit, glucose syrup and artificial enhancers.

PRODUCTION METHOD

Cooking in small batches results in jam having the same consistency throughout. If jam is cooked in a very large vessel, fruit can float to the top, which leads to parts of the mix being runny while other parts are too thick.

Copper bottoms and copper pipework inside the boiling pan helps the fruit and sugar mix heat-up quickly. Steam passed through the copper pipes transfers heat very well and, as a result, jams need only be boiled for a brief period. This makes for the best possible jam.

TRY BEFORE YOU DIE!

–

DUTRIEZ BAR-LE-DUC
£££££

This hand-seeded redcurrant jam has earned the intriguing soubriquet of the 'most expensive jam in the world'. It is made in Bar-le-Duc, a town in north-east France that has been making fine jam and preserves for grandees of the world for 700 years, winning plaudits from famous people across centuries, including Mary, Queen of Scots, who called it a 'ray of sunshine in a jar'.

What makes this product so special is that normally it is not possible to make redcurrant jam without including unappetising seeds. Extracting the juice to make a jelly is a pretty straightforward business, but a jam contains the skin and flesh of the fruits. So, sometime in the fourteenth century, local monks had the idea of removing the seeds of redcurrants before making the jam. One by one, with a goose quill.

TIPTREE LITTLE SCARLET STRAWBERRY CONSERVE
££

Tiptree Little Scarlet Strawberry Conserve has to be the signature English jam. It's even James Bond's jam of choice, as we learn in Ian Fleming's *From Russia With Love*. The Little Scarlet variety of strawberry has been grown for over a hundred years on the Wilkin & Sons farm at Tiptree, Essex. The berry is tiny – no bigger than the nail of your little finger. Little Scarlet is difficult to grow and very challenging to pick, but its jam has a deep, earthy, strawberry note to the very last drop. The tiny berries remain whole in the boiling pans, and thus there is an explosion of flavour with every bite.

TIPTREE 'TAWNY' ORANGE MARMALADE
££

While Little Scarlet is prized by connoisseurs with a sweet tooth, 'Tawny' is favoured by those with a more bitter palate. The secret is to use the very finest Seville oranges, chop the peel into sizeable chunks, and cook three times to develop that distinctive bitter bite.

Chocolate

If I was asked to pick one product in this book for which there is the greatest variation between the expensive and cheaper versions, chocolate would definitely be it. Here, there is a monumental difference between the taste of inexpensive chocolate, which we are used to from childhood, and the acquired taste required to savour the most expensively produced version. Once this taste has been acquired, though, few, given the choice, venture back.

I properly discovered artisan chocolate more than a decade ago during a visit to Rococo, a charming chocolate shop in Motcomb Street, Belgravia. They have a small courtyard garden and on a lovely fresh summer's day I sipped hot chocolate and ate my way through their range. Here is what I think you need to know to appreciate chocolate at its best.

A BRIEF HISTORY

THERE IS VERY little about the substance most of us now think of as chocolate that early lovers of cacao would recognise. Over the centuries it has transformed from being an extraordinarily healthy drink to being a sugary, fatty snack, which features on the watch list of public health experts worldwide. Throughout this chapter, 'cacao' refers to the plant and beans before they have been processed, and 'cocoa' to the product once processing has begun.

Chocolate was in fact a drink, not a solid food, for most of its history. The Mayans and Aztecs first turned cacao drinking into an art form. Packed full of antioxidants, vitamins and minerals, and containing theobromine, which makes the body produce endorphins, cacao was revered for its feel-good and life-giving properties. It became fundamental not only to these people's day-to-day lives but to their religious ceremonies, too. The elite were buried with bowls of frothy cacao drinks to give them the strength to make their way into the next life.

Europeans first experienced cacao in the sixteenth century when Spanish conquistadors went to South America. It was not long before the more adventurous among them started drinking it on special occasions. It was their equivalent of champagne and ladies would drink it out of golden goblets. Crucially, though, they began to adapt it to their European tastes by adding cane sugar and substituting cinnamon, black pepper and aniseed for chilli and achiote. They also found a way of making instant hot chocolate by manufacturing a tablet of ground cacao that could be dissolved with sugar in hot water. Cacao became more valuable than gold. One sixteenth-century chronicler noted that a rabbit was worth ten cacao beans and a slave could be bought for a hundred beans. Cash did actually grow on trees!

In the seventeenth century, chocolate houses were all the rage across Europe and, with advocates including Casanova and the Marquis de Sade, chocolate developed quite a racy reputation.

It was not until the mid-nineteenth century that Joseph Fry built the first chocolate-bar factory and the treat became known more as a foodstuff than a drink. Today, in this era of mass consumption, an average chocolate confectionery bar contains no more than 5–10 per cent cocoa liquor; the rest is mainly fat and sugar. As a result, around 85 per cent of all cocoa beans are bred to prioritise output and cost over flavour, which leaves chocolate companies ever more reliant on added ingredients to make their products interesting or appealing.

GEOGRAPHY

THE TREE THAT produces cacao is native to the northern Amazon basin and isn't at all easy to grow. It needs hot, damp conditions that can only be found 20° north and 20° south of the equator; it must be planted next to taller trees that protect it from direct sun; and it won't bear fruit until it's three to five years old. It is vulnerable to all kinds of diseases, too. Even in the best conditions, each tree produces just 1,000 beans a year, which is enough to make about a kilo of chocolate.

There are three varieties of cacao: criollo, forastero and trinitario. Multiple hybrids exist of each strain. Forastero is typically the hardier, more reliable strain but what it gains in higher yield, it loses in depth and variety of flavour. It is used to make mass-produced chocolate. West African farmers grow predominantly forastero and supply about two-thirds of the world's cocoa crop, nearly half of that coming from Ivory Coast.

Criollo is the variety that was prized by the Mayans and Aztecs. The beans are less robust or productive than forastero, but produce a much more interesting range of flavours and aromas. Today, criollo tends to be the preferred bean of chocolate connoisseurs. Trinitario beans are also highly valued for their depth and variety of flavour and were bred to be somewhat hardier than criollo.

Criollo and trinitario beans are most widespread in South America, particularly in Venezuela and Peru, but even there many farmers have been persuaded to plant faster growing modern hybrids, so finding the very best, most flavoursome beans these days is far from easy. Today, 'bean to bar' chocolate-makers are looking further afield to Madagascar, parts of Indonesia and even Vietnam.

Many things are compared to fine wines, but in the case of cacao nothing could be more apt. Like a Château Lafite Rothschild, great single-estate cacaos each have their own personality, made so by their unique growing conditions and the skill of the chocolate-maker.

'Single estate' means that the beans are from one single plantation or from a group of small farmers who have the same kind of cacao and who do all their post-harvest processing together. The alternative 'single origin' is like saying 'wine from France'! It simply means that the beans all come from the same country. It may or may not be good chocolate but it certainly isn't the very best.

HOW CHOCOLATE IS PRODUCED

CACAO FARMING is labour intensive and time consuming. Even today, every stage of the process, from planting, irrigating and harvesting to fermenting and drying, is done mainly by hand. That's why nearly all the world's cacao trees are grown on small family farms.

Cacao trees can be beautiful, strange things, with their multi-coloured pods jutting straight from the trunk and lower branches. Pods take five months to grow from the blossom bud to ripe fruit. The harvest happens twice a year and has to be done by hand, with machetes, taking great care not to damage the budding new flowers or cut the bean because once it dries it will break up. There are about 30–40 beans in each pod.

Fermentation is crucial to the taste of cacao: without it, cacao beans won't develop a chocolate flavour, but mess it up and you can ruin a great harvest. After the beans and pulp have been removed from the pod, they are placed in hardwood boxes, covered in banana leaves and turned twice a day to aerate them. Inside the boxes, beans soon become a big mulchy mass and juice leaks from the pulp. The oxygen in the air activates the enzymes in the pulp sugar, causing it to acidify, which changes the chemical composition of the beans. They give off a strong aroma as they reach temperatures of around 52°C.

Drying the beans is less complex than fermenting, but it requires care and attention. After fermenting for around 72 hours for finer cacao and up to 170 hours for forastero, beans are placed in the sun, first for a gentle dry, which means an hour in the morning and afternoon, when they need to be turned constantly. Exposure to the sun is then increased by the day until the beans are dried, usually over the course of a week. The optimum humidity of a dried bean is 7.5 per cent. A bean that's too moist won't keep, and a bean that's too dry will break up and be difficult to roast because the broken pieces could easily burn in the roaster.

The beans are transported in this form to the factories where they are turned into chocolate.

Chocolate-making starts with roasting beans, which brings out and enhances their flavour. Typically, lower quality beans with less natural flavour will be given a heavier roast to cover their shortcomings. Many people think they don't like dark chocolate because they have only eaten the cheap stuff that has slightly bitter burnt notes.

The shell is then sucked away to leave the cacao nibs, the edible part of the bean. Approximately 50 per cent of each cacao nib is cocoa butter and the rest cocoa solids. These nibs are ground into a liquid. This is the basis for all types of chocolate and different brands and chocolate-makers then create their own recipes.

In its simplest form, dark chocolate has just sugar added, so a 70 per cent chocolate contains 70 per cent cocoa solids and 30 per cent sugar. Milk chocolate also has milk powder added, while white chocolate is made from only the cocoa butter part of the bean.

Cocoa butter is included in the percentage of cocoa solids and many chocolates have quite a bit added to ease production. It gives a lovely shine to the bar, but means flavour washes very quickly away once you have eaten it.

The final part of the process is when liquid chocolate is tempered, cooled, deposited into shapes and wrapped. The tempering machine warms and cools the cacao mass to precise temperatures so the butter and solids set together perfectly. Tempering also prevents bloom, which is when the butter and solids separate and the chocolate develops an uneven colour and texture.

WHY THE PRICE VARIES

INGREDIENTS

The price of chocolate should be determined primarily by the quality of the beans and the degree to which manufacturing methods maximise flavour or minimise cost. Sadly, these factors are often distorted by clever marketing; beautiful packaging and imaginatively told stories can make people feel good about paying prices quite unwarranted by the quality of chocolate inside.

Of course, everything starts with the bean. Only 15 per cent of the world's beans have the depth and character of flavour to command a significant price premium, sometimes more than double the world cocoa prices.

When you get to the 'chocolate' used in confectionery bars, it is guaranteed that only the cheapest beans will have been used. The chances are that they won't have been properly fermented or dried either. The overall character of the bar is created from a whole host of other ingredients' flavours and textures.

You can tell much about the quality of chocolate by its ingredients list. Apart from cocoa solids, cocoa butter, sugar and milk powder (in the case of milk chocolate), no other ingredients are strictly necessary. If you want to taste a chocolate that really reflects the flavour of the bean, check the ingredients list. There are some things to look out for that to a greater or lesser degree should set your alarm bells going. Most obviously, you don't want added vegetable fats. They melt smoothly in the mouth, but are no more than cheap padding. You also need to take a view on soya lecithin, which emulsifies fat and makes chocolate more fluid – and therefore makes production easier – but it does have its own taste.

You will almost always find vanilla in chocolate. This might be a matter of preference, but it is typically used to give a constant back note for chocolate bars to hide the fact that they are made from a blend of cheaper beans. Chocolatiers using the best beans would not want to cover up their carefully nurtured flavour notes with something as strong as vanilla.

Cocoa butter, the other big ingredient in chocolate, is the most important ingredient in white chocolate. Almost all but a handful of chocolates worldwide are made using de-odourised cocoa butter, pressed out of the lowest quality beans. To avoid unpleasant flavours, all flavour and aroma is removed leaving a neutral white fat. It is worth looking for particularly white chocolates using natural cocoa butter pressed out of good beans.

Chocolate need not taste simply sweet and brown. If you pay just a little more for chocolates it will become clear why the official name of the cacao tree, *Theobroma cacao*, is derived from the Greek for 'food of the gods'.

PRODUCTION METHOD

The best chocolate-makers pay top prices to farmers whom they know will ferment and dry beans perfectly. They also pay a little more to be sure that in difficult years they get the first, or best, beans to guarantee supply.

Once in the factory, considerations of ease of production and cost weigh more heavily for mass-market producers than for chocolatiers. In the biggest, most commercial, factories a cacao bean can find itself in a bar within a few hours of entering a continuous production process. In artisan factories, a bean could take up to 16 days to do the same journey and that adds cost.

A chocolatier designing this second type of factory would start by choosing to roast in small, individually controllable batches because on different days with different temperatures and different levels of humidity even the same beans may need roasting for a few minutes more or less. Traditional ball roasters are generally considered to be the best by premium chocolate-makers because beans circulate among hot air inside the ball to give an even roast and perhaps less bean breakages than other forms of roasting.

It is in the conching that the biggest time difference between the two approaches occurs. Conching is like kneading and helps develop the desired flavour and texture. In continuous production the temperatures are turned right up so the volatile molecules that carry acidity but also create the aroma and flavour are driven off in a few hours. If you did this to a beautiful high-quality bean it would lose layers of flavour. This is why artisan chocolate-makers conch at low temperatures for days.

SMALL SCALE VERSUS MASS PRODUCED

HAVE YOU EVER wondered why so much chocolate tastes the same? It is because so many chocolates are not actually made by the brands themselves. Apart from the global companies, such as Cadbury or Lindt, most buy-in mass-produced liquid chocolate from one of the big two Belgian chocolate-makers, Barry Callebaut and Belcolade, and remould it into their own shapes.

Extraordinarily, you find chocolates, biscuits or cakes all round the world proudly trumpeting that they are 'made with Belgian chocolate', but that actually means they are made by one of two huge industrial giants.

In Belgium, Pierre Marcolini is the only known brand making any chocolate 'bean to bar' and this is said to be less than 5 per cent of his total production. In the UK, Willie Harcourt-Cooze of Willie's Cacao pioneered 'bean to bar' chocolate-making in 2008. A cacao farmer himself, his philosophy is to find the world's great single-estate cacaos and to make chocolate from them that perfectly captures the flavour of the bean. He has since been joined by smaller makers, including Pump Street Bakery and Duffy.

TRY BEFORE YOU DIE!

–

WILLIE'S CACAO VENEZUELAN RIO CARIBE 72 /MADAGASCAN SAMBIRANO 71
£££££

The grands crus of the chocolate world are single-estate bars, made from the bean by craft chocolate-makers such as Willie's Cacao. Look for ones with no vanilla and no soya lecithin as the flavour. Taste at least two types, one after the other, at room temperature, and preferably at the beginning of the day when your pallet is the cleanest. Break the chocolate, listen for the snap, savour the aroma, then let the chocolate melt slowly around your mouth so the layers of flavour unfold.

In these magnificent examples, you would find that the first has deep notes of nuts and coffee, and the second bursts with notes of lively, summer fruits. With both, the flavours are complex, pure and long, but as different from each other as it is possible to imagine.

If I were you, I would work my way through Willie Harcourt-Cooze's entire range to find your favourite type of chocolate. The last time I counted, he had 14 different varieties but the range keeps growing. If I had to pick my last square it would be his Venezuelan Gold Las Trincheras 72. Willie has his own cacao farm in Venezuela and there is no skimping on quality.

MADECASSE
£££

Madecasse is another fabulous brand of chocolate to try that really delivers on flavour. It is made from a heritage cocoa-variety grown in Madagascar and the whole production process from bean to bar takes place in Africa to ensure that the returns benefit local communities.

Patisserie and Pastries

I was completely baffled a number of years ago when a competitor to Waitrose reduced the price of its cakes and croissants at a time when raw material costs were going up. Retailing is a cut-throat industry, but this just didn't make any sense at all. I decided to investigate and couldn't believe what I subsequently discovered. The 'excellent value' chocolate cake being sold for next to nothing actually didn't contain any chocolate at all, but rather chocolate essence. The croissants, meanwhile, were no longer made with butter, which is certainly something that would give any French baker a touch of the vapours.

The experience really got me thinking about the wide price range in some of our favourite sweet treats.

A BRIEF HISTORY

THE **NUMEROUS** variations of pastries made today have evolved over centuries from a crude flour and water dough mixture invented by the Romans. This paste was wrapped around meat and game before roasting, but was not intended to be eaten; it was simply to help contain juices and aromas. As time went on, the pastry was enriched with fat and milk and by medieval times pastry-making was well-established, being used for elaborate creations containing fruit, meat, fish and game. Different areas began to develop their own signature dishes and by the seventeenth century both flaky and puff pastries were added to the mix. The decorative and intricate patterns made with the raw materials became almost as important as the taste of the delicacies themselves. It became a great honour to be given a cake and it still is, whether that cake is home-baked or bought.

The word patisserie is used for a type of French or Belgian bakery that specialises in pastries and sweets. It is a legally controlled title that can be used only by bakeries that employ a licensed *maître pâtissier*, or pastry chef.

CAKES

Within each country – and the UK is no different – every region has traditional favourites relating to the history of ingredients available at the time. Dried fruits and nuts were imported into the port of Dundee, leading to the development of the eponymous cake. The cooks of the north of England used more lard than butter, as the land was used more for the rearing of beef cattle than the keeping of dairy cows. So here we find a collection of flaky pastry tarts, such as Chorley cakes and Eccles cakes, and griddle cakes, such as Northumbrian singing hinnies and Scotch pancakes made with and fried in lard.

Other regional specialities were simply first produced in a certain place the name of which became linked to the product, such as Bakewell tarts, Shrewsbury biscuits and Grantham gingerbread.

Fruit cake isn't everyone's cup of tea, but maybe you just haven't tried the right one. A properly baked, doused, matured cake made with high-quality ingredients and by an experienced hand can be a delight.

With some cakes, freshness is everything. A very simple Madeira cake, still with a breath of the oven about it, served with sun-warmed fresh raspberries and a steaming hot espresso or cup of strong leaf tea – preferably on a balcony overlooking an azure sea – is bliss.

PASTRIES

Croissants are a French institution and every year lists are published by trade bodies and the press highlighting where consumers should go to treat themselves. And some Parisians have been known to walk half an hour or take four different Métro lines to sample the best croissants! These are some of the latest top bakeries in Paris from which to sample the best croissants or pains au chocolat:

- Le Grenier à Pain

- Blé Sucré

- Du Pain et des Idées

- Miss Manon

- Delmontel

- 134 RdT

WHY THE PRICE VARIES

INGREDIENTS

There is no way around it: good-quality ingredients, such as unrefined sugar, spices, nuts and butter, make good cakes and pastries expensive.

The trouble is that the possibilities are endless. Flour can be white, brown or wholemeal. Fat can be butter, margarine or oil. Sugar comes in every shade from white to dark to sticky brown, with the flavour varying significantly with the colour. Then there are the refined commercial syrups, adding sweetness and shelf life but nothing in the way of flavour. 'Other ingredients' could be fresh or dried fruits, nuts or seeds, or artificial additives, preservatives and flavour enhancers.

With so many possible variants, it is easy to see why the price of patisserie products can be anything from a few pence to many pounds. It is not hard to see that a cake made from free-range eggs, butter, good flour and treacly muscovado sugar, studded richly with plump dried fruits, will cost more to make than another made from the cheapest flour mixed with oil, syrup, chemical preservatives and battery-farmed eggs. This is all before we even think about decorating the finished article.

While the quality of ingredients can vary hugely, the relationship between price and quality or flavour is not always clear-cut. You can have an expensive margarine made from a high-quality oil, or a very cheap spice that really packs a punch. Flavour, nutrients or appearance can always be corrected with an additive: highly nutritious carotene was always added to margarine to give it a sunshine glow, for instance, rather than the fat's actual bland white. Fresh citrus zest may give less depth of flavour than an artificial alternative, and the current trend to remove salt demands that other flavours be added to avoid a 'flat' taste to our food. These additions can be made throughout the process, sometimes giving a cost saving, sometimes not. The talent of the commercial baker is to use the most appropriate ingredient, and combination of ingredients, to create a finished cake at the right price.

Take croissants as a specific example, since this is one of the foods that set me off on this trail. Croissants are traditionally made with flour, butter, sugar, water, yeast and salt. Some are made with margarine or a mix of butter and margarine. The quality of the ingredients and the percentage and type of butter will hugely affect quality and price – a croissant can be bought from several pence to several pounds. Usually croissants will use between 18 per cent and 24 per cent butter and its provenance can play a major part in its price. Butter from specific areas (Protected Designation of Origin butters), such as Brittany butter or Charentes butter, will be much more expensive. Cheaper croissants will be made using margarine, which is usually much less expensive than butter. The croissants will be paler in colour and will lack the buttery taste usually associated with good-quality croissants.

MADE BY MACHINE OR HAND

The principle behind making cakes and pastries is the same in a commercial bakery as it is at home, but the practical method can vary. Ingredients are weighed, mixed and baked. Toppings and fillings are prepared and everything is assembled and packed. Each of these processes can, and often is, completed automatically, without the touch of a human hand. This produces a uniform product every time. Then there is the semi-automated process, where machines assist with timed mixing and baking, or perhaps with sprinkling decorations from a conveyor, or with a computer-controlled wrapping and packing process. At any stage in a semi-automated process, the commercial baker can go back to basics and sort the ingredients by hand, spread the fillings, produce the decorations or pack the cakes carefully for the shelf.

DECORATION

This is often the most costly part of the process. It is completely possible for a finished cake to leave the production line with no direct human contact. From precisely placed decorations, to screen-printed images, textured toppings and evenly sprinkled sparkles, anything can be programmed into the right piece of machinery. The simplest of styles is to apply a shaking of sugar or cocoa, or a coat of poured icing.

The bespoke, luxury process is more likely to include at least some handmade elements and is related far more closely to the home baker, where decorations are cut from hand-rolled sugar paste, sugar flowers have each petal shaped and curled, figures are carefully formed and piping is applied from a carefully chosen piping bag and nozzle. This attention to detail creates a cake that looks like a one-off, for a special occasion when you want to feel that someone – rather than something – has made that cake just for you.

TIME

A final consideration is time. Whereas most cakes race through the production process so they are packed as freshly as possible, a really good fruit cake needs to mature first. The baker has to invest in producing the cakes in advance of demand (such as at Christmas time) so they can rest for anything up to six weeks or more.

TRY BEFORE YOU DIE!

–

Rather than attempting to select one cake over another, I have picked my three favourite places for patisserie.

OTTOLENGHI, LONDON

Where to start? Chef Yotam Ottolenghi's cooking style is rooted in the Middle East, but with a Mediterranean influence. His specialities include baked ricotta with fig and lavender honey, fig, yoghurt and almond cake, tahini and halva brownies, and mascarpone, cherry and grappa trifle. I could go on and on but it really is best to visit and try for yourself.

BETTY'S OF HARROGATE (AND NOW ELSEWHERE AS WELL)

For me this is the best place for a café-style afternoon tea. It is still a wonderful family business that is proud of its Yorkshire roots. The cake trolley always gets me in a spin, but I nearly always opt for a cream cake. Vanilla slice and eclairs are a favourite.

THE RITZ, CLARIDGE'S AND THE GORING

These are my three favourite hotel spots for afternoon tea in the UK. I like something different about each one of them, but they all offer the best quality and service in beautiful surroundings.

Ice Cream

My father loved ice cream. I distinctly remember the large yellow tubs it came in and, looking back, I think it must have been one of our staple foods at home when I was a child. That tub certainly seemed to come out a lot. Once again, it was the Italians who showed me that what I once believed to be a pretty decent treat paled in comparison to the real thing. When I lived and worked there for a time as part of my degree, I was introduced to the skill of the *'gelatiere'*. As with so many foodstuffs in this book, I discovered the truth that all ice cream is not born equal.

A BRIEF HISTORY

THERE ARE MANY elaborate tales about Marco Polo introducing ice cream from China to Europe, and King Charles I having his own personal ice-cream maker, but sadly these wonderful stories cannot be backed up with historical evidence. The earliest reference to ice cream was in China in the Tang period (AD 618–907), when buffalo, cow's and goat's milk was heated and allowed to ferment. This was then mixed with flour for thickening and (surprisingly) camphor for flavour, and chilled before being served.

In England, ice cream was served at a banquet for the Feast of St George at Windsor Castle in 1671. It was such a rare and exotic dish that only the guests on King Charles II's table had 'one plate of white strawberries and one plate of iced cream', while the other less exalted guests looked on with envy.

The honoured few were clearly in no hurry to share. Ice-cream making was a closely guarded secret for many years and the first recipe in English did not appear until 1718.

Ice-cream making became more straightforward with the introduction of the ice-cream making machine in 1843. It comprised a wooden bucket that was filled with salt and ice and had a handle that rotated.

The breakthrough in larger scale ice-cream production came when ice 'harvested' and imported from Norway, Canada and America in the early nineteenth century was made readily available to the general public. Ice was shipped into London and stored in ice houses, from where it was sold to ice-cream makers. The huge ice-house pits built near King's Cross by Carlo Gatti in the 1850s are still there and have recently been opened to the public at the London Canal Museum.

The invention of the electric refrigerator is what made the ice-cream industry what it is today. Huge quantities of imported ice were no longer necessary and ice cream could now be transported and stored. Mass production was born.

HOW ICE CREAM IS PRODUCED

THE ICE-CREAM BASE can either be made with milk, cream, eggs, skimmed milk powder, sugar and natural flavours, or cheaply with vegetable fats, skimmed milk concentrate or powder, water and whey protein concentrate, with added emulsifiers, stabilisers, colourings and flavours.

To maintain shelf-life ice cream is pasteurised and homogenised before ageing. Homogenisation breaks down the fat globules into smaller ones to give a smooth creamy texture. Emulsifiers are added to allow crystallisation of the fat. Premium ice creams use egg as a natural emulsifier; cheaper ice creams use chemicals that work to freeze the product more quickly and are more reliable.

Once the base is aged, up to a minimum of 12 hours in the case of premium ice cream, ingredients and flavours are added pre- and post-freezing. Air is then added while the mix is frozen down. In the trade this is known as 'overrun' and the quantity of air added can vary from around 30 per cent in quality ice cream to 200 per cent in cheap soft-scoop ice cream.

The recipe determines the amount of overrun an ice cream can hold. If eggs are used as an emulsifier, the overrun will be low. Chemical emulsifiers, however, allow a much higher overrun. Stabilisers are then needed to keep the ice cream from shrinking at these high overruns.

The ice cream is frozen through a number of different phases ending with a fast freeze in a freezing tunnel. This produces smaller ice crystals thereby creating a smooth-eating ice cream.

Once made, ice cream is stored at minus 18–22°C.

Artisan ice creams are produced in a slightly different way. The ice cream may not be homogenised and fast freezing might not be possible. As the ice cream takes longer to freeze you may well get larger ice crystals and a much less smooth texture. The amount of air used will be low, giving a dense texture.

Italian ice cream (*gelato*) is an exception to the standard process. Recipes tend to be lower in fat and are served warmer to get a soft eat. Originally designed for immediate consumption, unlike industrially produced ice cream, it does not need to be kept in a cold room.

WHY THE PRICE VARIES

THERE ARE TWO primary factors that affect the price of ice cream: the ingredients and production method.

INGREDIENTS

Better quality ice creams always use dairy fat and minimise the number of ingredients used.

Different breeds of dairy cows produce different types of milk. For example, Jersey cows produce milk with a high butterfat content, which makes for the creamiest milk and is ideal for ice cream. The quality of the sugar and ingredients adds to the taste and cost. Real fruit, Madagascan vanilla or single-origin cocoa beans (like Santo Domingo) give a rich chocolate taste. Ice creams made to this quality need to be allowed to warm slightly before serving.

Cheap ice cream is made using a vegetable fat, such as coconut oil; then milk, protein powders/concentrates and water are added, together with low-cost flavours and colours. Stabilisers and emulsifiers are then mixed in so lots of air can be added to make the product scoop-able straight from the freezer.

PRODUCTION METHOD

Air is free! The more that is added, the cheaper your tub of ice cream will be to produce.

A simple way to gauge quality, other than the price ticket, is to look at the weight on the pack as a guide to the amount of air included. Or, you could simply feel the weight of comparable-sized products. Generally speaking, the heavier the product, the better the quality.

Beware of misleading descriptions. The term 'Cornish ice cream' implies the ice cream comes from Cornwall, but there is no legal requirement for this to be true.

Check the ingredients panel to see if it is real dairy ice cream. In the UK, products that do not contain any fresh milk and cream can still be called 'ice cream'. The legal requirement is only that a certain percentage is butterfat, which may well come from reconstituted skimmed milk or whey powder/concentrate and water!

Lastly, most premium-quality ice cream may have a very small amount of stabilisers and emulsifiers added to help mix the product and protect against temperature fluctuations. Lower quality ice cream will have much more of these chemicals rather than natural ones.

VANILLA – A LITTLE BIT EXTRA!

Vanilla remains the UK's favourite flavour of ice cream, but there are several types of vanilla ingredients, ranging from real vanilla, to vanilla extract or vanilla flavouring. I think the best is usually the real thing: Madagascan vanilla.

Vanilla is very expensive, largely because it is difficult to grow as it needs a particular tropical environment to grow naturally. It is extracted from the seed pods of a variety of orchid. Originally from Mexico, the vanilla orchid is very difficult to cultivate artificially because of the way in which it needs to be pollinated. It wasn't until the nineteenth century that the hand-pollination techniques currently in use allowed for worldwide cultivation. Still, it's a laborious process, all of which makes vanilla one of the most expensive food items per-ounce in the world, right up there with saffron and truffles. It's a good thing a little goes a long way! Vanillin is the primary chemical component responsible for the unique aroma of vanilla beans, though natural vanilla also gets flavour from piperonal and several hundred other minor constituents, all of which add complexity.

Artificial vanilla, on the other hand, is made with pure vanillin diluted with water and alcohol, and while the vanillin is chemically identical to that found in real vanilla, it's extracted from coal tar or wood pulp as a by-product of paper production and is thus extremely inexpensive to produce. So check what is in your ice cream.

TRY BEFORE YOU DIE!

–

THREE TWINS ICE CREAM
£££££

The price of this ice-cream sundae (almost £40,000 at the time of writing) also provides the purchaser with a first-class airfare and transfers to Kilimanjaro, a guided climb of the mountain, accommodation and a five-figure donation to an African environmental non-profit charity. The company that serves this ice-cream sundae, made with glacial ice from Mount Kilimanjaro, did so to raise awareness of the mountain's glacier, which is expected to disappear within the next 10–15 years due to climate change.

barMASA TRUFFLE ICE CREAM
££££

The truffle ice cream served at barMASA restaurant at the ARIA Resort & Casino in Las Vegas is the creation of chef Masa Takayama, with the aim of achieving simplicity and purity using only fresh ingredients. It is made of seasonal truffles and gold flakes and served in a glass.

Regionally I would recommend:

SIMPLY ICE CREAM
££

This luxury ice cream is made in Bonnington, near Ashford in Kent, using British dairy products, Kentish seasonal fruits and ingredients from top suppliers sourced locally where possible. All Simply Ice Creams are made by hand. Try the Heavenly Honeycomb Crunch.

MACKIE'S OF SCOTLAND
£

The Mackie family have been farming at Westertown Farm, in Aberdeenshire, since 1913. Mackie's was formerly a milk retail company and in 1986 began making ice cream with its own milk. All the ice cream is still made on the farm.

The hallmark of Mackie's Luxury dairy ice cream is a smooth texture and especially creamy taste.

PURBECK ICE CREAM
££

Purbeck Ice Cream began with 60 Friesian cows feeding on 126 acres of lush green hillside directly opposite the historic remains of Corfe Castle in the heart of Dorset.

All Purbeck Ice Cream is produced in Dorset with local fresh milk, and thick double cream and is as 'natural' as it comes.

LAVERSTOCK ICE CREAM
££

Former World F1 champion Jody Scheckter makes the most amazing organic ice cream from buffalo milk on his Laverstock Park Farm in Hampshire. It's all wonderful but I particularly like the coffee and chocolate. There is no skimping on the quality of ingredients used.

Cheese

Cheese is, without doubt, my favourite food. If I could have been either a cheese or wine buyer for Waitrose I would have died even happier. In this vein, I have often pondered what I would choose if I knew it was going to be my last meal on earth, and I now know exactly what I would have. As a starter, the prawn cocktail that Mark Hix serves in his Oyster and Fish House in Lyme Regis. His delicious sauce is tomato-based but there's also a bit of booze in there. In this fantasy, I'd be able to eat the dish in the restaurant, looking out over the bright blue sea, watching the fishing boats returning with the day's catch.

My main course would be the Cotoletta alla Milanese, from Santini in Belgravia, London, with some sautéed spinach and I might also go for some of Heston Blumenthal's triple cooked chips. (A close second choice for main would be Heston's steak and kidney pudding from his Hinds Head pub in Bray. Trust me. I could play this game all day.) As it's my last meal, I'd indulge myself with an aperitif – one of Santini's famous negroni cocktails: gin, sweet red vermouth and Campari, with a large round ice ball almost filling the glass.

For dessert, the chocolate mousse on the menu at Michel Roux Snr's Waterside Inn in Bray. And then I would have a very, very large Waterside cheeseboard with fresh bread.

And if I could have just one course? It might surprise you to learn that I'd pick the cheese and bread.

One of my fondest childhood food memories is of eating crumbly, tangy Cheshire cheese bought straight from the farm. At dinners I generally skip desserts in favour of cheese and I have always taken great pleasure in visiting producers and tasting the results of their labours.

Since there are more than 700 named cheeses in the UK and more than 2,000 varieties worldwide, it would be impossible to write about the quality and price variations in them all in just one chapter. Instead, to help explain what's what, I have picked a hard, soft and blue cheese to write about.

A BRIEF HISTORY

THE EARLIEST evidence of cheesemaking dates back to 5500 BC in what is now Poland. It is thought that milk would have been stored in a ruminant animal's stomach. The rennet in the stomach would have split the milk into curds and whey by accident and the process of preserving milk as cheese began. There are pictures on the walls of Egyptian tombs showing cheesemaking, and it had become an art form by the time of ancient Rome. Cheeses from the Middle East would have been more like feta or cottage cheese, but those produced in the cooler European climate required less salt to preserve them, making them suitable for ageing.

Cheese is made by curdling milk to separate it into curds (solids) and whey (liquid). The curds are then made into cheese. The curdling process is started through the use of an enzyme, such as rennet, and starter cultures of bacteria that metabolise the lactose (sugar naturally present in milk) into lactic acid. The whey created as a by-product is used for a number of things, most commonly nowadays as a protein supplement.

Softer, fresh-tasting cheeses, such as goat's cheese or cream cheese, use much less rennet than harder cheeses, such as Cheddar or Swiss cheese, which are better for pressing and ageing.

Processed cheese, like the cheese slice you find on a burger, is made by adding other ingredients to cheese and cooking them together to change the textural and/or melting properties and increase shelf life.

Cheese can be made from any kind of milk; a farm in the Swedish town of Bjurholm is famous for its moose cheese!

SOFT CHEESE: BRIE, THE MOST FAMOUS!

THIS CHEESE IS named after the French region of Brie, Seine-et-Marne, where it was originally created several hundred years ago. Brie was one of the tributes that had to be paid to the French kings. Brie is situated just 35 miles from Paris, which helped build its reputation as the Parisians had both the money and the palate for this luxury cheese.

There are many different types of Brie, each with its own unique characteristics. Variations in the milk and the production and maturation processes result in differences in flavour and textures, from full-flavoured unpasteurised ripening cheeses to mild and creamy Bries.

HOW BRIE IS PRODUCED

BRIE CAN BE produced from whole or semi-skimmed milk. Raw (untreated), pasteurised or thermised milk can be used. Pasteurised milk is heated to destroy all pathogens (bacteria that can cause food poisoning), whereas thermised milk is heated to a lower temperature to reduce the number of these pathogens but this does not guarantee to destroy them all – bacteria are important in lending flavour to the cheese. Starter cultures and rennet or another coagulant are added to the milk and it is heated to a maximum temperature of 37°C. The curds are then cast into moulds in several thin layers and naturally drained for about 18 hours. The cheese is then taken out of the moulds, salted and sprayed with white mould culture. The cheeses are then dried for about 24 hours before transfer to *'hâloirs'* (maturation rooms) for 8–10 days. It is essential to control the humidity and temperature – around 98 per cent humidity at 12–14°C to allow the cheese to develop and the white mould coat to form. After around ten days the cheese is ready to be packed but not necessarily ready to eat. Mild and creamy pasteurised Brie will be ready to eat but ripening cheeses will be at the very beginning of their life and may need a couple more weeks to have the perfect texture and flavour.

Brie is a living product with active bacteria and ripening cheeses are best eaten towards the end of their shelf life. This can be between 45 and 50 days after making so that the cheese paste has softened and the flavours have developed into their full and distinctive character.

Young cheese that has not ripened enough will have a dry and/or chalky texture and may never 'break down' to become smooth in texture and develop flavour. Equally, some cheeses that have too high a moisture content can develop very quickly and become runny and very strong in aroma and flavour. They may develop 'slip coat', where the cheese immediately beneath the outer white mould coat becomes very liquid very fast, slipping off the central core of young curd.

Another fault to watch out for is black 'foreign' mould growing on the surface of the cheese, which occurs if the maturing rooms at the dairy have become infected with spores, and humidity and temperature conditions have not been carefully enough controlled.

Making Brie is not an exact science; every batch will be a little different due to minor variances in milk quality and ambient temperatures.

WHY THE PRICE VARIES

OFTEN **B**RIES on sale in the UK are not 'ready to eat' as they are too young and under-developed, but also watch out for the faults mentioned above.

If corners are cut in the sourcing of ingredients or at the manufacturing stage, the end result can be a big disappointment. Costs of production vary. An AOC (*Appellation d'origine contrôllée*) cheese, such as artisanal Brie de Meaux, which has provenance of many centuries from a specific geographical area east of Paris, is hand-ladled and dry-salted in small batches. At the other end of the scale is the mass-produced Brie made with pasteurised milk in a high-volume continuous vat anywhere in France, with very little labour involved throughout the process. Mass-produced Brie can be more consistent in quality, but will rarely have the flavours you would find in a premium Brie, which has been carefully nurtured through its production and maturation.

When shopping for Brie, think about how and when you intend to use it and who will be eating it. Is it for cooking? The cheeseboard? For children? Customers should ideally buy their Brie ahead of time and look carefully at the best-before code on the packet. This is especially true if it is a ripening Brie, which will get creamier in texture and develop more flavour the closer it gets towards its best-before date.

Brie should be removed from the refrigerator an hour before serving in order to allow it to come up to room temperature so that the texture becomes creamy and the flavour is expressed in all its complexity. A cold Brie will nearly always be a shadow of what it could be.

TRY BEFORE YOU DIE!

–

BRIE DE MEAUX
£££££

For a cheeseboard centrepiece, I would go for a ripening wedge of Brie de Meaux or Brie Pays. It is full-flavoured, rich, melts in the mouth and has lovely mushroom aromas. Serve with a crusty French baguette and a glass of red wine – absolute perfection.

Brie de Meaux is considered to be the best-quality Brie and is probably the most expensive. It has protected status cheese from a defined region. Brie de Meaux is made from unpasteurised milk with animal rennet to give more flavour to the cheese. It is an AOC-designated artisanal cheese, hand-ladled, dry-salted and matured on straw mats.

For children or adults who prefer a mild flavour, or for a sandwich, try a mild British Brie, such as Somerset Brie or Organic Cornish Brie.

HARD CHEESE: CHEDDAR

CHEDDAR CHEESE ORIGINATES from the village of Cheddar in Somerset. It takes its name from the dramatic limestone gorge on the edge of the village, which was used to store the cheese. Cheddar has been produced since at least the twelfth century when the King's accounts showed that Henry II bought 4.6 tons of Cheddar at the cost of a farthing per pound. Cheese was one of the few ways to preserve milk, which ensured its popularity in commercial centres, such as London, where it was enjoyed by the wealthy.

Today Cheddar is, by a long chalk, the most popular cheese eaten in Britain.

HOW CHEDDAR IS PRODUCED

THE MAKING PROCESS has changed little over the years. Be it on a large scale at a creamery or at a small artisanal producer, the basic process varies very little. It takes approximately 10 litres of milk to make 1kg of Cheddar.

Most milk used in Cheddar-making is, in the vast majority of cases, pasteurised. Milk is put into vats and starter cultures of bacteria are added. The main function of the starter cultures is to metabolise lactose (milk sugar), which is naturally present in milk, into lactic acid. This causes milk to become more acidic so that when rennet is added milk forms a set, which is a semi-solid structure due to the formation of casein (a type of protein) bonds. Once it has set to the required firmness, cutting commences.

Cutting results in solid particles, the curds, and liquid, whey. The aim is to achieve even-sized curds so that whey can escape easily to ensure that the correct moisture content is achieved in the final cheese. Curds are stirred in the whey to keep them in suspension and avoid them matting together, while the temperature of the mixture is raised, known as scalding.

Scalding is a cooking process that increases the amount of moisture lost from the curd in order to make a firm-bodied cheese. The curds and whey are 'pitched' or transferred from the vat to a drainage table where whey is separated and 'Cheddaring' takes place.

Cheddaring is the process whereby the curds knit together while whey is still being removed. It is vital that Cheddaring is well controlled to avoid pockets of trapped whey, which result in off flavours developing while the cheese matures.

After Cheddaring, curds are milled, or chopped up fairly small, and salt is added. Salt serves a fourfold purpose in cheese: to stop the bacteria from continuing to grow and produce acid, as a preservative, for flavour and for texture. So, the right amount of salt and good mixing throughout the curds are absolutely fundamental to good cheese.

Curds are then tightly packed together to form a close, dense structure with as little air as possible, either by being drawn under vacuum or pressed together. The cheese is then ready to be put aside to mature at a controlled temperature.

Cheddar is generally sold as mild, medium, mature, extra mature or vintage. There is no official definition of these terms and so the producer and retailer will have their own parameters for each category. At Waitrose, mild is classed as 4 months, medium 8 months, mature 15 months and extra mature 19 months. Some mild Cheddars elsewhere can be as young as four weeks old.

The recipe for each type is changed slightly depending on how long it takes to ripen. Mature Cheddar may also contain crystals, sometimes called 'crunch', which consist of calcium lactate and form within the body of the cheese when it is matured for more than six months. Historically, this was often perceived as a fault; however, today this is increasingly popular and adds another degree of texture. I much prefer my Cheddar that way. You just need to be patient while it matures as any artificial rushing affects the flavour.

WHY THE PRICE VARIES

INGREDIENTS

Although Cheddar is today produced around the world, its origins remain firmly in the south-west of England and it is certainly considered to be a British cheese. It is still widely made in the West Country where certain producers are licensed to make the EU Protected Designation of Origin 'West Country Farmhouse Cheddar'. This must be made with local milk on farms in Devon, Cornwall, Dorset and Somerset using traditional methods. This region is ideal for Cheddar production because it has mineral-rich soil and the ideal climate for lush pastures – plenty of rain and warmth – conditions that enable the cows to produce top-quality milk.

PRODUCTION METHOD

A small farmhouse Cheddar cheesemaker uses a lot of manual labour to make limited volumes compared to a large creamery that can make several hundred tonnes of cheese a day. The larger sites use highly mechanised, automated processes, thereby spreading labour and fixed costs over large volumes. Whey is a valuable by-product and large cheesemakers can invest significant capital into whey-processing facilities in order to maximise the value of the whey. However, for smaller producers, the value gained from small volumes means the investment in processing facilities isn't worthwhile.

RECIPE

A mild cheese, designed to peak in flavour delivery within a few weeks of being made, has a higher moisture content than a mature cheese that ages slowly over 18–24 months. If your mild Cheddar becomes like soft putty or rubbery in texture and lacks flavour and creaminess, it could be that the moisture levels in the cheese have been increased to make the cheese go further. This leads to a lower proportion of protein and fat.

TRY BEFORE YOU DIE!

—

KEEN'S, WESTCOMBE AND MONTGOMERY'S
£££££

The most expensive Cheddars are traditional farmhouse varieties, which are usually made using unpasteurised milk and in the characteristic 'truckle' cylindrical shape. They are often made from milk produced by the farms' own herds of cows, meaning only the freshest milk is used. The cheeses develop a natural coat, or rind, during the time they are maturing, normally for around 10–12 months, and this adds an extra dimension to the flavour. Great examples of farmhouse cheddars are Keen's, Westcombe and Montgomery's, which are all made with unpasteurised milk. Availability is limited since the milk comes from one herd and the making process is very labour intensive.

CORNISH QUARTZ
££££

Cornish Quartz, a favourite of mine, is a good example of a top-quality creamery Cheddar. It is made using milk produced only in Cornwall, a county renowned for its rich and creamy dairy products. Cornish Quartz is matured for at least 22 months, has a firm, flinty texture, with crunchy calcium lactate crystals, along with an intense taste.

BLUE CHEESE: STILTON

THERE IS EVIDENCE to suggest a cream cheese was made and sold in or around the English village of Stilton in the early eighteenth century. With the development of the coaching trade, the village became a trading post between London and the north and one of the innkeepers in the village sold cheese to passing travellers. To grow his business he agreed a commercial contract with a cheesemaker in Leicestershire, in the Melton Mowbray area.

As demand for Stilton cheese grew, so did production in Leicestershire, Nottinghamshire and Derbyshire. Blue Stilton cheese is the only English cheese to be granted a Certification Trademark (in 1966) and was one of the first to be granted Protected Designation of Origin (in 1996), which means it can only be made in the three counties and to specified methods of production and ripening.

HOW STILTON IS PRODUCED

BY CHEESEMAKING STANDARDS, Stilton takes a long time to make – 24 hours in fact – due to the slow development of acidity, which is necessary to achieve the characteristic texture of Stilton curd. The extended time limits the amount of cheese that can be made, which means Stilton is a more expensive cheese to produce. In contrast, Cheddar, other hard-pressed cheeses and most soft cheeses generally have a more economic making time of around four hours.

Milk for the cheese is sourced from within Leicestershire, Nottinghamshire and Derbyshire. It is pasteurised and then filled into cheese vats. Up to 78 litres of milk is required for a whole cheese. Small amounts of starter culture – *Penicillium roqueforti* mould culture – and rennet are added to each vat. After three hours clotted milk is cut and curds are left to drain overnight. The next day the curd is salted and placed in cheese moulds to drain for five days at a specific temperature. The cheeses are then removed from the moulds, their external coats sealed and placed on shelves for the traditional ripening process in special maturing rooms. After about five weeks, each cheese is pierced with stainless steel needles, which allow the growth of the blue veins. The cheeses are ripened for at least a further three weeks before they are ready to be graded and dispatched.

WHY THE PRICE VARIES

INGREDIENTS

The quality and composition of the milk, which varies with the season, has a noticeable effect on the cheese.

PRODUCTION METHOD

Stilton reacts to all the stages of its production, which means cheese quality varies between each of the six producers, in spite of all producers conforming to the production methods specified according to the Protected Designation of Origin. The conditions in a particular dairy will affect temperature, humidity and airflow. In addition, the control of moisture content in Stilton production is important to achieve consistent salt levels and curd texture. Even blueing of the cheese is vital to provide consistent quality.

The maturing process then has a further impact on quality. Cheese ripening depends on humidity, temperature and the microbiological composition of the curd. Many varieties of cheese are hermetically sealed, packed and then ripened, so the influence of humidity is lost. Stilton, however, is matured traditionally and this requires careful attention to humidity levels in order to achieve consistent flavours. Equally important is the age of a Stilton, since it has a limited period of time when it is considered to be at its optimum for flavour and texture. The best Stilton is carefully graded and selected and does not automatically get passed down the packing line just because it has reached a minimum age.

A good-quality Stilton should have a moderately firm yet slightly yielding texture, which melts readily in the mouth releasing layer upon layer of complex flavours. It should not be bitter or harsh or soapy. When a whole truckle is halved horizontally, blue veins should evenly radiate out from the centre to the edge of the cheese. A poor Stilton may have uneven blue veining and as a consequence the parts of the cheese lacking blue will be acidic and sharp in flavour, with a firm crumbly texture. If Stilton cheese is over-mature, it will start to discolour, particularly under the rind, where it will become brown and stained. The rind should not be sticky or weeping. A faint whiff of ammonia is normal, but very strong smelling cheese indicates that the maturation has probably gone too far for many people's tastes. The body of the cheese will darken in colour as it dries out, and the blue veining will lose its intensity of colour.

TRY BEFORE YOU DIE!

–

COLSTON BASSETT BLUE STILTON/
DUCHY ORGANIC CROPWELL BISHOP BLUE STILTON
££££

My favourites are Colston Bassett Blue Stilton and Duchy Organic Cropwell Bishop Blue Stilton. Both cheeses are made by hand-ladling curds from the vat into drainage tables. This is a very labour-intensive task, requiring a surprising degree of skill, but it is a very gentle method of transferring the delicate curds, resulting in a 'melt in the mouth' texture to the finished cheese.

The cheese produced by both Cropwell Bishop and Colston Bassett are traditionally 'rubbed up' by hand. This step seals the outside of the cheeses immediately after they are formed, before they are placed into the maturation rooms. Again, it is a highly skilled job.

Butter and Spreads

The butter versus margarine debate has always been a slippery one. For a long while butter was a bit of a pariah and we were all warned about the threats of heart disease and cholesterol if we slathered too much on our morning toast. Then we were told margarines have unhealthy trans fats (trans-unsaturated fatty acids) and may not be the healthier option after all. In fact, experts pronounced butter as the 'natural' choice – in moderation, of course. And so the argument rages on. This is all before you get into the fors and againsts in taste preferences, too.

I am happy to stand up and be counted as a butter eater myself. However, given the amazing growth in the sales of spreads over recent years, it is clear many, many people have come down on the non-butter side.

Without wishing to fuel the debate in either direction, I thought I would explain why quality and cost vary for both.

A BRIEF HISTORY

BUTTER IS THOUGHT to have originated over 10,000 years ago in central Asia, from where it advanced to India and Europe. In Greece and Rome, where it was in competition with olive oil, it was originally treated with suspicion, being considered an inferior foreign product.

Butter was originally produced from sheep's and goat's milk. Cream was skimmed off the top of the milk, which had been left to stand. It was then put into a wooden churn and the cream was vigorously stirred/shaken to bind the fat together to make butter, and the buttermilk rinsed away, or used in baking.

In Scandinavia, milk was allowed to sour before skimming off the cream, and the resulting lactic flavour persists in continental butter to this day. The lower pH acts as a preservative, and therefore salt is not a necessity. In the UK the preferred method of preserving the product was to scald/pasteurise the cream and then add salt to the butter.

Margarine owes its origin to war. Napoleon III offered a reward during the Siege of Paris to anyone who could find a substitute for butter. Margarine was patented and first manufactured in 1869 by Hippolyte Mège Mouriès, a French chemist, and shortly afterwards the Jurgens and van den Bergh families commenced production in Holland on a commercial scale.

There are three types of 'spreadable fats' and they are categorised by the origin of the fat used: milk-fat products, such as 'butter' and 'dairy spreads'; vegetable and/or animal fat products, such as 'margarine' and 'fat spreads'; and mixed fat products (milk fat with vegetable and/or animal fats), such as 'blends', and 'blended spreads'.

Traditional margarines or 'yellow fats' are spreadable fats that have a minimum fat content of 80 per cent and less than 90 per cent but this can change depending on which description is used. Most spreads/yellow fats are made using vegetable and/or animal fat. This type of fat also remains solid at 20°C.

HOW BUTTER AND SPREADS ARE PRODUCED

BUTTER HAS a minimum of 80 per cent fat. There are four types of butter available:

- sweetcream salted butter

- sweetcream unsalted butter

- unsalted lactic butter

- whey butter, produced from skimming off the fat from whey created from making cheese

Within the EU, butter can be produced only by 'churning' in a rotary churn or continuous butter-maker. Once the cream has been heat-treated, it is aged for between eight and ten hours to crystallise the fat globules it contains.

The churning process breaks open the fat-globule membrane, releasing butterfat through shaking/stirring of the cream. The released butterfat then sticks together and buttermilk is drained off. For lactic butter, salt or starter culture is added, depending on the type of butter being produced.

Butter varies naturally according to the season, region and breed of cow used. The feeding of silage in winter and the shorter summer period for cows to eat grass results in northern European butters being much firmer and paler. Butter produced from cows fed on fresh grass in early summer has more unsaturated fat and carotenes, giving a much softer texture and deep yellow colour.

Virtually all yellow-fat spreads are produced by blending vegetable oils and animal-fat ingredients together to form a 'water in oil' emulsion. Other ingredients, such as emulsifiers, are added to help stabilise the mixture during processing. In lower fat spreads, stabilisers, such as starch, lactic acid or citric acid, are used to reduce pH, and potassium sorbate can be added to help its preservation. Natural colours and flavours are added.

The mix is heat-treated and then cooled to crystallise fat and create a smooth spreadable product. Key to the process is the dispersion of water droplets in the spread for optimum shelf life and flavour.

Blended spreads are made by mixing butter and vegetable oil together to improve spreadability. The mixing of the ingredients and temperature control are both important in their effect on the final product quality.

WHY THE PRICE VARIES

INGREDIENTS
Good-quality butter starts with good-quality cream from good-quality milk. Welsh butter is characterised by a higher salt content of 3 per cent, compared to 1.5 per cent in most salted butters on the market. Legend has it this is down to a taste for salt developed over time by Welsh miners, whose hard manual labour meant they needed more of it.

With spreads, quality and price can vary significantly depending on the use of 'cheaper' vegetable oils and olive oils. The selection of ingredients is key to consistent quality.

PRODUCTION METHOD
Attention to detail in the production process is vital. Careful control of factors such as cooling the butter will have a big impact on the final product. Butter should have a close, waxy texture, a slightly matt appearance and be free from mottled streaks. There should

be no moisture visible to ensure it lasts. Poor-quality products may have an open texture, with too much aeration and free moisture. These defects will shorten the shelf life and the butter will go off more quickly.

A good spread should have a tight structure, a moderately firm texture that is spreadable straight from the fridge and a pleasant flavour. It should have no taints and should not leave any oily aftertaste.

Excess surface moisture is a sure sign of an inferior product that will not taste good and will have a short shelf life.

ETHICS

Recently published figures show that there is a significant difference in what dairy farmers are paid by various retailers and producers. At lower levels it is an unsustainable amount for farmers to survive.

ADDED BENEFITS

Many spreads include health benefits, such as supplementary vitamins and minerals, which add cost to the product.

TRY BEFORE YOU DIE!

–

WEST COUNTRY FARMHOUSE BUTTER
££

A number of farmhouse cheesemakers are producing whey butter, using the fat that would otherwise have been 'lost' in the whey (the liquid remaining when milk has been curdled and the curds removed). Some of these butters are of high quality with a unique acidic, cheesy flavour coming from the cheese starter cultures. This particular butter is a blend of fresh pasteurised cream and whey cream, and is churned on the farm in the Brue Valley in the heart of Somerset.

GUERNSEY BUTTER
£££

Guernsey Butter uses milk from pedigree registered indigenous Guernsey cows, and is produced on quality-assured farms within the Bailiwick of Guernsey. It is characterised by its exceptional richness from naturally occurring beta carotene. It has a rich creamy texture and deep yellow colour.

SALTED OR UNSALTED BEURRE D'ISIGNY
£££

These butters are made using locally sourced milk and are specific to this region of France. The cream has a starter culture added and must then be left to ripen for a minimum of 18 hours to allow the acidity to increase to the right level. The small quantity produced and lengthy process make the butter slightly more expensive than average.

Yoghurt

Yoghurt comes in many forms and can be made from the milk of cows, goats, sheep and even mares, camels and yaks. It has a great many uses, too. In Western Europe, we know it best as a sweetened fruity dessert or breakfast food. It's also consumed as a drink in India (lassi), used in baking to provide moisture and flavour and made into a kind of cheese (labneh). It's very digestible, even to people with lactose intolerance, as added bacteria converts the indigestible lactose into more accessible lactic acid. For the health conscious and dieters, there is a range of fat content on offer from full-fat versions with added cream to very low-fat versions. The market also offers a vast array of yoghurts to suit all palates and meal occasions. They come in a variety of textures (e.g. liquid, set, smooth) and flavours (e.g. natural, fruit, cereal), and can be consumed as a snack or part of a meal, as a sweet or savoury food.

With so many variables on offer, it is quite hard to get to the bottom of their true value. Here's what I learned.

A BRIEF HISTORY

RATHER LIKE CHEESE, it is generally believed that yoghurt was discovered by accident as a result of primitive storage methods for milk in warm climates. Most historians attribute the discovery of yoghurt to the Neolithic people of central Asia around 6000 BC. As people began the practice of milking animals and used dried animals' stomachs as containers, the enzymes contained within them curdled the milk, making a kind of yoghurt. It is said that Genghis Khan, the founder of the Mongol Empire, and his armies enjoyed yoghurt made with horse milk.

The word yoghurt is Turkish in origin. The Turks are also believed to have identified the health benefits of yoghurt, using it to treat intestinal problems. Its first industrialised production is attributed to Isaac Carasso in 1919, in Barcelona. His company was named 'Danone' as a tribute to his son, 'Little Daniel'.

Yoghurt is produced through the fermentation of milk by lactic acid bacteria, usually *Lactobacillus bulgaricus* and *Streptococcus thermophilus*. The milk is firstly pasteurised, then cooled, before the addition of bacteria. Given the right conditions, i.e. correct temperature, the bacteria ferment the milk sugar (lactose), producing lactic acid.

The milk proteins then coagulate and set to form yoghurt. The lactic acid gives yoghurt its distinct flavour. Yoghurt can be made from different types of milk, including skimmed, semi-skimmed, whole, evaporated or powdered forms. Different bacteria cultures are used to achieve different textures and flavours.

The way in which yoghurt is processed makes a big difference to the style, quality and texture of the end product. There are two main methods for producing yoghurt:

- **Stirred yoghurt** The milk and bacteria culture are added together and stirred very slowly to allow the mixture to ferment.

- **Set yoghurt** The milk is warmed, bacteria culture is added and the mixture is put in the pot it will be sold/served in. It is then incubated at a controlled temperature. The resulting yoghurt is very delicate, so cannot be pumped or moved around.

The majority of the UK yoghurt market is based on the stirred variety. How the yoghurt is handled is very important. Yoghurt is like a gel and the more it is stirred, moved or handled, the more it breaks down. There is real skill and expertise involved in knowing when to stop fermentation and which cultures are best to achieve particular tastes. Some yoghurt producers have passed these skills down through the generations.

Low-fat yoghurts have milk powders added to them to help achieve the thickness required of a yoghurt without the fat content. This increases the protein content and the sugar content (present in the lactose from the milk) as these powders are effectively concentrated milk. Really low-fat or fat-free yoghurts may have a bit of a powdery feel when eaten. This is because even more powders need to be added to achieve the thickness and there is a lack of fat to coat the mouth and give a creamy feel. Low-fat yoghurt has less than 3 per cent fat and fat-free less than 0.5 per cent.

Some yoghurts, for example artisan Greek yoghurts, are strained. This simply means that they are sieved or put through a centrifuge that removes more of the whey. With the whey goes a significant proportion of the sugars, which is why strained Greek yoghurts are higher in fat and lower in sugar than other styles.

WHY THE PRICE VARIES

INGREDIENTS

Some types of milk are more expensive and add cost to the product. For example, organic milk or milk from a specific geographic location, such as the West Country, which is renowned for the richness of its milk, commands a higher price. In addition, simply using British milk rather than foreign imports can add cost. By law, authentic Greek (rather than Greek-style) yoghurt must be made in Greece so it is not possible to use British milk.

- **Bacteria** All yoghurt contains live bacteria, but the term 'bio' can no longer be used in association with the live bacteria used to make yoghurt following an update in European legislation clarifying the requirements for claims on gut health. The best producers carefully select the bacteria used in their yoghurts. Cultures are chosen for the texture and flavour that they produce. Typically, a different set of cultures will be used for different styles of yoghurt, e.g. fat-free versus authentic Greek yoghurt. As with sourdough bread, there is a real history attached to specific cultures.

- **Flavourings** The quality and provenance of the fruits or other ingredients used to flavour the yoghurt impact significantly on cost. The proportion of additional ingredients used relative to the yoghurt itself also influences price. Of course, natural flavouring ingredients will cost more than artificial flavours. Sugar is naturally present in milk and forms around 8 per cent of yoghurt content, and fruits used to flavour the yoghurt will contain naturally occurring sugars, too. More sugar may be added where sharper fruits have been used to balance the flavour. How the fruits are handled will also affect quality and price: gently handled fruit compotes with large, unbroken pieces of fruit will be more expensive than industrially produced blocks of frozen fruit.

PROCESSING METHODS

The milk and bacteria need to be fermented with care and then very gently handled, processed and packaged to retain a thick texture. This requires skill and expertise. It is particularly important to be consistent in all production to avoid the need to rely on chemical additives.

Mass-scale industrial production involves yoghurt being pumped about, which destroys the thickness, so stabilisers, gelling agents or gums need to be added to hold the consistency together. Smaller scale batch production, where the yoghurt is gently handled, means the consistency of the yoghurt can be maintained without these additives. However, it is more labour intensive and the economies of scale are fewer, so the end product is more expensive.

STYLE

Authentic Greek yoghurts will be more expensive because they are strained losing whey, and therefore volume.

WHAT TO LOOK FOR WHEN BUYING YOGHURT

PRODUCTS CAN APPEAR to be first class to the customer through clever branding, copy and packaging. However, this is no guarantee of premium quality. The quality depends on the ingredients, provenance and production method. Customers cannot necessarily gain all of this information at a glance, but a good starting point is the information about ingredients and nutrition on the pack. If the story and ethics behind the product are also visible on the pack, this can give further guidance. The price point and where this sits among other similar products is also a key indicator of quality. Generally, with yoghurt, the higher the price the better the quality.

TRY BEFORE YOU DIE!

—

The very best has to be authentic, artisan-strained Greek yoghurt in a terracotta dish, topped with wild Greek cherries, or honey and fresh walnuts, or honey and dark fresh figs. However, some of the Greek-style yoghurts now available in the UK are fantastic quality, with the added benefit of being made with British milk, such as Tims Dairy below.

TIMS DAIRY
£££

All of the milk and cream used to make Tims Dairy yoghurts is British, in support of UK farmers, and is supplied fresh to the dairy on a daily basis. The farmers are part of the National Dairy Scheme and a fair price is paid to them. The yoghurt is made at the dairy and natural fruit preparations are added to create different flavours. The technical process of heating the milk and then cooling it varies according to the style of yoghurt, but the simple artisan principles remain very similar to the early days. It is all just done on a bigger scale.

YOOMOO'S CAVIARMOO
£££££

In 2012, Harrods Food Hall launched a frozen take-away yoghurt bar with a truly rare taste pairing. Caviarmoo includes naturally fat-free Yoomoo frozen yoghurt, topped with shavings of Harrods' own couverture white chocolate, 23-carat gold flakes and caviar. It was hailed as a 'must-try' by frozen yoghurt fans and food lovers alike, combining the flavour experience of salt and sweet to offer a revolutionary taste experience.

Eggs

Back in the 1960s the slogan 'Go to work on an egg – and be your best all day' did wonders for the Egg Marketing Board. Since then, scientists have proved it wasn't all advertising puff. Egg proteins, particularly those found in the white, help us stay awake. Indeed, they are far more effective than carbohydrates found in chocolates, biscuits and sweets, which many people rely on for a quick pick-me-up.

I am a huge fan of this most basic of foods. I think the omelette is a much-underrated dish. It's quick and easy to cook, and very nutritious. One of my favourite restaurant dishes is the lobster omelette at the Goring Hotel in London. They cook a very good, rich, creamy omelette at the Goring, but I think it's the luxury of eating lobster as part of it that makes it such a treat.

A BRIEF HISTORY

EGGS AND CHICKENS ARE somewhat interlinked but I won't pre-empt here the history of chicken given in a later chapter. What I can tell you is that the egg came first! Certainly in this book anyhow.

It is worth adding, however, that chickens were not always kept so their eggs could be used for food. Historically, 'fowl' were eaten more regularly than eggs – to eat an egg could potentially mean eating a future whole chicken and so the practice was considered wasteful. This may be where the saying 'he who steals an egg will steal an ox' comes from.

It wasn't until the twentieth century that we started to separate chickens into 'broilers' for meat and 'layers' for eggs. Animals have been selectively bred ever since to accentuate desired traits, whether those traits are fast meat production for chicken destined for your roast dinner or a regular egg supply from reliable layers.

To appreciate the importance of differences in quality, it is helpful to understand the recent history of eggs. In 1988, there was concern over salmonella in eggs vocalised by Edwina Currie, the then Under Secretary of State for Health. A decade later, the British egg industry reacted by establishing the 'British Lion' assurance scheme, which made certain that all 'Lion' hens were vaccinated against salmonella.

The Lion scheme is extremely successful and salmonella has been all but eradicated in UK egg production. However, imported eggs are often not produced to such strict quality standards. A government test in 2004 found nearly 7 per cent of imported eggs tested positive for salmonella, compared to none of the British Lion eggs tested.

In the UK all Class A eggs (that means for human consumption) have to be marked with a code showing the type of farming system used, country of origin and production unit. In addition, British Lion eggs, which are produced to a particular quality standard (90 per cent of Class A UK eggs are produced to this standard), have a best-before date on the shell and carry the Lion logo.

HOW EGGS ARE PRODUCED

THERE IS A range of different systems for producing eggs:

BATTERY PRODUCTION (0 PER CENT UK PRODUCTION – BUT WE IMPORT 16 PER CENT OF ALL THE EGGS WE USE)

In this system, each cage houses up to ten birds, each with just enough room to stand up. The cages usually have a sloping wire-mesh floor and are kept in rows stacked in several tiers. Each shed will typically house tens of thousands of hens and the largest sheds can contain more than half a million birds. These hens may never experience natural light or fresh air and do not leave their cages until they are gathered for slaughter at the end of their productive lives.

Barren battery cages were banned by the EU in 2012. This meant the minimum animal welfare production system would be 'enriched cages', which have more space and height. It was the first piece of legislation in the EU to ban a method of production over animal welfare concerns. This law was passed in 1999, and came into force in 2012, but allegedly it took longer than that for some EU countries to comply.

This method of production is still legal outside the EU and it is estimated that 60 per cent of laying hens around the world, and 95 per cent in the US, are kept in these conditions.

To avoid eggs laid in barren battery cages, consumers are advised to look for the British Lion mark on eggs and egg packs, which guarantees that the eggs are both legal and produced to the higher animal welfare and food-safety standards. However, many of these battery-farmed eggs are used as ingredients in products such as quiches and cakes.

LAYING CAGE SYSTEMS (52 PER CENT UK PRODUCTION)

These are the larger 'enriched' colony cages introduced by the EU. Colony cages provide 750cm^2 per bird (about 20 per cent more than in battery production) along with a nest box for the birds to lay their eggs in, perching space for the birds to sleep on and a scratching area. In the UK, most of the new enriched colony cages are designed to contain between 40 and 80 birds. Food is supplied in troughs fitted to the cages and an automatic water supply is provided. The units are kept at an even temperature and are well ventilated. Lighting provides an optimum day length throughout the year.

The UK Lion Quality Code of Practice states that 'Farm' descriptions, farmyard and countryside scenes or pictures of hens roaming freely cannot be used on the egg box of Lion eggs produced by hens in cages.

BARN EGG PRODUCTION (3 PER CENT UK PRODUCTION)

In the barn system, hens are able to move freely around the hen house. In the EU, there is a maximum of 9 birds/m^2 of floor space, a perch per hen, and litter for scratching and dust bathing over one-third of the ground. There must be one nest box per five hens, or communal nests, at the rate of 120 birds/m^2 of floor area. Feeding and drinking space is allowed for each hen. Water and feeding troughs are raised so that the specially prepared food is not scattered. Electric lighting is provided to give an optimum day length throughout the year.

The advantage of this system is that it allows the hens much greater freedom of movement. They can stretch, flap their wings and fly. They can also perform other natural behaviours, such as pecking, scratching and laying their eggs in a nest.

The Lion code stipulates that for Lion Quality barn hens the maximum flock size is 32,000 birds, divided into colonies of a maximum of 4,000 where flock size is over 6,000 birds in total.

FREE-RANGE EGG PRODUCTION (45 PER CENT UK PRODUCTION)

EU egg-marketing legislation stipulates that for eggs to be termed 'free range', hens must have continuous daytime access to runs that are mainly covered with vegetation and a maximum stocking density of 2,500 birds per hectare. Hen-house conditions for free-range hens must comply with the regulations for birds kept in barn systems, with a maximum stocking density of 9 birds/m^2 of useable area. Hens must be provided with nest boxes, perches and litter as per the barn-production legislation.

The Lion Quality Code of Practice stipulates the same additional standards for Lion Quality free-range hens as for Lion Quality barn hens, plus provision of outdoor shading in the absence of a veranda and one pop-hole per 600 birds open for eight hours daily to allow access to the outside. Maximum flock size is 16,000 birds, divided into colonies of 4,000 where the flock size is over 6,000 birds in total. There is a maximum stocking density of 2,000 birds per hectare. The width and height of the pop-holes is greater than required by EU legislation.

ORGANIC EGG PRODUCTION (2 PER CENT UK PRODUCTION – INCLUDED IN THE 45 PER CENT ABOVE)

Hens producing organic eggs are always free range. In addition, hens must be fed an organically produced diet and ranged on organic land.

Hen-house conditions for organic hens are set by the EU Organic Regulations and stipulate a maximum stocking density of 6 birds/m^2 of useable area and a maximum flock size of 3,000 birds. Hens must be provided with nest boxes and more perching and litter space than in other systems.

The higher standards for flocks producing British Lion organic eggs include the provision of outdoor shading, additional height and width of pop-holes, which must be open for eight hours daily to allow access to the outside, and a maximum range-area stocking density of up to 2,000 birds per hectare.

WHY THE PRICE VARIES

PRODUCTION METHOD

Checking eggs before you buy them is important. All eggs sold in the UK must be stamped with the method of production:

- 0=organic
- 1=free-range
- 2=barn
- 3=caged

The method must also be stated on the carton. The British Lion symbol tells you that the eggs are British-laid and the hens have been vaccinated against salmonella. Price is a good indicator of how the hens were raised. If you buy your eggs from a supermarket, the cheapest are likely to be from hens kept in enriched cages, while the most expensive organic brands are potentially related to the highest welfare standards.

Breed

Breed is the first determiner of quality. Brown-feathered hybrid cross hens, such as the British Blacktail, lay brown eggs, while white hybrid hen crosses generally lay white eggs: the colour of an egg is entirely down to the colour of the breed. Different breeds will produce different quality eggs. Eggs from novelty or very traditional speciality breeds will be more expensive because they are less common and lay fewer eggs. Traditional breeds stop laying eggs in late autumn, take a break over the winter – the moult period – and start laying again when daylight gets longer in the spring. To ensure that the customer receives eggs all year, hen houses contain lights that are kept at the spring day length. Hens think it's always spring and keep laying eggs all through the year.

Feed

The quality of feed used is important and quality hens tend to be fed quality feed ingredients. For example, British Blacktail hens are fed on a rich grain-based diet containing wheat, maize, beans and soya together with crushed seashells to provide calcium for the eggshell. Hens supplement their ration with grazing and scratchings from their grass ranges. The better the quality of the hens' ranging the more natural 'carotenoids' they consume from plants and the deeper the colour of the egg yolks produced. British Blacktail flocks are reared to range strongly and fully utilise their ranging area.

Cheaper eggs come from hens fed a lower quality diet, for instance wheat with less protein and less energy. Cheap feeds are formulated to the lowest cost; feed manufacturers may have 15 or so different raw materials available to them and will use the 8 or so cheapest each month to make up the feed. That means hens receive fairly frequent diet reformulations, which is good for keeping costs down, but not necessarily the right nutritional answer for the hen and the eggs they produce. Some high-protein ingredients are particularly expensive, such as maize and beans, and ensuring there is no genetically modified content in the hens' feed also adds significant cost (around 30 per cent at the time of writing).

FRESHNESS

All egg packs feature a 'best-before date', which will be a maximum of 28 days after the egg was laid.

TRY BEFORE YOU DIE!

–

LOBSTER OMELETTE AT THE GORING HOTEL
££££

Clarence Court hen eggs are used for this indulgent dish, which is a Goring Hotel stalwart. Or for something more unusual …

CLARENCE COURT OSTRICH EGGS
£££££

Ostrich Eggs are the size equivalent of 24 hens' eggs and are in season from late March to early September. They take 50 minutes to soft boil and two hours to hard boil but it's worth the wait. The shells retain their heat after cooking so plunge into cold water to stop them overcooking. Their large, smooth hard shells also make them ideal for decorating once blown. Carefully make a hole in the bottom and empty the contents into a mixing bowl to keep the shell intact.

Flour

Most people would be forgiven for believing there is little difference between the flour sold in one shop and another. Wheat is wheat, right? Wrong. The good news is that things are nowhere near as unpredictable as in the eighteenth and nineteenth centuries when unscrupulous shopkeepers diluted their flour mixes with anything from alum and lime to powdered bones. (The practice was blamed for the severe malnutrition prevalent at the time.) There is a marked difference in the quality of flour available today. While we are no longer in danger of ingesting some unwanted and unpalatable additions, it is well worth your while finding out more about this food-cupboard staple.

A BRIEF HISTORY

FLOUR, AS THE white powder we know today, was first noted in the Middle East approximately 10,000 years ago. In those days, early grass seeds were ground using rocks to create a rudimentary product.

Flour milling has undergone many developments since then. Rocks were replaced with pestle and mortars, and later flour was ground between hand-operated rotating stones called querns. In the Roman period, larger scale, water-powered mechanisation was introduced. Until the late 1800s, stone milling was the primary source of flour production and many UK villages had a watermill or windmill – many of which can still be seen today. Horsehair sleeves were used to sift out any unwanted material during the stone-milling process and pure white flour was considered superior because it was less likely to contain any general rubbish that might have come in with uncleaned wheat.

In the late 1800s, steel rollers were introduced into the milling industry and roller milling is the main process still used today. There are, however, a small number of commercial mills producing traditional stoneground flour using time-honoured techniques.

As well as developments in milling, wheat varieties have also changed over time. Early wheat varieties were 'long-strawed'; in the last 30 years, wheat has been bred to become 'dwarf', which means that the wheat is shorter in height, and a larger head of wheat can be carried by the plant. This halves the height of the plant and doubles the amount of grain.

GEOGRAPHY

WHEAT CAN BE categorised according to planting season as a spring or winter variety. Winter wheats are planted between September and December and lie dormant through the cold months. Spring wheat is planted between February and April. Both spring and winter wheat are harvested in July and August, weather permitting. Spring wheat varieties tend to have a lower yield and are generally of a superior bread-making quality (higher protein).

The best wheat/cereal-growing regions in the world have temperate climates and include Canada, North America, Australia and northern Europe, as well as the emerging areas of Kazakhstan and Ukraine. Climate is the major factor in determining the best growing locations; the crop doesn't grow when it is particularly dry or wet.

Canadian Red Wheat and Kazak wheats are superior varieties, renowned for quality in bread, pasta and pizza-making.

In the UK, the best growing areas are East Anglia and the south-east due to the climate and soil. Some flours display the Red Tractor symbol to demonstrate their British provenance. Smaller millers tend to source English wheat from local farmers in a commitment to help keep food miles to a minimum and reduce transport costs.

HOW FLOUR IS PRODUCED

AFTER HARVEST, WHEAT is stored and delivered into flour mills throughout the rest of the year. Wheat is traded globally as a commodity so the price paid by UK millers is based upon global supply and demand. The performance of harvests in Russia or Australia have a huge impact on the price a UK farmer receives.

Cereals can be produced using conventional or organic growing methods. Cereals grown on organically certified farms make flours that bear their organic certification. Organic farming predominantly uses natural methods, such as crop rotation, to strengthen the soil, and organic farmers encourage natural predators as pest control to minimise the need for pesticides.

The LEAF (Linking Environment and Farming) standard can be applied to cereals if they meet particular environmental standards in the way they are grown.

PRODUCTION METHOD

Wheat comprises three parts: the bran, germ and endosperm (the starchy white part of the grain). To make flour, the white endosperm must be extracted from the grain. To do this, the grain is gradually reduced, or broken down, by passing it through steel rollers, followed by sieving to separate the endosperm from the bran or germ. For white flour, only the endosperm is used. For brown or wholemeal flours, some or all of the bran is added back.

Some specialist flour mills still make some flours in the old-fashioned way, grinding the whole grain between horizontal French Burr stones. French Burr was quarried from the Marne Valley in northern France. When stone-grinding flour, the cleaned wheat passes into the middle of a set of millstones; the top one, or runner, rotates while the bottom one, the bed, stays still. As the wheat goes into the middle of the stone, it spreads and is cut and ground by the grooves on the stones. A chute takes grain into the stones and it is shaken by a shaft called the damsel. When the hopper of wheat runs low, a little bell still rings to warn the miller. The whole of the grain is ground to flour in one process; nothing is removed thus making a wholesome flour.

French Burr stones are nowadays very rare, and therefore they require significant care. Normally a miller will re-sharpen traditional mill stones every three months because over time they wear, slowly run smooth and then don't grind properly. This highly skilled job is done by hand using techniques that have remained unchanged since the earliest days of milling. The miller taps at the stone face with a traditional chisel to reintroduce, or re-emphasise, the shallow grooves. It is labour intensive. The work is referred to as dressing a set of stones and it can take a miller a week.

Traditional stones have a much smaller output than modern roller milling, and therefore stoneground flour tends to be more expensive than the mass-produced alternative. The milling process also gives stoneground wholemeal flour a characteristic and unique nutty flavour.

WHY THE PRICE VARIES

WHEAT QUALITY

The quality of flour is determined by the quality of wheat used and the skill of the miller in creating the grist (the milling recipe). UK wheat is classified from Group 1 to 4:

- Group 1 comprises of premium, high-protein bread wheats.

- Group 2 includes more general bread-making wheats.

- Group 3 is made up of soft wheat varieties used for biscuits and cakes.

- Group 4 includes wheats generally grown to be used in animal feeds.

Premium-quality flours tend to be made using the best Group 1 wheats. Value flour products will be made from lower quality grade wheats.

The best brands continually monitor incoming wheat quality and, if necessary, make adjustments to the grist to ensure the flour remains consistent year after year, even if there is a poor harvest.

The best-quality flours include white and wholemeal bread flours made from 100 per cent Canadian wheat. The quality and quantity of gluten in Canadian wheat results in flours that are very forgiving and tolerant; a novice bread-maker is less likely to have baking failures when using these top of the range flours.

CONSISTENCY

Quality flour performs consistently for a baker. Nowadays mills have stringent quality assurance procedures, with onsite laboratories where the wheat is tested for a number of variables (such as protein quality and content, and moisture levels) and the flour is checked throughout the milling process.

High-protein bread flours make doughs that are more forgiving and easy to handle. Bread rises higher with a better crust, colour and crumb, and a baker is less likely to have bread-making failures, than when using cheaper flours. Better quality plain flour is easier to roll out and has less shrinkage when baked. It also makes whiter and creamier coloured pastry (with a lack of bran specs), which many find more appetising. Better quality self-raising flour will produce a lighter, fluffier sponge and its whiteness will highlight the yellow colour of the eggs.

PRODUCTION METHOD

Traditional techniques are obviously more costly and time consuming than mass-production, particularly when the skill of the miller is key.

Techniques that millers can use to produce lower cost flour include milling wheat harder. This gives the impression when it is tested that the resulting flour is stronger in protein than it actually is; however, when this flour is baked it is more difficult to handle, particularly in longer baking processes. The miller can also mill what are called 'thinner wheats' in order to reduce costs. These include more bran in the flour in relation to the endosperm.

Both these measures will reduce costs but they do have quality implications.

Sustainability

The farming system that is used impacts on price: organic farming produces lower yields and organic wheat is therefore more expensive.

When shopping, you might find it difficult to assess quality between different flours that are for the same purpose. The best thing to do is to look at the nutritional information on the side of the pack and compare it for different flours. For example, if comparing Strong White flours for bread-making, the customer could look at the level of protein shown. The protein content refers to the amount of gluten that can be formed using the flour. Gluten provides structure and aids the texture of the bread. The higher the protein content, the better the flour will perform when making bread. It means the loaf will be bigger. You will probably notice a difference when baking with wholemeal or seeded bread flours as the protein is provided by the 70–80 per cent of the white flour in the mix, which is needed to lift the bran and seeds.

I would like to add a note of caution here. There is a relatively wide tolerance when it comes to nutritional on-pack data for flour so it should be used as a guide only.

On-pack marketing messages and product descriptions can be helpful when assessing whether a product is good quality. Statements such as 'Very Strong Canadian flour', '(traditional) Stoneground Wholemeal flour' and 'Organic flour' are all indicators of a superior-quality product.

TRY BEFORE YOU DIE!

–

DOVES FARM ORGANIC KAMUT KHORASAN WHOLEMEAL FLOUR
££££

When the world's most expensive cupcake was commissioned (in Dubai, need you ask), it was Dove's Farm Organic flour that was used for the $1,000 creation.

This Khorasan flour was originally made for the pharaohs in Egypt and reflects the growing popularity of ancient grains. The wheat variety is naturally high in protein and minerals, such as selenium. It is milled the old-fashioned way, using a stoneground process.

SHARPHAM PARK ORGANIC SPELT FLOUR ARTISAN
££££

Spelt was brought over from the Middle East around 9,000 years ago. In Britain it is first known to have existed as a main crop in 2000 BC but it had fallen out of favour by medieval times. After a brief revival in the nineteenth century, it was back out of fashion again in the twentieth century as crops producing higher yields took over.

Spelt is a cross between emmer wheat and goat grass, and has a distinctive, nutty flavour and unusual texture. Unlike common wheat, spelt has not been hybridised or chemically altered, and it remains as simple and hardy as it was when it was first introduced. Sharpham Park grows and mills spelt on its own 300-acre farm near Glastonbury. British spelt is versatile, delicious, nutritious and easy to digest, making it a fantastic alternative to conventional wheat.

Sugar

Sugar or, to be more precise, dietary sugars have been under scrutiny for years and have been blamed for everything from causing dental cavities to obesity to hyperactivity and a lot of other conditions in between. While some of the criticism is deserved, some of the assumptions are just plain wrong or, at the very least, based on incorrect interpretations of the data. It is bacteria that causes tooth decay, not the sweet stuff. Since 1997, no less than five leading scientific and health organisations, including the World Health Organization and the Institute of Medicine, have concluded that dietary sugars are not associated with causing illness or chronic diseases, including obesity. And, no, sugar is not addictive, even though it is very nice. We're just genetically programmed to like sweet things.

Of course, this is not to say it shouldn't be taken in moderation. For those with a very sweet tooth, a good philosophy might be to restrict your intake by treating yourself to a more limited quantity of the best-quality sugars. Here's how.

A BRIEF HISTORY

THE **SUGAR-CANE PLANT** is believed to have originated on the Polynesian islands and was first domesticated in New Guinea 10,000 years ago. It spread slowly from island to island, reaching the Asian mainland around 1000 BC. From there, it made its way to India where it was processed into a powder, and then to Persia. It was here that Arabs discovered sugar and fell in love with it. They perfected sugar refinement and turned it into an industry. As sugar cane grows in tropical or semi-tropical climates, Europe relied on trade from the East for supplies. This made it expensive and for the elite only, until Columbus took sugar cane to the West Indies on his 1493 voyage. Sugar plantations spread dramatically and, with their growth, demand for slave labour imported from Africa. As production increased, sugar prices fell and by the mid-seventeenth century, sugar had become an accessible commodity for all in the Western world. Before the slave trade was banned in Britain in 1807, it is estimated that 11 million slaves had been trafficked from Africa, around half of whom had worked on sugar plantations.

All this time, beet was being grown in Europe for animal fodder, but it had not been identified as a source of sugar. That breakthrough came in 1747 when Andreas Marggraf, a German chemist, succeeded in extracting sugar from beet in a form usable in cooking. During the Napoleonic Wars, the British Navy blockaded French ports, preventing goods, including cane sugar, from being imported. This led to a rapid increase in sugar-beet farming in mainland Europe. It then began to rival cane sugar and became the main source of sugar in Europe by 1880. The abolition of slavery during this time also increased the cost of cane sugar, making sugar from beet even more competitive. Britain became particularly interested in beet during the First World War, as the government encouraged farmers to grow it when German U-boats began sinking trading ships.

GEOGRAPHY

THE **KIND OF SUGAR** we buy today therefore comes from two very different sources; sugar cane, which grows in tropical areas, and sugar beet, which is grown in the UK and in other temperate parts of the world. They are suited to entirely different climates but once the sugar they contain is processed, you end up with the same product – 99.95 per cent sucrose.

Sugar cane is a bamboo-like plant the roots of which sprout new canes each year, and sugar beet, a relative of the red beetroot and turnip, looks like a large white turnip or beetroot. Sugar beet tend to be grown near sugar-processing factories in East Anglia and the Midlands in the UK. British Sugar buys and processes 100 per cent of the British crop and sells it to food manufacturers, retailers and Silver Spoon, the only brand to sell

100 per cent UK sugar. Just under half of the sugar used in the UK comes from cane sugar, and the rest from beet. In the rest of the world, by far the majority of sugar (around 80 per cent) comes from cane, although in Europe there is a much higher reliance on beet.

HOW SUGAR IS PRODUCED

BEFORE GETTING INTO the process I quickly want to explain the difference between white and brown sugar and refined and unrefined varieties. When sugar crystals have been extracted from the juice of the beet or cane plant, a strong-tasting black syrup (known as molasses) remains. When white sugar is made, it is refined until the molasses are entirely removed, whereas brown sugars will be refined less so the crystals retain some of this natural syrup. The more molasses there are in brown sugar, the stickier the crystals, the darker the colour and the stronger the flavour. However, beware, as many brown sugars are actually white sugars with an added brown coating for colour and a little flavour.

'Unrefined' sugar is entirely produced where the sugar cane is grown, not in a refinery elsewhere. Producers who do this are able to command a very significant premium over selling just the sugar cane, which in turn benefits the local community.

Unrefined sugars lock in, rather than refine out, the natural molasses of the sugar cane. It is this difference that gives the sugar a greater richness, depth of flavour and natural colour, which refined sugars, even if coated in molasses, do not possess. Unrefined sugar goes through a minimal amount of processing within its country of origin in order to maintain its superior quality.

SUGAR CANE

On average, a hectare yields about 50 tonnes of sugar cane, from which 7 tonnes of sugar can be extracted.

Once harvested sugar cane is taken to a mill, cut into small pieces and shredded. It is then crushed between heavy rollers and sprayed with hot water. Lime is added to clean the resulting juice. The brown liquid is filtered to produce a thin juice, which is boiled under vacuum to form a thick syrup.

The crystals (raw sugar) and syrup (molasses) are separated in a centrifuge and brown raw-sugar crystals are produced. The raw sugar is exported around the world for local refining. Refining removes impurities and traces of molasses to produce pure white sugar crystals.

SUGAR BEET

On average a hectare yields about 41 tonnes of clean, topped roots from which 7 tonnes of sugar can be extracted.

The production of sugar from sugar beet takes place in a factory. A sample from each delivery is tested to find out the quantity of sugar in the beet and the farmer is paid accordingly.

The sugar beet is washed and sliced into small pieces known as cossettes, which are sprayed with hot water. Lime and carbon dioxide are added to clean the resulting juice. The brown liquid is filtered and boiled under vacuum to produce a thick syrup. Crystals start to appear. Tiny sugar crystals called 'seeds' are added to encourage crystallisation. The pure white sugar crystals are separated from the syrup in a centrifuge.

SUGAR VARIETIES

As a result of the above two processes the following sugars are produced:

- **Golden caster sugar** This can be used instead of white caster sugar for sponge cakes or shortbread. It has a subtle caramel taste, giving baked goods a better flavour than white caster sugar. Caster sugar is better suited for baking than granulated sugar as it has smaller particle sizes, meaning it makes cakes lighter and airier.

- **Demerara sugar** This has a large particle size, which means it adds a crunchy texture to baking. It is ideal for crumbles and biscuits and is also perfect for coffee as it takes longer to dissolve, distributing the sweetness more effectively.

- **Light muscovado sugar** Muscovado sugar is the finest brown sugar you can buy, with a higher molasses content than soft brown sugars. Light muscovado is a great sugar to use in soft chewy cookies as well as chocolate cakes and puddings.

- **Dark muscovado sugar** Dark muscovado has a richer taste than light muscovado, meaning it is better for richer fruit cakes, brownies or chocolate cakes.

- **Soft brown sugar** This is both soft and moist with fine crystals and a distinctive caramel taste. It can be confused with muscovado but it has a smaller molasses content, meaning it does not possess the same flavour. Soft brown sugar can either be partially refined or be white sugar with molasses added.

- **Dark brown sugar** Darker in colour than light brown sugar, with a stronger molasses flavour, this can be used for gingerbread and rich fruit cakes, whereas light brown sugar has a more delicate honey-like flavour and is commonly used for making butterscotch and biscuits.

- **Icing sugar** Also known as powdered sugar or confectioner's sugar, icing sugar is made by sifting and grinding regular white granulated sugar, resulting in a fine powder. It is usually mixed with a small amount of anti-caking agent to keep it dry and free flowing. There is a variety of icing sugar you can use to suit your baking needs. Regular icing sugar is great for buttercream or you can use fondant icing sugar to make glossy, smooth fondant icing. Royal icing sugar is hard-setting, traditionally used for Christmas cakes or wedding cakes.

- **Golden icing sugar** This is an unrefined sugar with natural molasses, giving it a caramel flavour and natural honey colour. It is perfect for icing, buttercream or desserts, though the colour means some cake-makers prefer the whiter variety.

- **Jam sugar** This is a combination of sugar and pectin. The added pectin ensures that jam or jelly sets quickly, retaining its fresh fruity flavour and natural colour – perfect for quick and easy jam-making with fruits that are low in pectin, such as strawberries, raspberries and apricots. It even works with frozen fruit.

- **Preserving sugar** The large sugar crystals of preserving sugar dissolve slowly, producing a clear preserve using fruits that are naturally high in pectin, such as apples, plums and gooseberries. The sugar doesn't sink or rise up, thus reducing the risk of burning and the need for stirring. This allows impurities to rise and makes it easier for skimming.

- **Molasses sugar** Molasses is a sweet, thick liquid obtained from the sugar-refining process. The liquid is crystallised to make molasses sugar. It is the ultimate soft brown sugar, packed full of natural cane molasses, and has the deepest colour and richest flavour of all sugars. This, combined with the sticky texture and treacle-like flavour, makes it perfect for rich Christmas cakes and indulgent sticky-toffee puddings. It is also excellent for making chutneys, marinades and ethnic foods, where a rich colour and sweet flavour are essential.

WHY THE PRICE VARIES

SUPPLY AND DEMAND
Sugar is largely commoditised on a global basis, so the quantity of sugar being produced and consumed plays a very large part in price.

VARIETY
White granulated sugar is a global commodity but high-quality unrefined sugars, such as muscovado, command a premium due to the unique process that delivers such a sought-after product. Producing a true unrefined sugar is an art and only a handful of producers have mastered the technique. Expert producers carefully and painstakingly create these sugars and are therefore able to command a very significant premium over selling just raw sugar for refining.

ETHICS

There are many ethical schemes in place that can contribute to premiums on sugar pricing. Probably the most recognised is Fairtrade, which helps support local farmers and workers with better prices and fair trading terms.

TRY BEFORE YOU DIE!

–

UNREFINED MUSCOVADO SUGAR
££££

This is truly the king of sugars. Its rich caramel taste melts in your mouth to deliver the true flavour of real sugar and, once tried, is never forgotten. The name muscovado is thought to mean 'middle of the barrel' and references times past where molasses syrup would be dried in barrels under the heat of the hot sun to produce sugar. The top of the barrel would be a golden colour, the middle rich and moist, and the bottom of the barrel dark and sticky, like the molasses sugar we know today. Muscovado sugars lend themselves to rich recipes, such as fruit cakes and sticky syrup puddings. However, they can also be used in chocolate brownies and I can assure you one of these will be the best chocolate brownie you have ever tasted.

BILLINGTON'S
££££

Billington's unrefined soft sugars are made with sugar cane and grown, produced and packed in Mauritius. Their unique and delicious flavour elevates baking but can also be a surprising addition to your savoury dishes. Should you wish to treat your taste buds to these sugars, may I suggest a trip to a Paul A. Young store (www.paulayoung.co.uk)? Paul A. Young is an award-winning chocolatier who uses only the finest and simplest ingredients to make his world-renowned chocolates. Paul has been using only unrefined sugars in his chocolate creations for over 15 years.

Bread

If cheese is without a doubt my favourite food, bread is, I am afraid, my downfall. I could definitely eat far more than is good for me and if I was able to eat nothing more than bread and cheese, accompanied by a good red wine, I would be a very, very happy man indeed. So, the challenge for me in this chapter was how much to leave out.

Every country and region around the world has its own special way of producing bread. It is incredible that four simple ingredients – flour, water, yeast and salt – could yield such a huge variety of exquisite-tasting breads. Whether it is a Parisian baguette or an Irish soda bread, every community has bread with which it can be identified with and of which it can be rightly proud.

You can buy very cheap loaves of bread, and I will explain how that's done, but for me it's worth every penny to spend that little bit more and here I will share the secrets of my favourites.

A BRIEF HISTORY

WHEAT AND OTHER grains for bread-making have been cultivated for over 10,000 years, and in the British Isles from about 6,000 years ago. Some historians, and

I agree, think that without the cultivation of grains to make bread, villages, towns, cities and the great civilisations that have shaped our history would not have evolved. So bread, for me, is the foundation stone of the modern world.

The earliest breads were flatbreads, made from ground grain and water mixed to a paste and baked on a flat stone over a fire. Breads of this kind, such as pitta, tortillas and chapatti, can still be found all over the globe. The earliest archaeological evidence of leavened bread is from ancient Egypt.

All grains attract yeast spores to their surface, and wholegrain flour mixed with water that is left in the open in a warm climate will soon start bubbling away as yeast starts to feed on the complex starches in the flour and produce carbon dioxide. It was probably an accidental discovery of this phenomenon that led to the realisation that dough that is leavened (that is, allowed to 'rise' through the activity of yeast) before baking is less dense and more palatable than if baked straight away.

Pliny the Elder, the Roman statesman, noted that Gauls used foam skimmed from beer to produce 'a lighter kind of bread than other people's'. Beer and wine ferments have long been a source of yeasts for bread-making.

Bakers soon discovered that they could take part of their dough and use it as a 'starter' for leavening their bread the following day. Artisan bakers still use this method and prize their 'mother-dough' as a key ingredient. Many such doughs can be kept by bakers for years and they will develop their own distinctive taste over time. Some micro-climates encourage the growth of yeasts that endow bread with special taste properties. Examples of this are San Francisco sourdough and the breads of Altamura in Italy.

Today, most bread is made using baker's yeast produced on a large scale in ultra-hygienic facilities. We have all heard the expression 'the best thing since sliced bread' and over eight out of ten loaves we buy today are sold ready wrapped and sliced. Otto Frederick Rohwedder first started work on his slicing machine in 1912, but it was not until it was adopted by a bakery in Missouri, USA, in 1928, that the concept started to spread rapidly across North America and then Europe.

The next big development in bread was the Chorleywood bread-making process in 1961. This method, in which dough is mixed in a matter of minutes under a vacuum, proved for about 50 minutes, then baked in around 20, greatly reduced the process time from a day or more to a few hours. As the time reduces and the baking equipment is better utilised, so does the cost reduce. About 80 per cent of the loaves we eat today are made in this way.

And now we are turning full circle with a growth in interest in artisan breads, going back to the old ways of production, using sourdough and overnight fermentation and without the use of additives.

HOW BREAD IS PRODUCED

WHEAT REMAINS THE main grain for bread-making, although rye and other grains are often used, particularly in northern Europe. Wheat is widely grown and different countries and regions will produce wheat of varying qualities for bread. Bakers often say that the best-quality wheat for bread-making flour is grown in Canada, where the cold winters and hot summers are the perfect combination for making strong (higher and better quality protein) flour. The UK's climate, with mild wet winters and unpredictable summers, is not ideal for wheat production save in the south-east region. Britain has therefore imported wheat for bread-making for thousands of years.

Over the past few decades, however, UK farmers and seed growers have made great improvements in quality and now many bakers are able to use flour made from UK wheat.

There are so many different ways of producing bread that it would not be possible to cover them all here. All bakers have their own techniques and preferences, and many will debate whether baking is a science or an art form. Perhaps what might be interesting would be to compare the modern 'Chorleywood Process' with a more traditional approach, still used by many bakers today, even some of reasonable scale who supply major supermarkets.

Traditional Method	Modern High-speed Process
Use of 'mother-dough' or sourdough starters to leaven the dough, sometimes with some slow-acting yeast, too	Use of fast-acting liquid yeast
Dough mixed in slow-speed spiral mixers, a bit like a larger version of a Kenwood Chef, 10 to 15 minutes	Dough mixed under vacuum in a high-speed mixer, 2 to 4 minutes
Dough left to ferment for many hours, sometimes overnight. Often added to the final dough mix as what bakers call a 'sponge dough'	Use of emulsifiers and added enzymes (often called 'dough improvers') to produce a softer loaf with good keeping qualities while avoiding time taken by long fermentation
Dough divided by hand or in a bread divider	Dough divided by a high-speed divider

Bread proved (left to rise) naturally over a few hours Dusted with flour and cut or topped with seeds by hand	Bread fed from divider into an in-line prover for about 50 minutes Automatically dusted and cut by machine or topped with a lid
Baked for around 30 to 50 minutes	Baked in an in-line moving tunnel-oven for about 20 minutes
Cooled in racks	Cooled in in-line coolers, then sliced and wrapped automatically

The benefits of wholemeal bread as opposed to the white version are well documented. Wholemeal bread typically contains 7.1g of dietary fibre per 100g, as opposed to 2.4g for white. Studies have shown that white flour loses significant levels of vitamins and minerals during the milling process (Henry A. Schroeder, *American Journal of Clinical Nutrition*, May 1971).

Another American study in the *American Journal of Clinical Nutrition* in 2007 found that people who eat more wholegrains tend to weigh less, have lower cholesterol, a lower body mass index and have smaller waists. Wholegrains may also help lower the risk of heart disease and type-2 diabetes (*Journal of Nutrition*, 2011).

As I mentioned in the chapter on flour, to make wholegrain flour, the different elements of the grain are mixed back together again at the end of the process. A French study in 2005 (Chaurand *et al*, *Industries des Céréales*, no.142) showed that stoneground organic flour had a higher mineral level than 'roller milled' flour.

A sourdough loaf is made from a dough that has been kicked-off with a starter-dough leaven that the baker has nurtured for many years and fermented for many hours. After that it is folded and 'knocked-back' perhaps six times, before being divided, moulded, cut or decorated by hand, proved for a further hour, then placed into a stone-bed oven for perhaps 50 minutes.

WHY THE PRICE VARIES

AS A GENERAL GUIDE, price is usually a good indicator of quality in bread.

INGREDIENTS

When inspecting a loaf, bakers look for what they call a good 'bloom'. This describes the delicately shaded reddish-browns on the top of a loaf that merge into a golden yellow crust and then to a silvery cream colour on those areas of the loaf that have been protected from the direct heat of the oven. Without a good-quality bread-making flour, such an appearance is hard to achieve.

Bakers also look for good volume in a loaf. A loaf that has poor volume (that is, has not risen well) is too dense and not great eating. This can be caused by any number of things, but may be the result of a weak (low protein) flour, scalded yeast, a final dough temperature that is too low at the end of mixing or insufficient proving. At the other end of the scale, a loaf that has too much volume is difficult to slice and will rapidly fall apart when spread with butter.

As noted in the chapter on flour, in medieval times flour for bread-making was often adulterated by unscrupulous bakers wanting to make more profit. This led to some of the earliest food regulation by governments and some pretty tough punishments for bakers who broke the law. The Assize of Bread and Ale, a thirteenth-century statute, stipulated the price, weight and quality of bread and hefty fines for law-breakers.

PRODUCTION METHOD

The difference in costs between a loaf made by an artisan baker and one made by an industrial 'plant' bakery are easy to see. In the former, a skilled baker is using a starter-dough, fermenting the mix for many hours, sometimes days, before shaping, cutting and dusting by hand, and baking in small batches. In the latter, ingredients are automatically fed into a high-speed mixer and may not be seen again except by a maintenance engineer, or a quality-control operative, until sliced and bagged loaves emerge from the end of a bagging machine. That's not to say it isn't a good loaf.

Highly controversially, some writers and bakers, such as Andrew Whitley, the author of *Bread Matters*, believe that there is a correlation between the rise of high-speed industrial bread-making and wheat intolerance. The theory is that the fermentation process (during which bread 'rises') is too short to allow the breaking-down of wheat proteins and does not allow the development of naturally occurring micro-flora that may aid digestion. Many in the bakery industry reject these claims and, although some research has been conducted, more is required before we fully understand any connections between the two. In the meantime, various studies have lent some credibility to claims that sourdough breads have positive health benefits for sufferers from irritable bowel syndrome and coeliac disease, or have an impaired glucose metabolism.

TRY BEFORE YOU DIE!

–

There are four regional artisan bakers in the UK who make wonderful sourdough bread:

- Gail's Artisan Bakery, London

- The Long Crichel Bakery, Dorset

- Exeter Street Bakery, London

- The Bertinet Kitchen, Bath

POILÂNE BREAD
££££

One of the most expensive breads on sale in the UK is Poilâne. The Poilâne loaf was first made from a closely guarded recipe create by Parisian master baker Pierre Poilâne in 1932. The list of devotees of the rye sourdough bread, which weighs slightly more than 1.8kg per loaf and takes six hours to bake in an oak-burning oven, has included Robert De Niro, James Coburn and Catherine Deneuve.

ROYAL BLOOMER
£££££

The UK's most expensive loaf of bread is made from 24-carat gold leaf and champagne. It was created by Robert Didier, who trained with top chef Raymond Blanc, at his Orchard Pigs bakery in Wrexham, North Wales. To make the luxurious three-foot loaf, Robert replaced some of the water used in traditional sourdough breads with a few glugs of champagne, in this case a bottle of Charles De Cazanove, and mixed 24-carat edible gold through the dough. The loaves are made once a month and they are reserved for special occasions. They have even been shipped to New York.

Pasta

As I have said, my first experience of the world of pasta came when I worked in Italy each summer as a student. It was all a far cry from Vesta frozen lasagne on sale back in Lancaster. I found it truly incredible that three everyday, basic ingredients – water, flour and eggs – can taste so different. Of course, Italians have made pasta into an art form. After mixing and kneading together these somewhat boring ingredients, they cut, roll and squash the elastic dough into an endless range of shapes, before combining them with vegetables, fish and meat to make the most delicious meals.

This chapter should help you separate the durum wheat from the wheat. However, I should point out at the start that pasta production/usage/nomenclature varies significantly between the regions of Italy (and even within them!) so writing a concise, 100 per cent factually correct brief summary of pasta is very challenging.

A BRIEF HISTORY

THE EXACT ORIGIN of pasta is hotly contested. Some say Marco Polo brought it back to Italy from his travels in the Far East in the thirteenth century, and there is clear evidence of the use of a mixture of flour and water, dried and boiled, in China from 1100 BC. However, others (particularly Italians!) argue that pasta was invented in Italy and with some justification as fourth century BC wall paintings in an Etruscan cave do indeed show pasta-making. The philosopher and orator Cicero also referred to enjoying '*laganum*', thick wide strips of pasta. The word 'pasta' comes from the Italian word for paste, referring to the mix of flour and water, if you want to push the Italian case further. However, some believe the Greeks, Persians and Arabs can also lay claim to being the first inventors of pasta in the Western world. Lunching one time in the Florentine square outside the Uffizi Gallery I overheard an American tourist say it was invented in his native country and the Italians then imported it! Perhaps it's a good thing everyone wants to own it.

What we do know is that by 1400 pasta was being produced commercially in Italy and pasta would be hung in the streets, or anywhere there was space, to dry. The pasta industry developed around Naples because of the proximity of locally grown durum wheat (although cereals were also imported into Italy for pasta production) and because the climate of alternating dry and humid winds allowed pasta to dry at the right speed – not too quickly so it would crack, not too slowly so it would go mouldy. In the 1600s the first moulds were made to make shapes.

Pasta production really took off, enabling pasta to become a food of the masses, with the invention of kneading and drying machines.

HOW PASTA IS PRODUCED

DRIED **PASTA IS** made from '*semola*' (semolina), which is roughly milled durum wheat, a variety which is particularly high in protein and low in starch. Fresh pasta, however, will often be made with '00' flour, which is finely ground flour, and no *semola* at all.

On the face of it, making dried pasta is very simple; mix semolina and water, knead it, shape it and allow it to dry. However, the experience of centuries of production means that these days a huge amount of skill is involved in creating quality pasta.

Firstly, grains are milled to separate the semolina (endosperm) from the rest of the grain. The proportion of grain used impacts on quality – upmarket producers use only the best part of the grain (say 60 per cent).

The semolina is mixed with water. Artisanal producers use cold water and carry out the kneading at a low temperature; mass producers use warm water, but this can reduce the texture, aroma and flavour qualities of the pasta when cooked.

Once kneaded, the pasta dough is shaped. This is done using what is called a 'die'. The choice of die determines the shape of the pasta and the dough is forced through it at great pressure to give the resulting shape.

The pasta is then dried before it is packed.

Fresh pasta is considered to be an entirely different product. In fresh-pasta production eggs are usually added right at the start to give richness, protein and colour, and often '00' flour is used exclusively with no semolina as the pasta doesn't need to be as firm. This is why it is easier to make this sort of pasta at home. It is much more delicate, has the consistency of a soft dough and needs to be cooked for a very short time compared to dried pasta. When measuring fresh pasta you will need more than for dried pasta; dried pasta swells and absorbs a lot of water during the longer cooking process whereas fresh pasta isn't in contact with the water long enough to absorb much liquid.

PASTA SHAPES AND USES

ITALIANS MAKE PASTA in all shapes and sizes to suit various sauces. Ribbed pasta holds more sauce than smooth shapes so rigatoni will need more sauce than macaroni. Rich, creamy sauces are best with chunky shapes, such as penne, while if you are serving an oil-based sauce, such as pesto, choose a fine pasta, such as spaghetti. Sheets of pasta, such as lasagne, are good cooked with chunky sauces made from meat, vegetables or fish.

Types of dried pasta available include:

- **Cannelloni** Large pasta tubes that are usually served stuffed and baked in the oven.

- **Farfalle** These bow-tie or butterfly pasta shapes are often a popular choice with children due to their novelty shape. Serve cold in pasta salads. Use fusilli instead of farfalle in recipes.

- **Conchilige** Also known as shells these pasta shapes have a ribbed outer surface so sauce tends to cling to them. Rather confusingly, they are sometimes called gnocchi, which is the same name and shape as the light potato dumplings popular in Italy. Orecchiette can be used instead.

- **Lasagne** One of the most popular types of pasta, lasagne consists of sheets of either egg or plain pasta approximately 8 x 16cm in size. There is a variety of different types including classic lasagne, which is sheets of plain flat pasta made simply from durum wheat semolina. *Lasagne all'uovo* is egg pasta sheets. Spinach lasagne or *lasagne verdi* is dark green in colour and the sheets are flat. *Lasagne verdi all'uovo* is egg pasta with spinach to give it the characteristic green colour.

  The different types of lasagne are interchangeable. The spinach variety provides an alternative in colour to the classic plain variety, while egg lasagnes have a slightly richer flavour.

- **Linguine** A thin type of spaghetti with flattened edges. The name comes from the Italian for tongue.

- **Macaroni** These thin tubes of pasta are one of the most well-known types because of the popularity of macaroni cheese. Macaroni is a generic word used to describe short-shape pasta. In English the word has become synonymous with the curved elbow-shaped tubes but not for Italians.

- **Vermicelli** Vermicelli (literally small worms!) are very fine strands of pasta, like a thin version of spaghetti. Vermicelli is sold in coiled in nests (*nidi*). Don't serve with heavier sauces that will soak into the pasta making it soggy.

- **Penne** Slender pasta tubes that are cut diagonally, penne are also known as quills due to their quill or pen-nib shape. There are two types of penne: *rigate*, meaning ridged, or *lisce*, meaning smooth. Both are popular in Italy.

- **Rigatoni** Similar to penne (either can be used in a recipe), rigatoni are ridged tubes of pasta cut straight across rather than diagonally.

- **Spaghetti** Probably the most well-known of all pastas, the long strands of spaghetti originate from Naples and it is still one of the most popular varieties. Many types are available including *spaghetti tricolore*, which is a combination of plain, red (tomato) and green (spinach) pasta.

- **Tagliatelle** Long, straight pasta from Bologna in northern Italy. Tagliatelle is sold in nests or in straight pieces.

- **Tortelloni and Tortellini** These are pasta shapes filled with various ingredients, such as ricotta and spinach, cheese or cheese and ham. Tortellini are smaller than tortelloni.

- **Ravioli** This is the generic term for fresh, filled pasta.

WHY THE PRICE VARIES

INGREDIENTS

Quality dried pasta is made with semolina from durum wheat. Cheaper dried pastas mix semolina with '*farina*', softer flour. The Italians know the difference – Italian dried pasta, by law, can only be made from durum wheat, but mixed wheat products are legal for export. Artisanal pasta-makers pride themselves on the blend of durum wheat grains they use, which lends a particular flavour to their end product. For fresh pasta, if fresh eggs rather than frozen or powdered are used, this makes it more expensive; and with filled pastas the quality of the fillings have an impact on price.

PRODUCTION METHOD

Small-scale, artisanal production is much more labour intensive than mass-production and so commands a higher price. The big difference in production method is the type of die used to extrude the shapes. Most pasta-makers now use Teflon dies because they last much longer (1,500 work hours, compared to 400 for a bronze die), making them cheaper over their lifetime. However, the bronze dies create a rougher, more porous surface that 'holds on' to the sauce much better than the Teflon dies, which create a very smooth, slippery surface. The drying process also makes a difference. Cheaper pastas will be dried quickly in hot-air tunnels whereas more expensive pastas are often dried slowly at a low temperature. Some pasta-makers claim that this slow drying at a low temperature maintains the colour, taste, fragrance and firmness of the pasta during cooking though this is debated, with others claiming that hot drying helps maintain shape better, provided the air is not too hot.

TRY BEFORE YOU DIE!

–

VERRIGNI GOLD DIE CUT PASTA
£££££

Verrigni, imported from Abruzzo, Italy, is the only 'Gold Die' pasta in the world. The gold die gives the pasta a distinctive texture. Uncooked, the pasta has a raw look; when cooked, the texture is smoother, with a more intense wheat taste and richer yellow colour than other pastas.

Pastificio Verrigni uses only the best Italian durum wheat and the traditional drying process to create a truly exceptional pasta, which has been made in the same way since 1898.

. . . .

How to make and cook pasta properly

How to make fresh pasta at home

The beauty of making pasta is that you can cut it into any shape you fancy.

Serves: 3–4 as a main course or 6–8 as a starter

- 150g '00' flour

- 150g strong white bread flour

- Extra flour (of either sort) for rolling

- 3 large eggs

- Mix the two flours together and tip onto your work surface in a high mound. Make a well in the centre, plumbing down to the work surface for maximum depth and keeping the outer 'walls' of flour as high as possible.

- Break the eggs into the well and whisk together with a fork, then gradually draw in flour from the sides until the eggs have taken in all they can. Now go at it with your hands, working the flour and egg mixture into a soft but not sticky dough (you may need a little more flour).

- Knead the dough until it is smooth and even. Roll it into a ball, wrap in cling film and rest at room temperature for 20 minutes.

- Unwrap the dough. It will feel soft, silky and settled. Divide into six if rolling by hand or eight if using a pasta machine.

- Take the first piece, flatten slightly and dust with flour. If using a pasta machine, follow the manufacturer's instructions, being sure to dust the pasta with flour (and shaking off the excess) between each rolling. I find that for most purposes it is enough to take the pasta down to the penultimate setting. If you are rolling by hand, dust the work surface and rolling pin with flour, then roll the dough out as thinly as you can.

- Line three trays (or large baking sheets) with a clean tea towel, dusted with flour. Cut the pasta into shapes, then lay on the floured tea towels, dusting with more flour to prevent them sticking to one another.

- To cook the fresh pasta, boil in salted water in a large pan for just a minute or two. Some people add a little olive oil to the pan to stop either fresh or dried pasta sticking together but gentle stirring should suffice.

How to cook dried pasta

- Fill a large saucepan with 1 litre of water for every 100g of pasta. Bring it to the boil.

- When the water is at a rolling boil, salt it. Then add the pasta.

- Cover with a lid and raise the heat to bring it to the boil as quickly as possible.

- When it reaches a rolling boil, stir to separate the pasta and cook for the length of time stipulated on the packet.

- Taste the pasta near this time to check if it is *al dente*. The pasta will continue to cook a little once drained, so be sure to slightly undercook it.

Rice

Rice is the most widely consumed staple food for over half the world's population, providing around one-fifth of the calories consumed worldwide.

This guide will help you identify the different types of rice so you will be able to tell your long-grain from your wild rice, and everything in between.

A BRIEF HISTORY

THE DOMESTICATION AND cultivation of rice is considered to be one of the most significant events in history. However, exactly when and where it happened is unknown and has been long debated by botanists and archaeologists alike.

Korea, China and India all lay claim to beginning rice cultivation anywhere between 5,000 to 10,000 years ago. Rice cultivation travelled from there to the Middle East, Africa, the southern shores of the Caspian Sea and into the Volga Valley.

Rice was introduced to Greece by soldiers returning from Alexander the Great's military expedition to India around 344 BC to 324 BC and large deposits of rice from the first century AD have been found in Roman camps in Germany. The Moors brought Asian rice to the Iberian peninsula in the tenth century and there is evidence to suggest that rice was initially grown in Valencia and Majorca. The Ottomans introduced rice to the Balkans. Muslims brought rice to Sicily long before it was planted in the plains of Pisa (1468) or Lombard (1475). After the fifteenth century, rice spread rapidly throughout Italy and then France.

In the year 1694 rice was introduced into the south-eastern United States. Its cultivation was built on slave labour – the captives bringing knowledge of the crop from West Africa and Sierra Leone. When slavery was abolished after the American Civil War, rice production became less profitable but now it is again a major US crop.

GEOGRAPHY

TODAY, **RICE PRODUCTION** is the third most highly produced foodstuff worldwide, behind sugar cane and maize. Small-scale farmers with holdings of less than one hectare are the main growers. Only 8 per cent of the world's rice production is traded internationally.

The majority of all rice produced comes from China, India, Indonesia, Bangladesh, Vietnam, Thailand, Myanmar, Pakistan, Philippines, Korea and Japan. Asian farmers account for 87 per cent of the world's total rice production.

Different plants, growing conditions and regions produce different rice grains, all unique in their characteristics and uses. Rice plants, or to use their botanical name *Oryza sativa*, have been cultivated for thousands of years. They are extraordinarily adaptable and have developed different characteristics to survive in different climates. Environmental conditions play an important role in determining the nature of rice grown in a particular region.

Rice plants require a large amount of water at the beginning of the growing season, followed by a long and uninterrupted season of hot dry weather for cultivating and ripening.

As a great source of fibre and B vitamins, rice is extremely healthy and nutritious and is one of the purest, most natural products available on the market. Valued as a source of slow-release energy, rice is classified as having a low glycaemic index (GI) due to the starch content. It does not contain any 'bad' cholesterol, gluten or extrinsic sugar. It is also low in salt and fat.

HOW RICE IS PRODUCED

RICE SEEDS ARE SOAKED prior to planting in the fields and in many Asian countries these seeds are sown by hand. After 30–50 days of growth, the seedlings are transplanted in bunches from nursery beds into the fields or paddies. Traditionally, these are flooded while, or shortly after, setting the young rice plants. Flooding is not mandatory but it does help weed and pest control during the growing period.

After about three months, when the grains have a moisture content of around 25 per cent, the paddies are drained and the grains are left to ripen. In most Asian countries, where rice is grown by smallholders, harvesting is carried out by hand.

The plant is cut and threshed to separate the rice grain, or seed, from the stalk. This unmilled rough rice, known as paddy, is encased in a hard durable husk called the chaff, which protects the rice during this violent process. Much threshing is still carried out by hand but there is an increasing use of mechanical threshers.

The paddy needs to be dried to bring down the moisture content to no more than 20 per cent, ready for milling.

The first stage involves cleaning the paddy as it is passed through a number of sieves that sift out the debris collected from the field and the threshing process. A rice huller is then used to remove the chaff. More often than not, this part is done in a mill using a mechanical process rather than by hand, and involves rolling or grinding the rough rice between stones.

Once the chaff has been removed, the rice grain is left with the outer bran layers, making brown rice, which needs no further processing. For white rice, the brown grains are passed through two further hulling machines that remove the outer bran layers from the grain. The resulting white rice grains are polished to remove any bran residue, before being passed through optical sorters, which look at each individual grain of rice to check both the shape and colour. The aim is to guarantee uniformity and an average grain length.

In a modern-day rice mill there is a lot of technology, which will process thousands, if not millions, of grains per second to ensure the rice meets the highest quality standards. However, an experienced rice miller will know the quality of the finished rice by looking, touching and biting an individual grain.

The waste husks and bran that are removed from individual grains are used to produce oil for livestock feed. Hulls are used to produce mulch to recondition farm soil, and straw from the harvested rice plants is used as bedding for livestock.

DIFFERENT RICE GRAINS

Rice generally falls into three categories:

	Grain Length	Texture When Cooked	Subspecies	Origin	Varieties
Short Grain/ Round Grain	Approx. 4–5mm and 1½–2 times longer than it is wide	Varying degrees of stickiness	Japonica	California, Egypt, Italy, Japan, Korea, Spain, Portugal	Pudding, Sushi
Medium Grain	Approx. 5–6mm; thicker than long grain rice	Varying degrees of stickiness	Japonica	China, Egypt, Italy	Risotto, Paella
Long Grain	Approx. 6–8mm and 3–4 times longer than it is wide	Dry and separate	Indica	Indian subcontinent, Thailand, Vietnam, Mississippi	Thai Jasmine, Long Grain, Basmati

SHORT-GRAIN RICE

Short-grain or round rice is highly absorbent, creamy in texture and the grains cling together when they are cooked. It is traditionally used in dessert dishes, such as rice pudding.

SUSHI RICE

Sushi rice is another short-grain variety. It's relatively bland, therefore ideal to complement the flavours of sushi and wasabi paste. The rice with its super-sticky texture is perfect to mould into sushi rolls without forcing too much flavour into the dish.

MEDIUM-GRAIN RICE

- **Risotto rice** Round and plump in their appearance, these grains are extremely absorbent and high levels of starch create a creamy, smooth texture during cooking. To create the perfect risotto, add the liquid bit by bit in order to allow this creamy texture to develop. The constant stirring releases more delicious starch into the dish. To serve the perfect risotto the rice should be cooked until the grains are *al dente* (soft but with a firm bite in the centre). It is traditionally grown in Italy; there are many different types and each variety has its own unique qualities. Specialist varieties include Carnaroli, Vialone Nano and Arborio. Carnaroli is regarded as the King of Risotto because it is the largest grain from the risotto family. It is usually grown in northern Italy and tends to be hardier than the others and therefore difficult to overcook. Vialone Nano is grown in the southern region of Italy, Provincia di Verona. Vialone Nano is not a high-yielding plant, therefore availability tends to be an issue, which can drive prices up. It is more absorbent and will therefore cook slightly faster. Arborio is named after the region in which is it grown, Arborio in the Po Valley of Italy. The grains are slightly smaller than Carnaroli but they are extremely absorbent. Carnaroli is considered to be at the premium end, followed by Vialone Nano and then Arborio.

- **Paella rice** Paella is a plump, short-grain rice, which remains quite firm in texture, but with a distinct, moist, creamy edge. The Bomba variety is considered to be the best paella rice due to its superior cooking characteristics. Unlike other rice used for paella it will expand in width only, not in length, and Bomba can absorb three times its volume in liquid (other rice absorbs two times). Bomba is more expensive than other paella rice as it is grown only in a specific geographic area next to the Spanish Mediterranean coast in the Valencia region, where paella was initially created. The production methods are also fairly labour intensive.

LONG-GRAIN RICE

- **Thai jasmine or Thai fragrant rice** This rice is characterised by its wonderful floral aroma. The grains are long and thin in nature, but become sticky in texture once cooked. The variety Hom Mali is considered the best for taste. Thai jasmine rice is best enjoyed as close to the harvest as possible, when the grains are freshest and the fragrance is at its best. It is one of the main sources of carbohydrate in Thailand, where the climate and highly effective water irrigation systems mean it is possible to have up to four harvests per year.

- **Long-grain rice** Slender in shape and typically three or four times as long as it is wide, these white and semi-translucent grains have a very light, subtle flavour with a fluffy texture when cooked. The subtle flavour makes it the perfect accompaniment to most dishes and it can also be used for stir frying. Brown long-grain rice has the same characteristics as white rice but the rice germ and bran layers have not been removed so the grain retains more vitamins and fibre than white milled rice. It needs slightly longer to cook than white milled grains and has a distinctive nutty flavour. Long-grain rice needs rich fertile soil together with a humid tropical climate to grow. The key growing regions include China, United States, Thailand and South America where there are ideal conditions and there can be several harvests throughout the year.

- **Basmati rice** Basmati is considered by many to be the best rice in the world. When cooked it has a subtle aromatic fragrance and a unique delicate flavour. The pearly white grains almost double in length when cooked, separate easily from each other and become fluffy in texture. Like a fine wine, basmati matures and improves with age so the rice is usually stored for 12–18 months before it is sold, allowing the natural characteristics of the grain to develop. While the majority of basmati sold has been milled to become white, brown basmati is also available. Basmati rice tends to be more expensive than the other grains because the plant is very delicate and requires constant vigilance. Being a tall rice, with a relatively weak stem and droopy leaves, it is prone to collapse and fall in the water, destroying the rice grain. Perfect growing conditions can be found in the Punjab region of India and Pakistan, which lies at the foothills of the Himalaya mountain range where the plants are nourished by crystal-clear snow-fed streams. Due to the delicate nature of the plants and the specific climatic conditions required, there is only one harvest per year, typically around October/November. To try to increase yields less good hybrids have been developed, and so to protect authentic basmati rice against fraudulent misuse of the name, a code of practice on basmati rice has been drawn up, which details the four main 'pure line' basmati varieties. So seriously do growers take the issue that scientific analytical methods, including DNA testing, have been developed to confirm authenticity.

- **Easy-cook varieties** Basmati and long-grain rice are available in an easy-cook form. Easy-cook rice is grown and harvested in the same way but, once the grain has been removed from the plant, it is soaked in hot water for several hours and then steamed. It is for this reason that the rice is also known as parboiled rice. This process causes nutrients from the outer husk, especially thiamine, to move into the grain. The process also gelatinises starch, making the grain firmer and more durable. Easy-cook rice takes slightly longer to cook than the non easy-cook varieties. However, it is fool proof and therefore perfect for the less-confident cook. It is extremely difficult to overcook as the grains hardly ever become stodgy or sticky.

Other rice grains

- **Red rice** One of the most well-known varieties of red rice is Camargue, which is grown in the wetlands near the delta of the Rhône River in France. Distinctive in its reddish brown colour this rice is slightly chewy and sticky in nature with a delicate nutty flavour when cooked.

- **Wild rice** Although classified as rice, wild rice is actually a seed of a special aquatic grass typically native to North America. The seed is long and slender in appearance with a subtle nutty texture. Wild rice is usually mixed with easy-cook rice to add contrast to a dish.

WHY THE PRICE VARIES

Yield

Different varieties of rice have different yields. Long-grain plants have a higher yield than basmati, therefore more rice is generated per area of land and the price is lower. In addition, the growing period of the plant will have an impact on prices. Long-grain plants have a shorter growing period (120 days versus, 180 days for basmati).

Seed price

Different grains have different seed prices, and these prices impact the end cost.

Supply and demand

Availability of rice is affected by a range of factors. The weather during the growing season and harvest will affect crop quality and yield. The price the variety commanded the previous year will influence which varieties farmers decide to grow this year.

Take the basmati market as an example. If there is a relative abundance of this grain, market prices will be low, therefore farmers will be more likely to plant other varieties the following season, when they will be able to obtain a higher price for their crop. This will restrict the supply of basmati, which will drive market prices up. However, if the previous season's market price for basmati is high, many farmers will choose to grow this grain in the following season, therefore prices will be reduced as there is relatively more basmati rice on the market.

Where rice can be grown also restricts availability. For example, Bomba paella or Arborio risotto rice can be grown only in a certain region and basmati thrives in a relatively small geographic area, compared to long-grain rice which is farmed extensively across the globe with several harvests per year. If there is an abundance of grain, prices are generally lower.

AUTHENTICITY

While there is a code of practice for basmati, there is currently not one for Arborio. There are discussions about creating one in order to prevent producers passing off inferior grains as Arborio. However, the volume of Arborio sold worldwide is significantly lower than basmati, which raises the question regarding the commercial benefit of this research into determining the correct DNA of this grain.

Most rice millers rely on the farmers when buying Arborio and request information such as a certificate of origin and variety description. That said, most rice millers are easily able to determine Arborio from other grains and use various physical identification marks to ensure the product reflects the supporting paperwork.

PROCESSING

Generally, easy-cook rice is a little more expensive to buy than non easy-cook grains due to the additional processing involved. Other complexities with the parboiling grains include ensuring uniform grain colour, which also has an impact on price.

AGE

Different types of rice can and should be stored for varying amounts of time. Starch is key here, since it affects the water absorption of the grain and changes in form after harvest. If the rice is cooked soon after harvest, the higher starch content means that the water absorption will be lower, and therefore the grains will be stickier in nature. If the grains are stored for 9–12 months or more, the starch changes, which results in a greater water absorption rate, leading to more separate grains.

Thai jasmine rice (or Thai fragrant rice) is famous for its sticky nature, a desirable characteristic for those who enjoy the grain. Therefore, it should be cooked as soon as possible after the harvest. Basmati is known for its fluffy texture and separate grains; consequently it is best enjoyed after it has been stored for 9–12 months. Some members of the Asian community store basmati for two years or more since, like a good whisky, it gets better with age. Assuming the rice is stored in a cool, dry place, no harm will come to the grains.

TRY BEFORE YOU DIE!

—

Forbidden rice or black rice
££££

Black rice is high in nutrients and is a good source of iron, vitamin E and antioxidants (more than blueberries). The bran hull contains one of the highest levels of anthocyanin antioxidants found in food and it has a similar amount of fibre as brown rice. The taste is mild and nutty, similar to brown rice. Varieties include Indonesian black rice and Thai jasmine black rice. It is also known as forbidden rice and the legend states that only emperors in ancient China were allowed to eat this rice due its rarity and high nutritional value. Another story says that the name came from the Greeks, who banned the rice when they conquered the Middle East as they believed it helped their enemies in battle.

Goan red rice
£££

This red variety is grown and predominately eaten in the southern part of India, especially Kerala and Goa. It is a parboiled rice and the vibrant colour comes from the red husk during the parboiling process.

Domsiah
Currently not available commercially

Related to basmati, this long-grain variety is grown in the Gilan province of Iran. The grain has a black spot on the end and the name is Persian for 'black end'. It is especially valued for its aroma, which is more intense than basmati, and its fluffy light texture. Unfortunately, this rice variety is not available commercially and in abundance. Some say it is better than the best basmati you can buy.

Beef

I had to start the chapters on meat with beef. It's my favourite. One of my most treasured food memories is of eating a wonderful barbecued Argentinian steak with the Familia Zuccardi in the restaurant at their winery in Mendoza, Argentina., washed down, of course, with their finest Malbec – a perfect wine for red meat. Beef is the third most widely consumed meat in the world, accounting for about a quarter of meat production, after pork and poultry, which each account for over a third. But, as with all meat, there is a significant difference in quality between the best and the rest. You can tell straightaway when you eat it.

A BRIEF HISTORY

I LEARNED AS AN ARCHAEOLOGY undergraduate that Africans domesticated local cattle around 10,000 years ago and some time later the practice spread to Europe.

Cattle have been farmed in the UK since the first farmers settled and started clearing the forests over 6,000 years ago. Initially, the cattle were small dual-purpose animals, supplying both meat and milk.

Breeding cattle for meat, rather than for the dairy trade, appears to have been invented in Britain. Breeds were singled out for eating from the fifteenth century onwards. The classic breeds, such as Hereford, Galloway, South Devon and Aberdeen Angus, have now been adopted across the northern hemisphere.

In the early nineteenth century, the working class lived on plain food, such as bread, butter, potatoes and bacon. Butcher's meat was a luxury, and beef was eaten infrequently by the majority of the populace.

For wealthy Victorians, eating became the centre of social life, and meat was very much at the centre of eating. From cold cuts for breakfast to elaborate roasts for dinner, barely a mealtime would pass without some form of meat being consumed.

Beef continued to play an important role in the nation's diet throughout the Edwardian period. The arrival of the restaurant, the celebrity chef and exotic new dishes also occurred during this era. Although meat consumption dwindled during the rationing and price increases experienced during the First and Second World Wars, during the post-war decades it rose again steadily, reaching record levels by the 1960s. Beef-eating began to wane in the 1980s, when concerns over saturated fat led the UK government to change its public health advice, warning people to reduce their red meat consumption and eat more starchy carbohydrates.

GEOGRAPHY

CATTLE ARE FARMED in every region of the UK. Certain breeds are better suited to certain areas, for example the Angus and Highland breeds are well suited to upland and marshland pastures due to their excellent foraging ability. As beef in the UK is predominantly grass-fed, cattle will thrive in areas with high-quality grass.

Many countries lay claim to producing high-quality beef. The United States, Canada and Australia are all major players in the global beef market, owing to the vast amount of land available in these countries for finishing cattle. It is not uncommon to see feedlots of up to 150,000 cattle in these areas. The key difference with the beef in these countries is that, owing to the lack of grassland, the cattle are predominantly grain-fed. This leads to beef that is less flavourful (North Americans have been known to describe British beef as 'livery') but has a noticeably more tender texture. Grain-fed beef is cheaper to produce as cattle can be 'finished' (brought up to market specification in terms of weight and grade) much more quickly on this high-protein diet rather than by allowing them to graze on grass. The debate of 'grass vs grain' is one of the central discussion points of the modern beef industry.

Some people do finish cattle entirely on grass and there are potential benefits to this: 100 per cent grass-fed beef comes from animals that have grazed in pasture year-round rather than being fed a processed diet for much of their life. Grass-feeding improves the quality of beef, and makes the beef richer in omega-3 fats, vitamin E, beta-carotene and CLA (conjugated linoleic acid, a beneficial fatty acid).

South America is also renowned for its beef, in particular Brazil, Argentina and Uruguay, owing to the plentiful space and large areas of high-quality grassland in these countries. South American beef is among the most exported worldwide, and their butchery and cooking techniques, as well as 'gaucho-style' restaurants, crop up in nations across the globe.

While less of a major player globally, Japan is renowned for the development of Kobe beef, celebrated as one of the most decadent meats in the world. This beef is sourced from a strain of Wagyu cattle, which are bred for the exceptional marbling quality of the meat. They are kept in luxurious conditions, and enjoy a health regime that can include daily massages, and a diet featuring beer and sake.

HOW BEEF IS PRODUCED

MANY MAY THINK ME patronising saying this but here goes – beef is the meat from mature cattle, not dairy cows! However, as I will explain later, dairy cows do enter the beef supply chain as lower cost meat.

Cattle are slaughtered when they have reached a 'prime' age and weight. Beef calves can be born to a beef-cross dam and reared at foot until weaning age, or to a dairy dam and removed at a few days old and reared on milk replacer and calf ration. Veal calves in the UK are generally juvenile male dairy cattle, and are reared until about five to seven months before slaughter.

Cattle generally take between 18 and 24 months to reach maturity, with some breeds, such as Highlands, taking longer than others. During their growing months they are fed on a high-protein ration necessary for skeletal and muscle growth, and during their last three months the diet will require a high-energy content in order to develop muscle and condition (fat).

Some cheaper beef is obtained from 'cull' animals – animals that have previously been used as either dairy cows or breeding bulls. Cull beef is palatable, with a stronger flavour to the meat due to the maturity of the cattle, and today forms a significant component of the beef industry. However, the muscles in these older animals are more worked and thus the meat is significantly less tender, which means cull beef is mostly used for the mince and burger market. If you've ever bought a cheap burger from a van, it is likely to have been made out of this.

Beef is produced by slaughtering and dressing cattle and butchering the resulting carcasses to make a wide variety of cuts. By law, this must be done in a certified abattoir that has been built for this purpose. Each animal will be split into two 'sides', and each side divided into a hindquarter and a forequarter.

The forequarter consists of the flank and the shoulder. Much of the meat on the fore is heavily worked by the animal and better for longer cooking. Cuts from the forequarter include the brisket, which is traditionally slow-cooked for a succulent roast (and especially popular for a Jewish Passover supper), neck and clod, which are often used for stewing, and the thin rib, which is one of the cuts traditionally used for mince.

The hindquarter of the animal is where some of the most popular cuts come from, and is aged for a longer period to ensure the meat achieves optimum tenderness. The fillet is from the lightly worked inner loin, prized for its tenderness; then there are the rib, the sirloin and the rump. These cuts are typically sold as joints, which are roasted whole for a traditional Sunday roast or sliced down into steaks.

Beef carcasses also provide a wide variety of other products that are typically known as the 'fifth quarter' – the organs or offal of the animal. This includes tripe, which is made by dressing and bleaching the four stomachs of the cattle, kidneys, which are used in the classic steak and kidney pie, and oxtail, used for soups and stews.

In order to get the best-quality meat you need to start by assessing the genetics of the sire and dam, and picking those traits that offer favourable characteristics. Farmers often build up their breeding stock over many years, constantly striving to produce cattle that are healthy, easy to look after and offer excellent eating quality.

Once farmers have achieved the genetics they want, it is imperative that cattle are well looked after through every step of their lives. Diet is also extremely important to ensure that the cattle produce muscles that are full and have the right level of fat to deliver fantastic eating quality.

After five years of Waitrose benchmarking, the Welsh Black just pips Hereford and Angus into second and third places respectively. It presents a well-conformed eye muscle and just the right level of fat to allow a nice layer on the back (to protect during ageing) as well as the perfect amount of marbling within the muscle. Dry-age the rib and loin for a minimum of 30 days and take your pick from the ultimate ribeye or sirloin, griddled, rested and served rare.

WHAT YOU SHOULD BE AWARE OF WHEN BUYING BEEF

BEEF IS ONE OF the more costly proteins but this is unavoidable due to the comparatively lengthy process involved in rearing cattle to maturity. However, you can still eat quality beef as there are numerous cheaper cuts, such as the cheek, shin or oxtail, which can prove exceptional when slow-cooked. A lower priced cut does not mean the product is poor quality.

Look closely at the meat before you buy and use the advice below to help you pick a joint that will be good to eat.

When buying mince and burgers, think carefully about the fat content. Many customers are understandably wary of buying meat that is fatty, but a leaner mince will impart less flavour due to the lack of fat. Mince and burgers should be a uniformly deep-red colour, with thick, equal strands. If burgers have been pre-seasoned, check the product for a good distribution of seasoning – too much can lead to an overpowering flavour.

A final factor to consider is cooking. Many customers have been put off beef after experiencing products that have been poorly cooked; excessive cooking can quickly ruin a good piece of beef. There are many tricks to cooking beef to perfection. One of the most forgotten is to let joints and steaks 'rest' after cooking, this will keep juices within the meat and make the finished product more flavourful.

WHY THE PRICE VARIES

HUSBANDRY

Good-quality beef is usually a deep, dark-red colour. This indicates the animal was in good health and in a comfortable environment when it was killed. Supermarket beef often appears bright red in colour. This is due to stores placing the meat under a bright light when on display, as it is thought consumers associate the bright colour with 'freshness'.

Depending on the breed, the best beef will often have a good level of 'marbling' within the muscle. Marbling refers to the distribution of intramuscular fat, and is evident in the raw meat as threads of creamy white fat running throughout the meat. When the beef is cooked, this fat will melt and ensure the beef is succulent and flavourful.

On the other hand, poor quality beef can be identified in a number of ways.

If the animal is under stress when it is processed, which can occur due to excessive periods of transport, poor handling or an unsettling environment, adrenaline is released into the muscle, creating a higher pH than usual, which leads to a purplish-black meat.

Although good beef will have a certain level of fat, animals that are overweight will yield beef that is overly fatty, less palatable and less value for money. This is clearly visible on meat with an excessive fat/beef ratio.

Conversely, if an animal is too lean, fat levels will be minimal, which will result in a less flavourful beef.

Gristle comes from elastin, a connective tissue within the muscle, which, unlike collagen, does not break down during cooking and is chewy and flavourless. Gristle is easily removed from cooked product and does not tamper with the flavour of the beef, but is best avoided if possible. It can be easily identified as darker portions of hard fat within the beef.

FEED

Cheaper beef is reared intensively and fed large amounts of non forage-based foodstuffs, promoting rapid muscle growth. The quicker an animal can be finished the more economically efficient it is for the farmer. However, if animals are finished too quickly, beef can be excessively fatty and unpalatable.

AGE

Be aware that cheaper beef can incorporate meat from cull animals, which will have a different flavour and texture. Remember this is beef from animals that were not bred for beef but rather for use as dairy cows or beef dams. After the end of their useful life, which could be as long as 15 years, they are regularly sold into the trade for meat. Bull beef can also be included (from animals either at the end of their breeding career, or bull calves surplus to the dairy sector), since this can be purchased cheaply. Certain processors will mix beef from cull animals into mince to lower production costs.

I believe eating quality to be at its best around 24–30 months of age and from prime beef steers and heifers. It is worth checking when you buy what kind of cattle have been used in the product.

GEOGRAPHY

Cheaper beef is often imported. UK minimum welfare standards and traceability are generally higher than other countries, including those within the EU. For example, a few years ago DNA of Zebu cattle (a subspecies of the domestic cow notorious for poor eating quality) from Brazil was being found in steak on pub-chain menus in the UK.

PROCESSING

Cheaper meat is not hung and is processed through the factory as quickly as possible, often making it tough and bland. Dry-ageing is considered the best ageing process. However, there is no legislation around the term, so many producers may dry-age the meat briefly for a few days before maturing in a vacuum pack for the remaining days. This prevents moisture loss, which helps weight (so more can be charged) but doesn't produce a dry, aged steak with authentic eating quality.

TRACEABILITY

Cheaper beef is often bought in primals, which are large, wholesale cuts of meat, such as rump of sirloin, or even big bags of trim. The downside to this, rather than buying the whole animal, is that it is not always possible to trace the origin of the beef back to the farm and how it was produced.

When buying a whole carcass a retailer has a relationship with the farmer and knows exactly where it comes from. Conversely, those that buy individual cuts, or quantities of trim, can often be buying them several stages down the chain and through a number of intermediaries across numerous countries. This was certainly behind some of the issues exposed in the UK horsemeat scandal that emerged in 2013.

Ethics

Buying a whole carcass gives greater security to the farmer, but has significant cost implications for the butcher or retailer who has to make use of the whole animal to ensure nothing is wasted, even the parts of the animal for which there is lower demand.

Buying beef that has been reared to a high standard and slaughtered under humane conditions is essential, not just for ethical assurance, but also for quality. Animals that have been subjected to stressful conditions will yield a less palatable, visually unappealing beef, owing to the release of adrenaline into the muscle.

It is worth knowing as much as possible about the supply chain. Never hesitate to ask in-store about where beef has come from or research online information about supermarket supply chains. A Red Tractor logo on the packet gives assurance that the animal has spent at least the last three months of its life on an Assured Farm and has been reared to certain standards.

Cheap beef is produced without strict protocols and not to the minimum Red Tractor standards.

Packaging

Cheaper beef will be sold in packaging to halt the maturation process at the point of packing. Look out for 'skin-packed' beef packaging, which allows the maturation process to continue, creating greater tenderness and flavour.

TRY BEFORE YOU DIE!

–

THIRTY-DAYS ABERDEEN ANGUS DRY AGED WING RIB OF SIRLOIN ON THE BONE
££££

From a native British breed, the meat is naturally marbled with fat and is exceptionally tender and full of flavour. The dry-aged Aberdeen Angus is matured on the bone for 21 days.

SHORTHORN
£££

Shorthorn, my favourite steak, is aged for 28 days and sold to some of the finest restaurants across Europe. The Shorthorn breed grows well when reared in a grass-based farming system and produces lots of fine meat with a delicious marbling of fat.

WAGYU BEEF
£££££

The meat from Wagyu cattle in Japan is known for its quality and commands a very high price. The best grade of Wagyu beef (A5) can cost upwards of £200/kg (that's about five times the most expensive beef you will find in a supermarket) and will have very intense marbling, a rich flavour and soft buttery texture.

Others regard the finest steak to be from traditional breeds, but dry-aged to extreme lengths. I have eaten steak matured for more than 100 days and it was very good!

· ·

How to cook perfect roast beef

Serves: 8 approx.

- 2.5–3kg Aberdeen Angus bone-in rib of beef (300–375g per serving, including the bone)
- 1 tsp mustard powder

For the gravy:

- 1 small onion, finely chopped
- 2 tbsp plain flour
- 200ml red wine, such as Merlot or Cabernet Sauvignon
- 500ml hot beef stock
- 1 tbsp horseradish hot sauce
- 1 tbsp mustard
- Salt
- Freshly ground black pepper

Preheat the oven to 180°C, gas mark 4. Weigh the beef to calculate the cooking time: for medium, this should be around 25 minutes per 500g, plus another 25 minutes. Place the beef bone-side down in a roasting tin, rub the mustard powder and seasoning over the fat crust and place in the oven. When the beef is cooked, transfer it onto a warm plate, cover loosely with foil and rest for 20 minutes.

To make the gravy, place the roasting tin with the meat juices on the hob, add the onion and fry gently for 2–3 minutes until softened. Spoon off any excess fat and stir in the flour. Turn up the heat, then gradually stir in half the wine and stir to loosen all the bits from the bottom of the tin. When the wine has nearly evaporated, repeat with the remaining wine. Finally, stir in the hot stock, horseradish sauce and mustard, and simmer gently for about five minutes. Check the seasoning. Serve immediately in a warm jug.

· ·

Pork/ Bacon/ Sausages

If you've ever tried to fry a rasher of cheap bacon and it shrinks to nothing in the pan, you'll know something is up. Mind you, you may have twigged that all was not well when you took it out of the packaging. If there is too much water in it, the stuff will feel soaking wet. Then, the second you pop it in the pan a grey, watery sludge will appear. Economy sausages don't behave much differently either.

While EU rules, which came into force at the end of 2014, compel firms to label their products 'with added water', that may not clear things up completely. Under the changes, producers and retailers have to mark their produce if it contains more than 5 per cent water. Previously, the ceiling for added water was 10 per cent. Many producers have cried foul because some production methods rely on brine, which is not viable at added water levels of 5 per cent or less. They have called for a return to the 10 per cent limit, which they say is a good enough deterrent to the over-watering of bacon. Meanwhile, as ever, the poor consumer is in the dark. What does it all mean? How can you be sure your morning fry-up is a respectable size?

A BRIEF HISTORY

THE FIRST PIGS evolved from wild boars in the Far East and China and were domesticated around 7,000 years ago.

Pigs were kept mainly for food but were useful in other ways, too. Their hides were made into shields and shoes and their bones used for tools and weapons. They also had an agricultural benefit, since their rooting helped to churn up the soil and made it easier to plough.

Before pork became widely popular, it was traditionally eaten in the autumn months. The pigs would become ready for slaughter at this time after being born in the spring and fattened during the warmer summer months. They would have fed well on windfall fruits from orchard trees and acorns that are abundant during this time.

In the twentieth century, pig farming became a big industry helped by the ease with which pigs are bred and kept. Curing techniques were also developed, which led to the widespread introduction of bacon and ham.

GEOGRAPHY

IN THE UK, East Anglia has a reputation for outdoor pig production, particularly in the counties of Norfolk and Suffolk. The relatively flat landscape of the region, its light, sandy, free-draining soil, cool summer air and extensive arable production make it ideally suited. Pig farming works well combined with arable production – the pigs are fed on the home-grown grain, while the crops benefit from the organic matter produced by the pigs!

Historically, each UK region reared pigs that were beneficial to their landscape. Gloucester Old Spots, for instance, were originally reared in Gloucestershire among apple orchards. The tale goes that the spots on their backs were caused by the falling apples.

Nowadays a great deal of care and science go into creating the right mix of breed for the desired end product and the native farming environment.

HOW PORK, BACON AND SAUSAGES ARE PRODUCED

THE MANY DIFFERENT WAYS of rearing pigs in the UK include free range, outdoor reared, outdoor bred and, by far the most common, indoor born and reared. Here's what that all means;

FREE RANGE

These pigs are born outside in fields and remain outside until they are sent for processing. They are provided with food, water and shelter and are free to roam within generous boundaries. Breeding sows are also kept outside under the same conditions.

OUTDOOR REARED

These pigs are born outside in fields and spend approximately half their life there (defined as being when they weigh at least 30kg). If there is a problem with the ground or weather, such as heavy rain flooding the fields, producers can apply to keep gestating sows in barns, on deep straw bedding, for a maximum of seven weeks at the start of each production cycle. Pigs are provided with food, water and shelter with generous minimum space allowances.

OUTDOOR BRED

This stipulates that the pigs are born outside in fields with the same conditions outlined above. They are kept there until weaning. After that they can move into any one of the other production systems. The point here is that the breeding sows live outdoors for their productive lives and the piglets spend their first few weeks growing naturally outdoors. Once the piglets are weaned, they are moved to another farming system. The pork and pork products labelled as 'outdoor bred' also contain a statement about how the pigs were subsequently farmed after being weaned from their mothers. You might want to check the seller's website for details.

INDOOR BORN AND REARED

An inseminated sow will typically be kept in a small concrete pen with a slatted floor (not every pen is slatted but many are), which allows dung and urine to fall through. Gestation time is three months, three weeks and three days. When the sow is due to give birth, she is moved into a farrowing crate with steel bars in a V-shape, which she lies in. This allows her to stand up and sit down, but she cannot move around freely, so preventing her from rolling on her piglets and potentially suffocating them. The sow and her piglets stay there for around 28 days, at which time the piglets are weaned and moved to their own pens, (again, usually slatted). The sow is re-inseminated after a few days, and the cycle starts again. This production system meets the 'Red Tractor' standard.

In the EU, the use of sow stalls (where the sow is housed permanently in a stall that restricts movement to standing up and lying down only) is still legal for the first month of pregnancy. Sow stalls were outlawed in the UK in 1999 but their use in the EU was only restricted from January 2013. It is believed that some EU producers are still using sow stalls, though. Broadly, about half of the pork products in the UK are imported from Europe.

ORGANIC

Pigs farmed organically are fed an organic diet and allowed to roam freely on land farmed to organic standards, which means they are outdoor reared for at least 80 per cent of their lives, with breeding sows and boars being kept outside throughout their lives. The farms are independently monitored by the relevant organic accreditation bodies. However, organic pigs in other countries may not be reared to these standards.

WHY THE PRICE VARIES

INGREDIENTS

Some processors inject their meat with a brine solution to keep it tender when cooking – this also increases the water content, but as long as this is under 5 per cent it doesn't need to be declared on the pack. This does mean that some customers can be misled into buying 'fresh' pork, without knowing that it has been injected with additional water.

When you buy bacon look for 'air-dried' bacon. This is the traditional way of producing bacon, without adding water/salt brine.

Where possible, you should avoid pork that has a declaration of 'added water', as this can be a ploy to sell water in the place of more expensive meat weight.

With sausages, customers should look for a high meat content product; ideally 80 per cent and over if it is plain pork. If there are added ingredients (leeks or apples for example), the meat content may drop down to make room for them. It doesn't mean the quality is any worse, just more ingredients. In lower quality pork sausages, meat content is usually anywhere from 42 to 60 per cent. However, the meat content can sometimes dip as low as 30 per cent in other sausages where government food labelling legislation allows.

The cuts used for sausages are important. Usually a mix of belly and shoulder is preferred so you get the flavour from the fattiness of the belly with the meatiness of the shoulder. Poorer quality sausages use lower grade cuts of meat or even a mixture of pork trimmings and fat in their make-up. Although some use proper cuts of meat, they are often cuts with greater fat levels than those used in higher quality sausages.

The lack of meat content is often offset with water and this is bound into the sausage using a selection of fillers, such as starches, pork rind and vegetable fibres, along with a large percentage of rusk. However, it is worth noting that rusk is a common functional ingredient in high-end sausages, although used in far smaller percentages to stabilise texture over the product's life, rather than to fill the gap where meat content is low. Permitted food additives are also used to help 'fix' the water in place, so that the sausage does not shrink when cooked. To achieve this with consistency, high-speed mechanical cutters are used to create a rough paste, which is then filled into casings.

Lower quality sausage seasonings are usually less authentic than those used in quality sausages and some even use flavourings to impart a more meaty flavour than the meat content would actually produce on its own. Premium sausages use fresh additional ingredients, such as herbs.

FARMING AND WELFARE

How your pork, bacon and sausages have been farmed and the welfare of the animal have a significant bearing on price; better feed and working practices cost more.

GEOGRAPHY

Welfare standards are lower outside the UK so it is possible to produce cheaper pork abroad. Customers wanting good-quality meat should look for 'British' as a minimum standard. Ditto if you have any concerns about saving animals from thousands of miles of travel.

BREED

Different breeds of pig offer different characteristics. Those that convert feed into meat the fastest will tend to be the cheapest, but are probably not the best eating quality.

The predominant indoor pig breed in the market is a cross between Large White sows and a Landrace boar. This combination is highly prolific, producing large litters, but not as robust as you would want for a breed being farmed on an outdoor system. It produces lean but not particularly tasty meat. The Landrace was imported from Sweden in 1949 and is now one of the UK's most popular breeds. As it copes well living outdoors, it is often crossed with another hardier breed suited to living outdoors, such as a Duroc. This breed's tough skin and thick coat allows it to survive the British winter.

ETHICS

Some retailers buy just the parts of the pig they want to sell, which is a bit of a problem for the poor old farmers because they can sell whole pigs only, not parts of pigs. Fair returns and long-term relationships are more expensive to maintain than buying when the price is right on the open market.

TRY BEFORE YOU DIE!

–

MANGALITSA
£££££

One of the most expensive breeds of pig to rear is the Mangalitsa. This is a rare breed, which was the result of a nineteenth-century Austro-Hungarian experiment, cross breeding a wild boar with a pig raised for lard. It has a distinctively woolly coat and can grow much larger than the average pig. It was near extinction in the 1990s before being brought back by a Hungarian breeder. Nowadays it is much more common in Europe. Its slow growth means that it is expensive and time consuming to rear, but its buttery, lardy meat makes it absolutely delicious. If you see it on a menu or find it on your travels, try it!

DUCHY ORIGINAL PORK SAUSAGES
£££

Free-range and organic production systems are more expensive, but these are highly prized products. Indeed, in my view, the production system influences the taste of the product. These sausages are made from prime cuts of organic free-range pork shoulder and belly, seasoned lightly with herbs and spices including nutmeg, ginger, thyme and sage.

BERKSHIRE AND HAMPSHIRE PORK
£££

Both meats have a reputation for their excellent taste and texture. In the case of the Berkshire, it is associated with higher fat levels. In addition to the pure breed, Berkshire boars are used to produce a 'sired by Berkshire' pork, which scientific tests have shown to be of the highest eating quality but expensive to produce!

How to cook perfect roast pork

- For successful crackling, choose an even-shaped joint with a good layer of fat beneath the rind.

- Preheat the oven to 180°C, gas mark 4 (it is vital that the oven reaches temperature before the meat is added so allow 20 minutes or more). Place the pork in a roasting tin, pat its skin with kitchen paper and leave for 30 minutes for the skin to dry. Check that the skin is evenly scored, adding more using a very sharp knife, if needed.

- Lightly rub or brush the skin with oil and sprinkle with a thin, even layer of salt and a little pepper. Rub the seasoning into the scored skin. Calculate the cooking time: 35 minutes per 500g, plus an extra 35 minutes.

- Transfer the cooked pork onto a serving plate or board. Cover loosely with foil and leave to rest for 15 minutes. Resting the meat before carving gives it time to relax, which will make carving easier and give you moist, tender results.

- If you do not get even crackling by the end of the cooking time, remove the crackling from the joint using a sharp carving knife and place on a baking sheet. Increase the oven temperature to 220°C, gas mark 7, and return the crackling to the oven for a further 15 minutes while the meat is resting. When ready, cut the crackling into pieces.

- Thinly slice the pork and serve each portion with some crackling, gravy and a generous spoonful of apple sauce.

British Ham

Strictly speaking, ham might have been included in the previous chapter on pork, bacon and sausages. However, since people in Britain seem to love it so much and buy such a great deal, I've singled it out for a little extra scrutiny. Prices for ham vary hugely and it is very useful to know why.

A BRIEF HISTORY

THE CURING OF MEATS FOR preservation can be traced back to around 2000 BC and the Egyptians. Cato the Elder talked about salting meat in his *De Agri Cultura* around 160 BC. The modern word 'ham' is derived from the Old English *ham* or *hom* meaning the hollow or bend of the knee, and it began to refer to the cut of pork derived from the hind leg of pigs around the fifteenth century.

GEOGRAPHY

PORK CURING HAS NATIONAL and regional specialities throughout large areas of the world as people have used salt and local ingredients to create hams with unique flavours and textures.

The Wiltshire cure, for example, is a traditional English technique thought to have been invented in the eighteenth century in Calne, Wiltshire, by the Harris family, who ran butcher's shops. It was originally developed as a dry cure and changed to the wet cure that we know today around the time of the First World War. Historically, it is thought that the pig-curing industry developed in Calne because pigs reared in Ireland were delivered to Bristol and then herded through Calne on drovers' roads (routes for driving livestock on foot or horseback) on their way to Smithfield in London.

Today, to be called Wiltshire ham, the product must use a Wiltshire cure. In 2010, supermarkets signed a voluntary code of practice agreeing that pork products sold in the UK labelled 'Wiltshire Cure' should have been sourced from the UK only. Out of all the big supermarket chains, Waitrose is the only one that currently sources all of its Wiltshire ham from a Wiltshire-based factory, sited just ten miles from Calne.

HOW HAM IS PRODUCED

CURING CHANGES THE composition of meat. As salt, sugars and spices are added, liquid is displaced, which delays decomposition and extends eating life.

Ham refers to meat from the leg of a pig, which has been cured and then usually cooked. In the UK, country hams are dry-cured by rubbing or tumbling in salt, or injecting a brine. The leg is then cooked and roasted.

Across Britain most regions have their own recipe for ham, each with a local twist influenced by plentiful ingredients and traditional preparation methods. Two of the most popular methods remain the York and Wiltshire recipes.

York is traditionally a dry-cured ham. From 11 November, St Martin's Day, which is traditionally the first day of curing, pigs fattened from a summer of foraging are slaughtered and laid on a bed of salt in a cellar, turned every few days and massaged regularly. They are then typically hung to dry for a minimum of two months.

Wiltshire ham undergoes a traditional wet cure in which the ham is soaked in brine and then hung on the bone for up to two weeks before being processed.

Ham can be made in three different ways. 'Ham' is meat that comes from one whole cured leg of pork. 'Formed ham' is made of several pieces of meat from more than one leg of pork, shaped into a joint before cooking and slicing. 'Reformed ham' is meat that has been 'rearranged' and comprises muscles of more than one leg with the addition of finely broken-down meat or meat emulsion, before being shaped and cooked.

WHY THE PRICE VARIES

BREED AND FARMING SYSTEM

The finest hams are produced using the best pig breeds, either outdoor bred and reared, or free range. The animals are slaughtered with compassion, ensuring minimal stress is placed on them. This maintains the delicate PH balance of the meat, ensuring it is delivered to the curing process in prime condition. Cheaper imported EU pork, processed into hams in the UK, is often less expensive as the animal welfare standards of pork production may be lower than those in the UK.

PRODUCTION METHOD

Ham from one whole cured leg of pork is the most expensive. Formed ham is the next costly, followed by reformed ham as the cheapest.

Added water versions of formed or reformed hams will be cheaper still. Phosphates can be added, which allows more water to be retained in the cooking process. Better quality hams will cook and roast off the water added during curing, and they have a meat content of 100 per cent displayed on the pack. In contrast, cheaper hams with additional water, often highlight a meat content of less than 100 per cent. Adding water remains the main way that producers create lower cost hams. However, there are merits in adding water to ham; primarily it creates a softer, moist texture that's often good for children's sandwiches.

Thanks to the time involved, the most expensive hams are traditional cures, such as Wiltshire and York. Also costly, but good, are other cure methods that use whole legs hung on the bone, which leads to the best flavours and textures as the bone intensifies the cure.

Seek out traditional cures from good-quality butchers, delicatessens and deli counters in good supermarkets. Experiment with different cures and glazes, such as honey, molasses and fruit chutneys, or different hams smoked in wood chips from hazelwood, beech, oak and even spruce.

TRY BEFORE YOU DIE!

—

YORK HAM
££££

Legend has it that the construction of York Minster provided the oak sawdust for the smoking of York ham. The area was also known for its brewing industry, the waste from which provided cheap feed for pigs, leading to an abundance of larger-than-average animals. It is believed that Robert Burrow Atkinson's butcher shop in Blossom Street was the birthplace of the original 'York Ham'. The ham had a distinctive taste due to the fact that it had been cured in the cellars for between one and three years. The flavour of York ham became so popular in that time that shoppers in other regional markets asked for ham 'like the ham in York'. Other producers tried to copy it on a larger scale, which led to Mr Atkinson's son Edward fighting a legal case. He successfully obtained an injunction to prevent anyone calling their product 'York Ham' unless it had been cured within two miles of the city boundary. Try it. It was worth the fight.

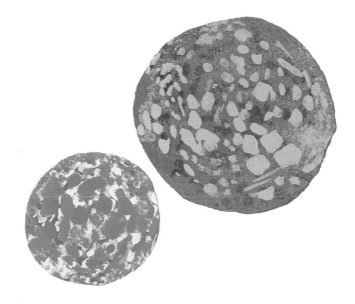

Charcuterie

The British love cured meats such as salami, Parma ham, lomo and chorizo, and we import lots of it every year from across Europe. There is even somewhat of a charcuterie revolution happening on these shores, with a number of farmers and smallholders entering the fray with their own versions. Products such as wild red deer salami, seaweed and cider salami and bath chaps (hot smoked pigs' cheeks) easily give their European counterparts a run for their money.

I would need several books to do justice to the meats of each country. So here is a whistle-stop tour, which I hope gives you a better idea of why there is such a huge variation in price points.

A BRIEF HISTORY

THE **SMOKING AND SALTING** of meat and fish have been practised in Mediterranean countries since biblical times. The Greek word for sausage (*orya*) was first recorded in 500 BC and the word salami has Latin origins (*sal* = salt). The process of preserving meat spread to the rest of Europe in the fourteenth century, when salting and drying of meats became common practice. This method of preservation helped use the whole of the animal after slaughtering.

Until the development of refrigeration, the production of dry-cure hams occurred in the winter months. The process follows the seasons of the year (modern processes replicate the traditional temperature and humidity.) While charcuterie is mainly associated with pork, the same method of curing is also used on beef, lamb, poultry, salmon and fish.

HOW CHARCUTERIE IS PRODUCED

CHARCUTERIE IS SPLIT into four main areas: sausages, which can be fresh, cooked or cured/dried; cured and air-dried meats; cooked meats; and lastly pâté. Here, I focus on sausages and cured and air-dried meats.

SAUSAGES

Fresh sausage has already been covered in the pork/bacon/sausages section. However, in cooked sausage, the meat is often minced into a finer consistency and uses raw or cooked meat depending on the recipe. Meat is then put into a casing, which is cooked (and sometimes also smoked). Frankfurters, mortadella and extrawurst are examples using raw material, while liver sausage, brawn and haggis use cooked meat.

For cured/dried sausages, raw meat is chopped or minced. Salt is added to the mixture, sometimes along with herbs or spices. The sausage is then dried over a period of time and normally we call this product salami.

Making salami has traditionally been a way to utilise small pieces of meat and fat by drying them in a natural casing. The English word salami is the plural form of Italian *salame*, while in France it is known as *saucisson* and in Spanish as *embutido*.

As with cheese or wine, salami can be fermented. This is either done naturally or with a starter culture. Traditionally, in northern Europe the product is often smoked, while in southern Europe, where the climate is warmer, pepper or spice, such as paprika, is added. Some salami are also mould-ripened (similar to Camembert). This metabolises the acid produced during fermentation, which changes the taste and flavour.

Salami can be coarsely cut with large pieces of meat and fat visible (*saucisson sec*), while others are finely minced (*Milano*).

Maturation time depends on the diameter of the sausage being produced, combined with the recipe and techniques used.

Just as in the production of cheeses, salami hang in a 'bodega' where naturally occurring microbes, which have built up over hundreds of years, ferment the meat. The bodega often comprises a number of rooms over several storeys, which allows producers to capture the air by opening and closing the windows.

Since the 1940s, starter cultures have been developed to replicate this process and the natural wind has been replaced by fans to make the products more consistent and safer. However, if incorrectly done, the speeding up of the process leads to greater water loss, which often results in a dry 'ring' around the outside of the salami, affecting the eating quality. Not only is it dry around the outside, it also creates a blockage that stops the centre drying correctly and makes it mushy.

Here, in my view, are the best regions for making salami:

- **For smoked:** I favour Germany or northern Spain for a smoked chorizo.

- **For slowly matured:** the Auvergne region in France for *saucisson sec*, and Parma in Italy.

- **For spicy:** northern Spain or Calabria in Italy.

CURED OR AIR-DRIED MEATS

When meat is cured or air-dried, the leg or muscle is preserved. It is covered in salt and left for two to seven days, then washed and hung up to cure over months or years, depending on the weight and the region. Typically, a pig would be slaughtered in the autumn and then hung until the following winter. It is not only the rear legs (called *jamón* in Spain and *jambon* in France) that are cured/air-dried. You can also find cured shoulder (front legs) called *paleta* in Spain and also the loin (*lomo* in Spain) or bresaola from topside of beef.

In my view the best cured or air-dried meats are:

- **From Spain:** *ibérico de bellota* made from free-range, Black Iberian pigs, which feed naturally on acorns, and matured for three years. Also, Teruel, which has a robust flavour and is from a bigger breed white pig, such as a Duroc.

- **From Italy:** Parma ham, sweet and flavoursome, but beware not all Parma hams are equal! And bresaola, a cured beef from the north.

WHY THE PRICE VARIES

PRICE DEPENDS ON the pork, production technique and expertise of the producer.

INGREDIENTS

In the UK, our biggest selling lines are bacon and ham, so pigs are selected to best suit these products. This means that they are often smaller and bred quicker than charcuterie pigs, which need to be much larger to create the optimum combination of meat and fat that is required within the long production process. To reach the required maturity, a charcuterie pig must be fattened well past the size of a traditional UK breed and has to eat twice as much in order to achieve the right weight and size.

Ibérico, from Spain, is ideal for making cured meats. There are different qualities of raw material based on age, feed and conditions of space/life. While they are all called *ibérico* some are intensively bred and some are free-range (*cebo*) with a natural diet of cereals. The highest quality is *bellota*. To be called *ibérico de bellota*, the pigs have to be free range and to have grazed in the *dehesa* of western Spain with a minimum space of six hectares each. They will be double the size of the intensively reared *ibérico* pig and for the final months before slaughter they live off foraged acorns (*bellota*), of which they will consume 6kg per day. The legs are then hung for over two years (which takes the total age to over three years). Acorns give the finished products a unique taste and flavour.

Ibérico pigs are expensive. They have smaller litters, yield less meat per head and take time to mature, which is why many ham producers around Spain cross-bred them with other varieties. Up until recently, ham made from pigs that were as little as half-*ibérico* could be sold as *jamón ibérico*, but legislation introduced by the Spanish government in January 2014 requires *ibérico* ham to be labelled according to the percentage of the pigs' Iberian ancestry and a number of other factors.

The biggest factors to affect the quality of pigs used for charcuterie products are better farming standards, which are more expensive; whether there is a higher/lower fat content; and if fresh or frozen meat has been used. Artisanal small-scale production versus mass production also has a significant bearing on price. The former allows greater attention to detail and for skills to be passed through generations.

PROVENANCE
If you buy an Italian *prosciutto crudo* or *pancetta*, you may find it surprising that the pigs may actually have come from the Netherlands, Denmark or Germany. This means that they will be cheaper and produce smaller legs, which will impact on the flavour/ texture.

MATURATION
Traditionally, meat is cured on the bone, but if you remove it you can speed up the maturation process and cure with three months versus the standard of ten-plus months. The longer a product is aged the more it will cost to store and look after through the ageing process.

TRIM
Leaving more of the fat on offers a higher return to the supplier and retailer.

PREPARATION
Better producers remove the very fatty centre of the meat, others don't. Retailers who want to speed up slicing freeze the block before doing so. This does impact on the flavour.

QUALITY STANDARDS

When shopping look for protected products with PDO (Protected Designation of Origin) or PGI (Protected Geographical Indication) marks. There are 150 charcuterie lines that have been awarded this status, which means that they are produced in a certain way and in a defined area across Europe. However, due to the important role of the individual producer and their expertise, the quality of each product is not the same.

FAT CONTENT

In sausages, the more fat added or the fatter the cuts of meats used, the cheaper the recipe.

PRESERVATIVES

Some products use preservatives to extend shelf life or add colour or to reduce the cost of the ingredients, although most cured or fermented products use nitrites as a safety control.

TRY BEFORE YOU DIE!

–

The most expensive commercially available *ibérico* ham, according to *Guinness World Records*, was sold by Selfridges in 2010. The 7kg Albarragena Jamón Ibérico de Bellota, which went for £1,800, had its own DNA certificate as proof of authenticity.

A considerably more affordable, yet nevertheless extremely wonderful, alternative is:

IBÉRICO DE BELLOTA JAMÓN
££££

The wafer-thin slices of the ruby-red wonder that is *ibérico de bellota jamón* has been described as one of the greatest food items in the world.

Lamb

At my home in Dorset, I look out over water meadows where spring lambs are brought for fattening. It is an idyllic setting, which gives no hint of the huge challenges upland farmers face to eke out a living while preserving some of the country's most precious and beautiful countryside. I hope in this chapter I can properly convey their endeavours to produce their wonderful product.

A BRIEF HISTORY

PEOPLE HUNTED WILD SHEEP from the beginning of the Stone Age, wore clothes made out of their wool, drank their milk and ate their cheese. By 10,000 BC, people in west Asia began to keep tame, domesticated sheep.

In medieval times, wool became big business and many people who had land, from peasants to major landowners, raised sheep. The grass-rich British landscape made for ideal conditions and exported English wool received top prices.

Until the twentieth century, the eating of sheep meat was largely based around mutton to maximise the number of crops of wool before the animal was used for meat. The definition of lamb is a young sheep under 12 months old; culling young lambs for meat, before they had delivered an income, was only possible for a wealthy minority.

It wasn't until the second half of the twentieth century that a market for lamb developed because by then it could be enjoyed and consumed by the masses.

The decline in the demand for wool due to the growth of synthetic materials, the development of 'frozen' technology and shortage of food after the Second World War created the market for lamb for meat, rather than sheep for wool.

GEOGRAPHY

AROUND **60** PER CENT of UK farmland is suitable to grow grass. Sheep and cattle farming is the most efficient way of converting this land into food. Different parts of the UK are suitable for different types of sheep, and these are classified into three types of geography: hill, upland and lowland.

Hardy hill sheep occupy the UK's highest and roughest terrain. Hill sheep include the Swaledale (Yorkshire), Cheviot (Scottish Borders), Shetland, Hebridean, Welsh Mountain and many other breeds that are perfectly adapted to live in the rough, exposed areas of the UK. They are thick-coated, which enables them to survive such hostile conditions. The female adults (ewes) make excellent mothers and give birth to a baby lamb (or very occasionally twin lambs) every spring. The father of these lambs (the ram or tup) will usually be the same breed as the mother, meaning their offspring are pure-bred. If the lamb is a female (a ewe lamb) she will grow up to join her mother in the flock as a breeding female. If the lamb is a male (a ram lamb or wether) he will stay with his mother for the first few months and then be sent to lower ground, like the meadows I look out on. Hill ground is too harsh to fatten lambs for meat.

After a few years, older ewes on the hill are moved to upland ground as draft ewes. Upland farms are found on hillsides and other high ground, but the land is lower and easier than true hill terrain. Draft ewes continue to have a baby every year, but this time the father is a different breed from the mother. The fathers are longwool upland breeds, such as the Bluefaced Leicester and Border Leicester, so the lambs that are born are cross-bred and referred to as mules. You can get all sorts of mules, including the Scotch Mule, North of England Mule and Welsh Mule. A female mule lamb will grow up to be a prized mother on lowland farms, while a male mule lamb will be reared for meat either on the upland farm where it was born or a lowland farm where more grass grows.

Lowland farms do not have the same tough terrain as hill and upland farms, are less exposed to bad weather and have lots of grass for sheep to eat. A mule ewe on a lowland farm will stay in good enough condition to have twin lambs every year (and sometimes even triplets, quadruplets or quintuplets). The father of these lambs will always be a different breed, so the lambs are all cross-bred. The father is usually chosen so his offspring will have lots of meat on them for the food chain, and lowland terminal sire breeds, such as the Suffolk and Texel might be used. The lambs do not have to withstand difficult terrain or weather, so they grow faster than hill or upland breeds and can afford to have a heavier frame. These cross-bred lambs get the very best start in life: their mum has excellent mothering abilities, including lots of milk to feed them and an instinct to protect and care for them, which is inherited from their hill-breed relatives, who are adapted to nursing their young on harsh hill ground; their dad is big and strong and passes on his genes to makes them grow fast and produce lots of delicious lamb for our dinner tables.

More than 40 per cent of our breeding flock is based in the uplands of the UK. It is no accident that our strong sheep areas are also our biggest tourism areas, since sheep have created and maintain our iconic landscapes.

When lamb is mentioned, people automatically think of Welsh lamb, and for good reason. The lush, green grass, rich soils and a temperate climate all come together to produce meat that is succulent and tender. Welsh lamb is held in such high esteem that since 2003 it has held Protected Geographical Indication (PGI) status. This status was also bestowed upon West Country lamb in 2014. The PGI mark allows Welsh and West Country lamb to stand out in the market as a product that is certified as being born, reared and slaughtered in that geographical area.

The UK tradition of eating lamb is actually out of kilter with the British lamb season as in March and April British lamb will be generally nearly one year old, stronger in flavour and less tender than 'best in season' lamb. Or it will have been born very early during the winter and finished on concentrate feed rather than grass, which will only have just started growing by that time of year.

Out of the British season, New Zealand provides the ideal environment for the production of quality lamb. For customers who prefer to support British lamb in the winter months (December to May), some British lamb is now available year round.

HOW LAMB IS PRODUCED

LAMB IS A SEASONAL MEAT. Ewes are mated in the autumn and lambs are born in spring when grass is lush and plentiful, allowing the ewe a nutritious diet from which she can provide milk for her young. Sheep farmers lamb their ewes both indoors and outdoors, depending on a variety of factors, including land topography, breed and weather conditions.

Once born, a lamb is dependent on the ewe's milk for three weeks. After this point it will begin to graze but only as a supplementary part of the diet. As a lamb ages, the balance of milk to grazing switches to a heavier reliance on grass as the main feed source, until the lambs are weaned at 12–14 weeks. Weaning is the process of separating the lamb from the ewe. This date is dependent upon factors such as the ewe's body condition, how much grass is available and how fast the lamb is growing.

Once weaned there are several options on which lambs can be finished, the term producers use to indicate an animal is ready for slaughter. Grazing on grass is a common diet for growing lambs, and often this is supplemented with creep feed. This is a concentrate feed with a high level of protein and energy, which maximises growth rates, but only when lambs are young as it is at this point that they have the most efficient feed conversion ratio. Alternatively, lambs can be finished with protein crops, such as red clover, chicory, plantain or brassicas, such as stubble turnips, swedes and kale. Protein crops, if utilised correctly, have the same ability to provide fast growth rates to lambs. For the modern market, lambs would typically finish at 40kg live weight. Once slaughtered, this will produce an 18–20kg carcass.

For clarification:

- **Lamb:** an animal up to a year old.

- **Hogget:** a sheep between one and two years old. The animals have developed a strong flavour but are less tender.

- **Mutton:** the meat of sheep older than two years. The majority of mutton comes from breeding animals that have reached the end of their productive contribution to the flock. Mutton has a bad name and fell out of favour after the Second World War when imports of New Zealand's cheaper, young lamb arrived, but younger mutton, hung to tenderise it and cooked slowly, is delicious. In fact, we probably eat more mutton than we realise. It often finds its way into Indian restaurants where it is suited to the slow cooking style and heavy spices.

WHY THE PRICE VARIES

SEASONALITY

Lamb is a seasonal product and supply and demand therefore have a bearing on price. The price is generally higher early in the season, when the product is less available. Geography really determines when ewes are 'tupped' and when lambs are born. The first lambs are born in January in the south-west and in Pembrokeshire and the Llyn Peninsula, and then births spread up the country and the last lambs are born in Scotland in April. The earliest new season lambs are ready at four months, so around mid-May. Most Welsh lambs are born from February to the end of March.

The UK exports about a third of its lamb crop every year and imports about the same amount from New Zealand to balance the seasons.

WEATHER

The impact of the weather starts right from the breeding season, when unseasonal weather can affect whether the ewes become pregnant or lose lambs. As sheep are generally fed on grass the growing season for grass is significant, too. Lots of lush, nutritious grass means lambs grow larger and more quickly, making them cheaper to rear. If it is a bad year for grass growth, farmers will have to supplement the lambs' diets with additional feeds, which can be expensive.

Feed

Concentrates allow lambs to be finished faster, allowing producers to sell their lambs at the peak of the season when demand is highest. The proportion of concentrate required versus grass has a big impact on the cost of production: 70 per cent of the cost is attributed to feed costs. Utilising home-grown protein crops is a good way for farmers to control their costs. New Zealand has a milder climate than the UK, which leads to a longer growing season, more grass and therefore the ability to produce cheaper lamb because less bought-in feed is required.

Breed

There are thought to be more breeds of sheep in the UK than anywhere else in the world – around 300 – which reflects the diversity of landscapes and weather, and therefore farming systems, we have. Each one is suited to a slightly different geography.

Carcass grading

When lambs go to slaughter, the carcass is graded, which is a legal requirement in the UK. Farmers who can hit the 'sweet spot' on a grid that measures fatness and conformation (muscle/bone ratio, size of prime muscles, etc.) are paid a better price. That can mean a 20 per cent difference in price, depending on how much meat is on the carcass. Farmers aim to avoid too much fat from heavy lambs, or chewy meat from older lambs, or lambs that are all bone and no muscle. However, some retailers buy at the lowest price and so will accept a much wider variation in specification from the abattoir.

Ageing of the meat

Some lamb will be aged on the bone for a few days to help develop flavour and tenderise the meat, but not for too long as the sweetness and mild flavour of lamb is lost. Ageing even for a short time adds to production costs.

Farming standards

When buying lamb look out for the Red Tractor logo or regional logos, such as Welsh Lamb, Scotch Lamb, the Quality Standard Mark England or Farm Quality Assured Northern Ireland. These logos mean each step is independently inspected to ensure the lamb is produced to a quality standard. As always, better standards cost more.

ETHICS

Some retailers buy directly from farmers and commit to taking the whole carcass. This means they negotiate the price upfront and stick to it, regardless of changes in the market. This gives farmers greater security and provides greater traceability of the meat. Others will buy on the open market, which means they can take advantage of low prices as the market fluctuates, but have no control over where or how the meat was produced.

TRY BEFORE YOU DIE!

—

NEW SEASON LAMB
£££

For the most tender, sweetest lamb, new season lamb from the lush finishing pastures of Wales or the south-west is the best.

HERDWICK LAMB
£££

Our hill and upland breeds are mainly kept as breeding stock as they offer useful traits for farmers, such as hardiness and easy lambing. However, they do not gain enough muscle, or finish, quickly enough to be sold as young lamb. As they take longer to mature, they tend to have a stronger flavour, more akin to mutton, but certainly interesting to try. Herdwick lamb, native to the Lake District, is a breed growing in popularity among celebrity chefs and is certainly worth a try.

LAMB'S BRAINS
££££

If you are feeling very adventurous, how about trying lamb's brains? They are delicious when prepared skilfully. They are considered a great delicacy and a favourite of the chef Fergus Henderson. He features them in his cookbook *The Whole Beast: Nose to Tail Eating* or you can go to his famous restaurant, St John's, in London and eat it there when it's on the menu.

How to cook perfect roast lamb

- Preheat the oven to 180°C, gas mark 4.

- Place the joint in the preheated oven, allowing 25 minutes per 500g for medium or 30 minutes for well-done meat, plus a further 25–30 minutes. If you are cooking potatoes in the roasting tin, stir them around and turn them occasionally.

- To test if the lamb is cooked, insert a skewer or carving fork into the centre of the flesh, remove it and allow the juices to run – the pinker the juice the rarer the meat.

- After the required cooking time, remove the lamb from the oven and the roasting tin. Place on a carving board and cover with foil. Allow to rest for 10 minutes before carving.

Chicken

A roast chicken dinner with all the trimmings is a guaranteed crowd-pleaser in most households and it is certainly the out-and-out number-one choice for a family meal in mine. Since it is also the personal favourite of the three Michelin-star chef and restaurateur, the great Michel Roux Snr, I feel we are in good company.

A BRIEF HISTORY

CHICKEN CAN CLAIM the oldest heritage in this book because it is the closest living relation to the Tyrannosaurus rex! Galliformes, which are heavy-bodied, ground-feeding birds, have been around for about 40 million years and include chickens, turkeys, pheasants, grouse, partridge, quail, guinea fowl and ptarmigan. The genus *gallus* or red jungle fowl is more like the domesticated fowl we know today and probably dates from about 8 million years ago.

We archaeologists believe the chicken was first domesticated in south-east Asia by 6000 BC. The Egyptians and Chinese were keeping chickens by 1400 BC.

Chickens were probably taken north from China via Russia to Europe by 700 BC. In Britain the chicken predates the Roman invasion since Julius Caesar records that they were already here. The Romans made an industry of chicken breeding.

Early breeding and selection introduced traits that are of little relevance today. These would have included a cock crow for alarm calls, feather colour and appearance for sacrificial purposes and aggression for cock fighting. Sad to say, the early domestication of chicken was for cock fighting. Indeed, so influential was cock fighting that boxing today still uses chicken-related terms, such as bantamweight and featherweight.

The chicken trade in London was significant enough for a poulters' livery company to be established by the thirteenth century.

Constant commercialisation through the twentieth century means there are now more chickens in the world than any other bird. In fact, more than 50 billion chickens are reared annually as a source of food, for both their meat and their eggs.

Back in 1950, chicken was such a treat that most British people ate less than a kilo in a whole year. Now, they eat more than 2kg per month (25kg in a year on average).

HOW CHICKEN IS PRODUCED

THE BROILER CHICKEN, developed in the United States in the 1950s, is a fast-growing strain of hybrid chicken used almost exclusively in commercial production.

Today, with so many advances in technology, such as X-ray, blood testing, computer programming and analysis and genome sequencing, many criteria are used in the selection of stock for breeding and development.

Pure breeds are more difficult to rear in volume and take longer to grow, and so have no real commercial value. As a result they are kept by hobbyists.

Birds are bred either indoors or outdoors as free-range or organic. This has a significant impact on price and quality.

INDOOR BIRDS

Around 80 per cent of chickens raised for meat globally are raised in intensive indoor industrial farming systems. This includes the majority of chickens in the UK, Europe and the United States, as well as rapidly increasing numbers in developing countries. Intensively farmed chickens are bred to reach their slaughter weight in less than six weeks. This is half the time it would take to grow to maturity traditionally. According to the University of Arkansas, if humans grew at a similar rate, a 6.6lb new-born baby would weigh 455lb (32 stone) after two months. Of course, this puts pressure on the bones and respiratory systems of the birds, causing health issues.

Stocking densities permitted vary from country to country. In the UK, the maximum density allowed by law is 39kg/m^2, which, if you assume a kill weight of 1.75kg, equates to nearly 22 birds/m^2. However, in continental Europe it can be as high as 42kg/m^2, or 24 birds/m^2 based on the same calculation. Most of the chicken produced in the UK is to Red Tractor standard, which allows a density of 38kg/m^2, just below the UK legal maximum.

Chicken can be produced indoors to higher welfare standards than those described above. In these systems the stocking density will be much lower, at 30kg/m^2, or around 17 birds/m^2. Diets are better and non GM (genetically modified) feed, which at the time of writing is around 30 per cent more expensive, may be used rather than GM. The barn may have natural light as well as perches and play bales to allow the birds to exhibit natural behaviours. Systems such as RSPCA Freedom Food and products such as Essential Waitrose Chicken are farmed to these standards.

OUTDOOR BIRDS

These can be divided between free-range and organic systems. In the free-range system birds need to be a minimum of 56 days old at slaughter and have outdoor access for half of their life, with roaming space of 1 bird/m^2 outdoors.

Organic birds need to be a minimum of 70 days old and have access to outdoors for at least a third of their life, with a roaming space of 1 bird/4m^2 outdoors. An organic diet is fed to the birds.

WHY THE PRICE VARIES

HUSBANDRY

Cheap chicken comes from intensive farming systems with high stocking densities, as described above. Intensive systems are cheaper to operate but severely compromise animal welfare. They will also tend to use high-protein soya feed with GM.

The more farmers allow their birds space in an environment that lets them display their natural behaviours, such as scratching and perching, the 'happier' the chickens are when they are sent for processing, which some say improves texture. But production costs are higher.

DIET

The diet fed to the birds has an impact on taste and texture. Maize-enriched diets tend to produce more succulent and coloured birds. Older outdoor birds tend to have a stronger 'chicken' taste but cost more to grow.

PRODUCTION METHOD

In the UK, chicken production is legislated and monitored using external independent bodies, e.g. Assured Chicken Production (ACP) or Red Tractor standard. Standards of production in the UK are much higher than elsewhere in the world, so cheaper chicken is often imported. However, even UK standards involve intensive rearing of chickens with the associated welfare concerns. Higher quality reared chicken will have more space per bird then the ACP standard, as well as access to natural light, enhanced bio-security and probably a GM-free diet.

If these things concern you, look for, as a minimum, UK-sourced chicken. Compassion in World Farming recommends RSPCA Freedom Foods or similar for the highest ethical standards.

If buying a whole bird, leg health (i.e. clean with no marks) is a good indicator of the farm's hygiene standards. When the litter is infrequently removed, a build-up of ammonia can damage the bird's hocks.

TRY BEFORE YOU DIE!

—

FREE-RANGE BRITISH CORN-FED WHOLE CHICKEN
£££

For the very best chicken you can't beat British, corn-fed, free-range birds.
Or for something more unusual …

LABEL ROUGE
££££

Label Rouge is a slow-growing bird and will be at least 81–110 days in age compared to around 35–56 days for a normal chicken. Stocking density in the chicken houses is low and the houses are large, with no limit on ranging space. A maximum of four houses per site is permitted under the Label Rouge scheme.

Label Rouge was developed by farmers in 1968; chicken production had become more industrialised following the Second World War and the French demand for the taste of traditionally farm-reared chicken grew. Label Rouge chicken now accounts for over 30 per cent of French poultry sales despite the higher price.

How to cook perfect roast chicken

- Fresh corn-fed, free-range British chicken, weighing approximately 1.5kg
- ½ unwaxed or organic lemon
- ½ small onion
- 2 bay leaves or a sprig of rosemary
- 25g melted butter

Preheat the oven to 190°C, gas mark 5. Remove all the wrapping from the chicken and snip the elasticated string that ties the chicken together. Wipe the chicken all over with kitchen paper to dry the skin.

Place the chicken in the roasting tin and season inside the cavity. Push the lemon and onion inside with the herbs. These will produce steam to keep the chicken moist as well as provide flavour. Brush the chicken all over with melted butter, then season. The salt makes the skin crispy and the butter will keep the chicken moist. Tie the legs back together with kitchen string to give a good shape.

Roast the chicken in the centre of the oven for 1½–1¾ hours. To check that it is cooked, pierce the fattest part of the thigh with a fine skewer. If the juices are pink or show traces of blood, cook the chicken for a further 10–15 minutes, then check again. If the juices are pale golden, the chicken is cooked.

Using two forks, lift the chicken from the roasting tin onto a large plate and reserve the cooking juices. Cover the chicken tightly with foil and leave for 10 minutes before carving. This allows the juices, which have risen to the surface during cooking, to be reabsorbed into the meat to give a moist texture.

Cook's tips

To add more flavour, sprinkle the breast with any of the following before roasting:

- 2 tsp dried mixed herbs or oregano
- 1 tsp paprika and a good pinch chilli powder
- 1 tsp each of mustard seeds and cumin seeds.

Carving the chicken

Hold the chicken steady with a fork, then insert a large sharp knife between the body and leg. Cut off the leg. Divide the leg in half at the joint to give a drumstick and thigh portion. Cut away the wing on the same side. Carve down the breast in thick slices. Repeat on the other side of the chicken.

How to make gravy

Drain all but three tablespoons of the juices from the roasting tin. Set the roasting tin on a hob and reheat the juices. Sprinkle in two teaspoons of plain flour and stir well with a wooden spoon. Gradually stir in 300ml of chicken stock. Bring to the boil, stirring until thickened and smooth. Season well. If the gravy is bland add a little mustard and a splash of soy sauce. For a special gravy, some of the stock can be replaced with red or white wine.

A WORD ABOUT TURKEY

TURKEYS HAVE AN interesting history. Unlike the chicken's ancestors, they are native to the Americas and have been around for 10 million years. American Indians hunted them from around AD 1000 and they are believed to have first been brought to Europe in the 1500s. The name 'turkey' was the result of a mistake as Europeans incorrectly thought they were the same bird as the guinea fowl that had been imported from the Ottoman Empire many years beforehand. The guinea fowl had been named turkey after its origins in the land of the Turks and although they are in fact different birds, the name stuck.

Turkeys are believed to have been brought to Britain in 1526 by Yorkshireman William Strickland, who acquired six birds from American Indian traders on his travels and sold them for tuppence each in Bristol. Henry VIII was the first English king to enjoy turkey, although it was Edward VII who made eating turkey fashionable at Christmas. However, most English households lacked ovens and the utensils necessary for complicated dishes. Food preparation was achieved by slow boiling in pots hung over the hearth fire, so the Christmas turkey or goose had to be carried to the baker's for roasting. When ovens became a more common feature in the home, roast turkey could be cooked in the house as part of the traditional festive meal.

There are 43 different breeds of turkey and the most commercially produced are White Hollands, with white feathers, although the Bronze turkey is the original breed.

WHY THE PRICE VARIES

THE REASONS PRICES vary between different types of turkey are similar to those for different types of chicken. The way they are reared makes a huge difference to price. Firstly, turkeys are always more expensive than chickens as they take much longer to mature and, obviously, they are much bigger. A turkey can take around 24 weeks to grow to maturity, which means the crop for each Christmas is carefully planned out around a year ahead, with the chicks destined for your Christmas dinner hatching in the summer.

More expensive turkeys will be free range. They will be fed on non GM food. Less expensive turkeys are farmed more densely, in barns, and the cheapest have a lot less space and no natural light.

Unlike chickens, the processing method also impacts on quality and expense. Some top-quality turkeys will be dry-aged. That means the feathers are removed and they are 'hung' for around 10–14 days with the guts in. This allows the meat to develop a deeper flavour. They are then 'drawn' to remove the guts and are ready to cook.

Another reason turkeys cost more than chickens is because turkeys vary in size a lot more. This makes them more difficult to process mechanically and so the processing is much more difficult to mechanise and is therefore expensive.

If you want the very best turkey for your dinner table, choose one that has had the best quality of life and has been dry-aged for the very best flavour.

Salmon

While we still love cod and haddock in the UK, at present we love salmon more. In 2014, approximately £1.00 in every £3.50 spent on fresh (or chilled) fish was spent on salmon. A whopping 97 pence of this £1.00 was spent on farmed Atlantic salmon, mainly from either Scotland or Norway. No wonder there has been such a rapid growth in aquaculture, or fish farming, over the past 20–30 years. It is now estimated that 51 per cent of the world's annual fish production comes from aquaculture and this will only increase over the next 50–100 years.

Meanwhile our wild-fish population clearly needs careful management. There are growing concerns around the long-term sustainability of wild Atlantic salmon. While there is currently a £25 million market for chilled wild Pacific salmon in the UK, it is a market under pressure. Wild Atlantic salmon has had to be heavily protected as stocks are low.

When it comes to fishing policy, nations can be extraordinarily parochial. We all need to think very carefully about the fish we eat and what it means for the depletion of the world's oceans, and start putting sustainability at the heart of everything we do when it comes to food production. I recommend looking out for fish that has been certified as sustainable by the Marine Stewardship Council and carries an MSC label.

A BRIEF HISTORY

THE ANNUAL MIGRATION of wild salmon has been a central part of both northern Pacific and Atlantic coastal communities for thousands of years. In many parts of Alaska, salmon are a key element in the traditional subsistence economy and cultural lives of native people. Salmon have long been respected, not only as a food source but also as spiritual beings that should not be overharvested or wasted.

However, by 1900, fish traps, overfishing for canneries, clear-cut logging, mining, dams and other habitat changes all took huge tolls on the once-prolific Pacific salmon runs. It was only when the US Congress approved Alaska statehood in 1958 that the newly established Alaska Department of Fish and Game was charged with bringing salmon back to their former abundance. Happily, they've been successful.

Fish were first farmed as early as around 3500 BC in China, where mainly carp were held in artificial ponds after river floods. In 1970 around 5 per cent of the fish we ate came from farms compared to around 50 per cent today.

GEOGRAPHY

THERE ARE TWO DIFFERENT genus of salmon; Atlantic and Pacific. Almost all farmed salmon is Atlantic salmon and almost all wild salmon caught is Pacific salmon. Wild Atlantic salmon stocks exist in varying numbers in and around Canada, Denmark, England and Wales, the Faroes, Finland, France, Greenland, Iceland, Ireland, Norway, Poland, Portugal, Russia, Scotland, Spain, Sweden and the United States but are heavily protected. There is only one species of Atlantic salmon but there are five species of Pacific salmon and the difference in taste and texture varies considerably.

The bulk of wild Pacific salmon imported into the UK is from Alaska, which is considered to be one of the most sustainably managed fisheries in the world. The five species of Alaskan Pacific salmon are caught in various locations around the state from the Kotzebue and Yukon rivers up towards the Arctic, right around to Ketchikan and Prince Rupert in south-east Alaska. The region, water temperature, feed and catch methods can all have a significant influence on the appearance, texture and taste of the fish. A good wild-salmon buyer will understand how all the varying conditions and variables determine the end fish.

The largest of all the commercial salmon fisheries in Alaska is Bristol Bay. Each summer, as many as 40 million Sockeye salmon return to the nine rivers that feed into Bristol Bay. As well as Sockeye, the bay is home to King (also called Chinook), Silver and Chum salmon. The fishery in Bristol Bay has more than 130 years of commercial fishing history.

Farmed salmon, on the other hand, is produced all over the world, but animal welfare standards and feed vary hugely, impacting the environment, cost of production and the quality of the salmon. The Atlantic species are primarily used for salmon farming.

Salmon are predators that need a high-protein diet and there is a significant cost in feeding them. Most are fed on a pelleted feed using small fish, such as anchovies and sardines, which are made into fish meal and oil. Due to concerns about the sustainability of this approach, much research is going into developing suitable plant-based feeds.

HOW SALMON IS PRODUCED

PACIFIC SALMON ARE anadromous; they start their lives in freshwater rivers and lakes and after one to four years migrate to the ocean, swimming thousands of miles to their feeding ground, feasting on ocean krill, shrimp and other small fish. This natural diet, combined with the rigours of swimming through icy waters, gives wild salmon their unique flavour, colour and superior texture.

Although the lifecycle and spawning characteristics of the species of salmon differ, each maintains the same timing year after year, returning to the exact place of their birth. How they know where to go is one of the wonders of the natural world.

Before the salmon return to spawn, they build up reserves of fat and nutrients to carry them through their rigorous journey upstream as they do not eat in freshwater as adults. It is at this point of peak quality, just before they reach freshwater, that the salmon are harvested.

Salmon that enter freshwater early in the season are more brightly coloured than those that arrive later, but all salmon turn darker as the time to spawn approaches. Pronounced morphological changes take place, particularly in the spawning male. The female selects a suitable patch of gravel and excavates a shallow hollow, known as a redd, where she will lay her eggs. When she is ready, she allows the male to fertilise her eggs, which are then covered with gravel and hopefully protected until they are ready to hatch.

While the new salmon are preparing to enter the world, their parents die, usually just days after spawning. This amazing cycle of life ensures that all of the salmon's nutritional value is returned to the river and the surrounding land for another generation to follow.

HOW WILD SALMON IS CAUGHT

The majority of the commercial wild salmon harvested in Alaska is caught using one of the following three methods:

- **Gill nets** As the name describes, these catch the fish by the gills or, more accurately, by the shoulders. Gill nets tend to be set like a curtain, perpendicular to the oncoming fish. They can be drifted downstream into the path of the fish heading for freshwater or they can be strung out from beaches and banks creating a 'set net' that intercepts fish swimming close to shore. These nets can then be pulled aboard a boat and the fish removed shortly before being iced on board. This method is responsible for 80–90 per cent of the Sockeye harvest in Alaska.

- **Purse seiners** These catch the majority of the Pink salmon harvest as well as a healthy proportion of the Keta salmon. Purse seining is when a long net is drawn around the fish in the ocean before the purse strings are tightened, capturing the salmon inside. The fish are then lifted into the hold. This method is very effective for Pink salmon, because they return in large shoals.

- **Trolling** The final major commercial method is trolling, principally used to catch King, Coho and some Keta salmon. Typically, four to six main wire lines are fished behind a slow-moving boat. Each line has multiple leaders primed with natural bait or lures. Each fish is retrieved by hand, resulting in a lower volume of extremely high-quality fish.

WHY THE PRICE VARIES

WILD SALMON SPECIES

The five species of wild Alaskan salmon vary in size, colour, texture and taste. This is one of the main factors that drives the difference in price. King salmon are the most expensive, followed by Sockeye, Coho, Pink and Keta, and the eating quality is believed to follow the same order. However, it is not quite that simple – a Keta salmon caught in the right place at the right time of year can be excellent to eat. So the knowledge of the fish buyer is important in understanding these variations.

Sockeye is recognisable by its distinctive bright-red flesh, which is a result of the rich diet of krill shrimp and other crustaceans. It is a much leaner fish than its farmed competition and will deliver a much richer and gamier flavour. Some might say that comparing Sockeye salmon to farmed Atlantic salmon is a bit like comparing duck to chicken – they are both delicious in their own right but very different eating experiences. Keta salmon are recognised as producing the best eggs (or ikura). In the UK, the meat is sold as an entry-level wild salmon product and has a pale flesh colour that is close to that of farmed salmon, although the texture is firmer and meatier. Coho salmon are typically higher in oil content than Sockeye and Keta and are often preferred for smoking.

ABUNDANCE

The abundance of each species dictates the price. Consider these harvests: in 2014, 487,000 King salmon were caught compared to 44 million Sockeye, 6 million Coho, 44 million Pink, and 11 million Keta. Rarity always commands a higher price.

SIZE

A King salmon typically weighs around 9–18k, although much larger ones are often caught. A Pink salmon weighs around 1kg. The smaller salmon are therefore much more suitable for being processed into cans or sent to Asian markets for further processing into very affordable salmon portions.

For all these reasons combined, a fisherman can be paid from 25 cents/lb for a Pink salmon and up to $2.50/lb for a King salmon.

FARMED SALMON

In Europe there is only one species of farmed salmon, Atlantic, so the species and abundance factors that dictate the price of wild salmon are irrelevant. Farmed salmon tends to be more expensive than wild Keta and Pink salmon, but cheaper than Sockeye, Coho or King salmon.

TRY BEFORE YOU DIE!

–

KING SALMON
£££££

Few, if any, fish are more prized by fishermen, whether commercial or recreational, than this giant of the salmon family. The Chinook or King salmon can grow to the size of a human and weigh more than 45kg. It also bears the highest fat content of all the five Pacific salmon species. It is generally considered the most delicious, and its secondary name King salmon is absolutely appropriate in more ways than one. A barbecued steak of King, lightly salted, peppered and drizzled with lemon juice, takes seafood lovers into epicurean heaven. Such a cut provides a cross-section of the entire creature from its crispy-when-grilled skin, to the firm back muscle, to the velvety soft and succulent belly meat often named as the very best part.

Sadly, it is almost impossible to source in the UK so you would probably have to add the price of an air ticket to Alaska to your budget! Waitrose is, however, one of the few outlets where it is still possible to buy wild salmon in Britain. I would very much recommend the Alaskan Keta and Sockeye fillets.

· ·

How to cook perfect salmon

I think poaching produces the best, moist, tender fish. Pour water, milk or stock over the fish to cover and add a little butter and white wine. Poach on the hob or in the oven until the fish is just done. In fact, all fillets and steaks, skate wings or whole fish, such as trout, sole and sea bass, are superb poached, as is smoked fish.

· ·

Tuna

Tuna are one of the most remarkable creatures in nature. Their name is derived from the ancient Greek verb 'thynno' meaning 'to rush' and rush they can. Indeed, they can accelerate faster than a Porsche 911 and are among the fastest swimmers in the sea. There are eight commercial species, averaging between 3kg and 300kg, and as a migratory fish, they navigate the oceans of planet earth.

Every day, several thousand tonnes of tuna are consumed around the world in hundreds of different formats and dishes. Tuna is truly a global fish that sits at the centre of our global food economy and culture, whether it is tuna-mayo sandwiches from a UK sandwich bar, or *salades Niçoise* served in European brasseries, or ceviche eaten by sunny South American beaches, or curries in the Maldives, or highest quality sashimi skilfully made in sushi restaurants in London, Paris and Tokyo.

My favourite tuna-based meal is a humble tuna sandwich and my favourite place to eat it is the Florida Keys, to be precise, Key West. It might sound a horrible waste of a beautifully fresh tuna steak, which is my preferred main-meal protein, but there is nothing that comes close to a fresh tuna sandwich, cold beer and view out over the Gulf of Mexico from around Mallory Square as the sun sets.

A BRIEF HISTORY

WE THINK THAT TUNA FISHING dates back to pre-Roman times. Phoenician settlers industrialised tuna fishing almost three millennia ago, founding multiple cities, such as Gadir, Lixus and the Port of Menesteo, setting up their factories in the area of the Strait of Gibraltar. They traded tuna along the Atlantic coast.

Almadraba fishing, an ancient artisanal technique of net fishing, was used. It involves constructing a maze-like trap to snare the tuna, which was then salted and dried (known today as Mojama) for preservation. These methods are still used today on the south coast of Spain and in other Mediterranean regions.

Over the centuries, many more tuna fisheries emerged. They were always based around coastal communities and fished seasonally, based on the migratory patterns of the tuna. As the fisheries developed, so did fishing methods, from the pole and line fishing off the northern Spanish coasts, to harpoon fishing off the coast of Norway and handline fishing off the tropical islands.

The emergence of canning as a viable preservation method played a significant role in the tuna industry's development.

In the late 1800s, the primary canned fish was sardine. The major sardine fisheries were in southern California, particularly San Diego. In 1903, due to a combination of overfishing and ocean conditions, the catch of sardines was exceptionally poor. Albert P. Halfhil, who canned sardines from San Pedro Bay, saw that he was going to have lots of empty sardine tins, so he figured out a way to fill them. He experimented by packing the empty sardine cans with locally caught albacore tuna. And so the American canned-tuna industry was born.

The rise of more industrial fishing methods, such as long line and purse seine, as well as ever-improving refrigeration have transformed the tuna industry over the last 60 years.

HOW TUNA IS PRODUCED

TUNA HAVE A TORPEDO-SHAPED body designed to swim at high speeds and cover vast distances. They swim over 35 miles every day even when young. In fact, they never stop swimming, as although their hard head allows them to swim fast and efficiently, it doesn't allow them to pump water to their gills to breathe, so they need to move continuously in order to have oxygen. Fish are generally considered cold-blooded animals – their body temperature is the same as the water in which they are swimming. Muscles are more powerful when warm and, unusually, most tuna can raise their body temperature several degrees above the water temperature due to a vascular heat interchange system developed during their evolution (although they cannot truly be considered warm-blooded animals as they cannot keep this temperature constant). This and a high metabolic rate result in an extraordinary growth pattern.

Tuna can live close to the surface and to depths of 100–500m. They are opportunistic predators, feeding on a great variety of fish, crustaceans and squid. That said, they can be very selective when they are not hungry. Owing to their size, adult tuna have few predators, although billfishes, sharks and toothed whales, such as orcas, carry the main threat (it is not uncommon to find small bites in the belly area of tuna).

The most common and valuable tuna species is Northern Bluefin, so named because of the blue strip along the side of its body, which helps to camouflage it. This is the biggest tuna of all, with the world record standing at over 670kg. High in fat, it is a favourite of the Japanese for sashimi. Unfortunately, this magnificent animal was overfished for many years at the start of the millennium and the population was declared endangered in 2011. Tuna is a very resilient species, however, and it is encouraging to see that conservation efforts are leading to a recovery of stocks.

Southern Bluefin tuna looks very similar to its Northern cousin, and for many years was considered to be the same species. It is smaller, with the maximum size recorded at around 260kg. This species is critically endangered and urgent action is needed to protect it.

Bigeye tuna is so named – you might not be entirely astonished to learn – for the size of its eyes. It lives deep in cool subtropical and equatorial waters, as opposed to Bluefin tuna, which prefers more temperate waters. Bigeye can reach 210kg, has deep-coloured flesh and can have a high fat content, but the flesh is not as red and fatty as the Bluefin. The Yellowfin tuna looks for warmer surface waters, and has a much leaner body. Yellowfin tuna can reach up to 200kg.

Albacore tuna and Skipjack tuna are smaller. Albacore tuna can reach 60kg, but most fished sizes range from a few kilos to 20kg. Albacore is unique because its flesh is much paler than other tuna species. It goes from a pale red to a pinkish white. It prefers temperate to tropical waters and its flavour is much more delicate than other species. Skipjack is the small cousin in the family. Its name comes from the dark longitudinal stripes on its silvery belly. It can reach 30kg but 10kg is considered a large size. The flesh is the darkest of all the tuna, and due to the high myoglobin (a particular muscle protein) content, it does not keep for long once caught. For this reason and for economic reasons Skipjack is most commonly processed and canned.

Fishing method

In recent years more attention has been given to how tuna are caught. Methods such as purse seine, where a large net engulfs a school of tuna and pulls in a big haul in one catch, have been criticised because high levels of other fish, turtles and marine mammals are caught at the same time. It is, however, efficient and therefore can lead to lower prices per tonne than pole and line fishing, where one hook and one line pulls in one fish at a time. Pole and line is considered to be more sustainable.

WHY THE PRICE VARIES

TUNA PRICES VARY according to catches and availability, regional and local species, preferences and taste.

TYPE OF TUNA

We can divide the global market for tuna into three main areas: canned tuna; fresh tuna for which the price is primarily dictated by the value of the fish for the Japanese-style market (sushi and sashimi) and fresh steaks; and regular frozen steak.

Canning is the cheapest form of tuna. The highest value species for canning is Albacore as it is succulent, has a more delicate flavour than Skipjack and has no metallic taste. It is very white when cooked and is often dubbed the 'chicken of the sea'. After Albacore is Yellowfin, with a lighter meat than other tuna except Albacore. It has a slightly more pronounced flavour and a lightly metallic taste. Skipjack is the most common species found in a can, as it is much more abundant than other species and has a higher reproduction rate.

FLESH COLOUR AND FAT CONTENT

When it comes to sashimi, price discussions move from price per tonne to price per kilo. Canned tuna is a commodity, whereas fresh tuna is a treat. Price is heavily dictated by the colour of the flesh. Buyers look for a deep-red, translucent colour. The fat content also has a huge impact on the value of the tuna, as fat represents flavour and succulence. Here the big winners are the Northern Bluefin tuna, followed very closely by their southern hemisphere cousin. However, stocks are still low and the Marine Conservation Society has given the species its strongest rating for lack of sustainability. Bigeye comes next, with its deep-red colour and a good fat level, followed very closely by Yellowfin tuna, which has a red colour but is very lean and with a much lower fat content. Yellowfin tuna is preferred in the European market because of its sustainability credentials and its uniform red colour.

THE LUNAR CYCLE

In some countries, prices fluctuate significantly at different times of the month because catch rates and quality change depending of the behaviour of the tuna. For example, tuna is more active and tends to follow the abundance of food to the surface during a full moon. Fishermen take ample advantage of this period, when catches are higher, so there is an abundance of fish on the market in the days immediately afterwards, which typically leads to lower prices for buyers. The opposite happens before a full moon or during bad weather when fisherman cannot land fish. It is not uncommon to see prices fluctuate by 100 per cent either way during the course of a month.

Individual quality grading

As well as the broader market trends and catch dynamics, the value of each tuna caught is individual and links to its specific quality credentials. In the raw-fish market, each tuna is graded one by one. Slight differences in quality can mean a huge difference in price. Freshness, colour, fat content, body shape, flesh and skin, and size all dictate prices. Tsukiji market in Tokyo holds the record for the highest priced tuna ever sold. In January 2013, a single 220kg fish was sold at auction for almost £1.1 million! This equates to £5,000 per kg. This was the first tuna auction of the year and attracted huge attention. While these prices are as much about PR and marketing as economic value, they provide an indication of the value that the Japanese attach to the very best tuna.

TRY BEFORE YOU DIE!

–

Raw tuna sashimi
££££

If you have never eaten raw tuna sashimi, you simply must. It is fresh, meaty and has a surprisingly neutral taste that surprises many people who have never considered the possibility of eating raw fish. Simply dip in a soy sauce and add some wasabi if you wish and you will be hooked!

Bigeye tuna cheek
£££

If you are feeling a little more adventurous, the real prize is to try the cheek of a large Bigeye tuna. In common with many delicious cuts of meat, it won't win first prize in a beauty contest but when you try it, you will be glad that you are in on the secret. Like most tuna, this cut is best served raw. The first bite has real texture and you will feel a healthy crunch. On the second, your mouth will experience an overwhelming sensation combining sweetness and succulence as the juices, fat and meat combine to melt in your mouth. Again, a dash of soy and wasabi complement this perfectly. You will have to look hard to find this cut and may even need to take a trip via Tsukiji market in Tokyo. After all, every fish has only two cheeks!

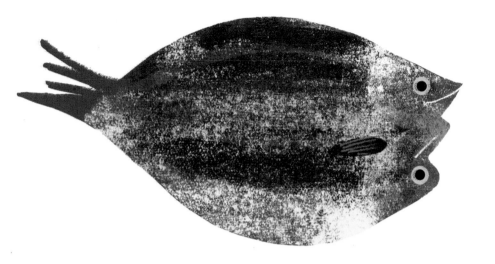

Smoked Fish

I haven't covered smoked salmon in this chapter because it deserves a chapter in its own right. This chapter covers smoked cod and haddock, which are both underrated treasures in my opinion, as well as my all-time favourite breakfast treat, the Craster kipper. Just in case you have yet to embrace the pleasure of a perfect kipper, I have also included some instructions on how to cook a kipper to encourage you to try one, and the same for smoked fish.

A BRIEF HISTORY

ONE OF BRITAIN'S great food traditions is 'cold' smoking fish using long-established methods. It is only possible thanks to this country's cold climate. Grimsby's traditionally smoked fish and the Craster kipper are as important and iconic as cheese from Brie or Parma ham.

The oldest smokehouses still operating in Britain are generally 100 to 200 years old and many of the buildings are now listed. However, the roots of fish-smoking are much older than that. There is evidence to suggest that the practice goes right back to prehistory. Often, fishermen had a smokehouse next to their cottage to extend the life of perishable fish by up to two weeks.

The arrival of railways in the nineteenth century allowed fresh smoked fish to be transported quickly from the coast to large cities inland and, as a result, a huge new market opened up for this distinct delicacy.

Kippering means to preserve by rubbing with salt or other spices, before drying in the open air or in smoke. The technique was originally used for the preservation of surplus fish (particularly those known as 'kips' harvested during spawning runs). Since then kippering has come to mean the preservation of any fish, poultry, beef or other meat treated in this way. The process for fish involves cleaning, filleting and butterflying or slicing the fish to expose maximum surface area to the drying and preservative agents.

It is said that kippering herrings originated in the village of Craster, Northumberland, although its near neighbour Seahouses holds a rival claim.

In 1939, the Torry Research Station in Aberdeen developed the first mechanical kiln, but it was only after the war that it began to come into use. In 1965 the same research station published a book that many say was severely biased in favour of the mechanical kiln. It declared that 'although in Britain most smoked fish is still made in traditional smoke houses, the mechanical kiln is being rapidly adopted.' In truth, most people within the industry knew that kilns had serious limitations in turning out products similar to those produced by traditional smokers.

It was, however, not the mechanical kiln that was responsible for the dramatic drop in numbers of traditional smokehouses from the pre-Second World War high, but the development of the fish finger, which was to revolutionise people's eating habits.

The success of the fish finger and the breaded fish fillet ensured two things. Firstly, an increasing level of indiscriminate fishing of the North Atlantic's already depleted stocks ensued. A thick coating of breadcrumbs covers many inadequacies in a fish, which encouraged fishing for quantity, rather than quality. Secondly, traditional products containing skin and bones, as smoked fish does, were suddenly shunned by consumers susceptible to slick marketing in an age that was still lax about product claims.

Today, the majority of smoked fish is produced in modern kilns. Those traditional smokehouses that have survived in England are mainly found in Grimsby. The port has been granted special recognition by the European Union for its long history of curing. Grimsby traditional smoked cod and haddock are now protected by a PGI (Protected Geographical Indication) meaning only fish cured in the traditional process can be called 'Grimsby Traditional Smoked Fish'.

For generations, smoked fish was referred to as 'cured', but with the advent of mechanical kilns, traditional smokers adopted the term 'smoked' to emphasise that their process was entirely dependent on the smoke produced from the smouldering embers of wood shavings. Mechanical kilns are electrically heated using a minimal amount of smoke in their process. However, kiln curers also adopted the term 'smoked' for their process to mask the difference between the two products. Thus it became necessary for the original process to be known as 'traditionally smoked'.

HOW SMOKED FISH IS PRODUCED

SMOKED COD AND HADDOCK

Fillets are immersed in saltwater brine for a maximum of five minutes, depending on the size of the fish and the season of the year. For dyed fillets, the brine will contain the natural pigments turmeric and annatto. Fillets are then left to drain (dreep) on stainless steel rods called speights. Once drained, the speights of fillets are placed in smokehouse chimneys to be smoked overnight. These chimneys are one metre by two metres square and up to ten metres high. They have openings at top and bottom to allow a draught of cool fresh air to mingle with the smoke as it rises, creating the special 'cold smoking' that the process requires. A door part of the way up each chimney allows the smoking process to be monitored and fillets to be moved and removed as necessary. The walls of the chimneys are allowed to gather a coating of tar over many years – essential in imparting the unique flavouring that cannot be produced by any other method.

A shallow pit at the base of each chimney is filled with sawdust. The amount of already smouldering sawdust added to the fresh sawdust to start the burn alters considerably with the season and weather, with less needed in summer. This variability, caused mainly by changes in temperature and humidity, can also be regulated by altering the amount of air in the laid sawdust. This is done by removing trapped air; the more the sawdust is compressed the slower the burn.

The expertise required to smoke fish successfully in the traditional way can only be learned over many years, with the knowledge often being handed down through families. This is in contrast to the modern mechanical kiln, which is a sealed electric oven regulated simply by turning dials. This is a great advantage to people with little experience of fish-smoking, but the product never achieves the same distinctive taste and aroma. Traditional fish-smoking is an overnight process, taking much longer than a mechanical kiln. The first speights of fillets are removed from the chimneys early the next morning. Speights nearest the fires are taken out first, and the higher ones removed in batches over the next few hours. An experienced fish-smoker can tell when fillets are ready simply by touch.

The mixture of smoke and cold air passed over the fillets means there is little heat involved in the process and it only takes a short time for them to cool. Once this has happened, fillets are packed into shallow cartons and rapidly chilled to below 5°C. The finished product is then transported overnight to its final destination.

KIPPERS

The smoking process begins with herring being split by machine. Any remaining gills are removed by hand before the fish are placed in brining tanks. 'Curing' them extends shelf life. Once brined, the split herrings are hung on tenterhooks and allowed to drain.

The fish are then ready for smoking, and the tenterhooks are placed in the chimneys. White wood shavings and oak sawdust make the perfect fire, but once again controlling the heat and smoke is a skill passed down from generation to generation. Once lit, each fire smoulders for about three hours before it has to be relit, but this is dependent on the direction and strength of the wind. Shutters in the roof of the smokehouse control the circulation of smoke.

It's important to build up the fire gradually so that the herrings, which are quite wet when they are first hung, have time to 'set on the hooks'. If the fires are too hot, they will fall off the tenterhooks.

The whole process takes between 14 and 16 hours and the finished product still looks like a fish. The head is preserved and the natural colours of the skin are tanned golden by the smoke. The flesh has a deep chestnut-brown colour, glistening with oil, and the kipper has a wonderful smoky aroma.

WHY THE PRICE VARIES

QUALITY (FRESHNESS) OF THE FISH

Both poor- and good-quality fish can easily be recognised with the naked eye, if you know what to look for. Good-quality, traditionally cured fillets look glossy, feel soft and springy to the touch and have a gentle aroma. Undyed fillets will be cream in colour with a glossy shine.

Dyed cod and haddock fillets will have an even distribution of colour with a high shine. Originally, smoked fish was produced from fresh fish coming to the end of its life – the fillets are dried to a certain extent during the smoking process, thereby prolonging the shelf life. The fish was dyed to hide the fact that the quality of fish was not as good as fresh. It was also a way to give the fillets a smoked appearance without smoking it for hours, thereby reducing drip loss and increasing yields. However, nowadays dying is simply a matter of personal taste.

Poor-quality fish are 'dull' (similar to a matt finish in paint), usually indicating that the fish was frozen at sea and defrosted prior to smoking. There will usually be little or no aroma, or there could be a heavy 'smell' and a rubbery feel to the fillet. Dyed fillets may show a tie-dyed effect, i.e. not an even distribution of colour. This, again, is usually due to the fish being previously frozen so colour is unable to adhere to the fillet. Sometimes there will be a speckled effect down the whole body of the fillet, which usually indicates that old fish has been used.

The quality of fish used has an obvious effect on the price you pay. To produce lower cost fillets, fish coming to the end of its life is used, as well as previously frozen raw fish.

SMOKING METHOD

One of the main differences reflected by price is whether the fish has been smoked in a mechanical kiln rather than the traditional way.

ETHICS

To ensure you are buying good quality, look for fish with a PGI and MSC (Marine Stewardship Council) accreditation. This proves lines of traceability and chain of custody, and that best practice has been followed.

TRY BEFORE YOU DIE!

–

CRASTER KIPPER
£££

The Craster kipper (sometimes called by aficionados simply 'the Craster') is produced using high-quality fish, and is still smoked in the traditional way by L. Robson and Sons in Craster, Northumberland. The smokehouses are more than 140 years old.

Neil Robson is the fourth generation of the family to be involved in the business, which was originally started by his great-grandfather, James William Robson. To begin with, the kippers were only eaten locally, but by 1937 they were being dispatched to various markets and private customers throughout the country. Today they are exported all over the world.

LIGHTLY GRILLED LOCH FYNE KIPPER WITH POACHED BURFORD BROWN EGG
£££££

My favourite restaurant for serving kippers is the Goring Hotel, London, which to my mind offers the best breakfast in town.

How to cook kippers

Here's how I enjoy them.

- Preheat the grill.

- Line the grill pan with foil and dot with a little unsalted butter. Lay two Craster kippers on the foil, skin-side up.

- Grill for 1 minute, then turn over and spread the kipper generously with unsalted butter.

- Grill for a further 4–5 minutes until the butter is sizzling.

- Serve immediately with a poached egg and lemon wedges to squeeze over.

How to cook smoked fish

It couldn't be simpler. Either poach as I set out in the salmon section or ...

- Preheat the grill.

- Brush the smoked fish with a little melted butter and grill for 3–4 minutes each side until the flesh is opaque and cooked through.

- Keep warm if preparing other ingredients.

Smoked Salmon

Smoked salmon is often my starter of choice, covered with freshly squeezed lemon juice and a generous dash of ground pepper. Over the years, though, I have become increasingly conscious of a wide range of tastes and textures in the dishes I am served.

A BRIEF HISTORY

WHILE THOROUGHLY EMBEDDED in Scotland's history, smoked salmon was first introduced into the UK from Eastern Europe. Jewish immigrants from Russia and Poland brought the technique of salmon-smoking to London's East End, when they settled there in the late nineteenth century. They smoked salmon as a way to preserve it, since refrigeration was very basic. In those early years, they were not aware that there was a salmon native to the UK so they imported Baltic salmon in barrels of saltwater. However, having discovered the wild Scottish salmon coming down to the fish market at Billingsgate each summer, they started smoking them instead. The smoking process has changed over the years and many contemporary smokehouses have left traditional brick kilns behind in favour of commercial methods. Only a handful of traditional smokehouses remain, such as John Ross Jr in Aberdeen and the Stornoway smokehouse on the Isle of Lewis.

Today's smoked salmon producers use mainly farmed salmon.

GEOGRAPHY

ATLANTIC SALMON IS predominantly farmed in Scotland, Norway and Chile. Over 2 million tonnes of salmon are farmed worldwide, and of that, 150,000 tonnes are farmed in Scotland.

Most Scottish salmon farmers are regulated by various third-party accreditations that control the welfare and quality of fish being produced. Having a lower stocking density is more expensive but the welfare of the fish is improved as they have much more room to swim freely. The fast-flowing waters around the west coast and islands of Scotland also ensure that the salmon are working harder swimming against the current, which produces good-quality, lean fish.

HOW SMOKED SALMON IS PRODUCED

MOST SMOKED SALMON PRODUCERS follow a similar process of curing, conditioning (or drying), smoking and maturation. The length of time the salmon spend in these processes will determine the level of smoke taste, texture and density of the finished smoked salmon.

The curing process uses a unique blend of salt and sugar, which is sprinkled onto the fillets. This is then left to do its work for up to 15 hours before being rinsed off, and the fish is left to dry before it's ready to go into the kiln. Some producers use only salt in this process. In traditional dry-curing, moisture is removed from the salmon, giving a firm-textured flesh. Although a longer and more labour-intensive process compared to wet curing (or brining), the extra effort is worth it to achieve the best product.

Most smoked salmon is cold-smoked, typically at 37°C. The cold smoking does not cook the fish, but rather flavours it, resulting in a delicate texture. Although some smokehouses go for a deliberately 'oaky' style by prolonging exposure to smoke from oak chips, industrial production favours less exposure to smoke and a blander style, using cheaper woods.

Originally, prepared fish were hung in lines on racks, or tenters, within the kiln. Workers would climb up and straddle the racks while hanging the individual lines in ascending order. Small, circular woodchip fires would be lit at floor level and allowed to smoke slowly throughout the night. The wood fire was damped with sawdust to create smoke; this was constantly tended as naked flames would cook the fish rather than smoke it. The required duration of smoking has always been gauged by a skilled 'master smoker', who manually checks for optimum smoking conditions. Too long and the salmon can have a strong 'tar' taste and too little can mean a milder smoked flavour than required. Traditionally, smoked salmon usually remains in the kiln for up to 24 hours.

The materials used to smoke salmon are varied. Traditionally, oak has been used as it's a robust material that smoulders rather than burns. Oak can be mixed with beech chips to help give a more delicate flavour. To create a more artisanal flavour the traditional kilns can use more indigenous Scottish flora, such as sweet gale, Scottish heather and peat, as well as chippings from whisky barrels and other local woods to help enhance the taste. In recent years, smokers have become more experimental with smoking materials – for instance, tea!

More mainstream, milder smoked salmon is generally smoked in mechanical kilns. While this can sound very clinical it actually ensures that the smoked salmon has a more consistent flavour as the state-of-the-art kilns regulate the amount of smoke. The fillets are usually laid onto racks, rather than hung, which means more fillets can be smoked in one kiln, therefore reducing the cost of the product. For a mild smoked salmon the smoking time is 8–12 hours.

The next stage in the process is maturation, which helps the flavour to develop. Maturation can take from one to six days depending on the level of flavour required, the size and thickness of the fillet and time of year.

Once the fillet has matured, it's then sliced. Smoked salmon can be sliced into a number of formats. Most commonly used is the 'D-shaped slice'. Fillets are skimmed with an angled cut, which ensures a consistent level of flavour is achieved in every slice. You can also buy long-sliced smoked salmon but this is sliced horizontally from the top of the fillet to the bottom, which means different levels of smoke are present in each slice.

WHY THE PRICE VARIES
PRODUCTION METHOD
Prices of smoked salmon vary depending on the production method and how long each stage of the key processes of curing, conditioning, smoking and maturation

takes. To produce the most cost-effective smoked salmon it would have to go through the process quickly to ensure the least amount of yield is lost from the fish. Mild smoked salmon can take three or four days to produce, including up to ten hours in the kilns, and is matured for at least one day to develop the flavour. However, more specialist products, such as peat- and heather-smoked salmon, for example, will spend 24 hours in the kilns and could be matured for three to five days.

QUALITY

Ethical producers ensure that salmon farms meet the highest standards and monitor feed and stocking density (the number of fish per cubic metre) to ensure fish have plenty of room to move around. This also helps them to stay lean and healthy, and so creates a better product. The lower the stocking density the more expensive the fish are, since producers' costs are spread over fewer fish.

Always remember that, like a good red wine, smoked salmon should be brought to room temperature before eating.

TRY BEFORE YOU DIE!

–

HANSEN & LYDERSEN SMOKED SALMON
££££

One of the most expensive smoked-salmon products available and no wonder. The rather eccentric Ole Hansen plays live piano jazz to the fillets that are drying. His customers claim that it makes the smoked salmon taste better. Maybe you should judge for yourself. Available from farmers' markets across London.

HESTON'S LAPSANG SOUCHONG TEA SMOKED SALMON
£££

I recommend that you try Heston's Tea Smoked Salmon because of its unique use of tea. The smoky tea leaves' natural tannins give the smoked salmon added depth.

LONDON CURE SMOKED SCOTTISH SALMON
£££

London Cure Smoked Scottish Salmon has established itself thanks to its delicate taste and texture. It has been smoked in the East End of the city since at least the late 1800s – the curing process uses only rock salt and oak smoke to bring out the taste of the salmon without leaving a strong smoke flavour. H. Forman & Son, based in London's Docklands, are the UK's oldest salmon curers.

BALIK SMOKED SALMON
£££££

This salmon is exclusive to Caviar House & Prunier, who bought the rights to supply it from its Swiss producer in 1992. Switzerland might seem an unusual location for producing smoked fish, but the makers claim that the combination of crisp alpine air and the local spring water and wood creates a unique flavour. The salmon is prepared using Norwegian salmon according to a secret recipe from the court of the Russian tsars, which was entrusted to Hans Gerd Kübel in 1978 by Israel Kaplan, the grandson of the purveyor of Balik salmon to the imperial court.

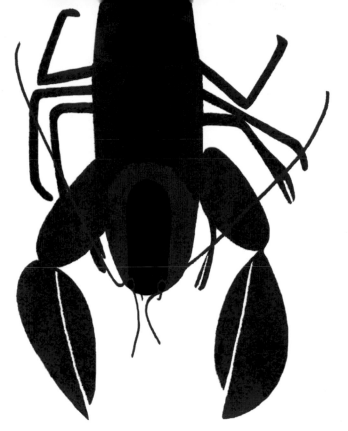

Lobster

In doing my research over the years I have frequently been surprised at how often food we consider to be posh today was once the staple of the poor. Oysters are a good example. They were eaten by the poor of London in their millions and their discarded shells can still be seen today piled high on the banks of the Thames. Lobster, you might be surprised to read, is the same. Before lobster became popular, the Canadian children who were sent to school with lobster sandwiches were from poor, working-class families.

Over recent years lobster from North America has become more affordable. Thanks to warming waters, lobster populations there are booming, bringing prices down. In the summer of 2012, the Maine lobster prices collapsed from around $4 per pound to just $2 per pound, which led Maine's Lobster Advisory Council to throw $3 million of marketing money into convincing Americans to eat more lobster and encouraging exports of frozen lobster into overseas markets. At the same time, the Scottish lobster industry has been dealing with smaller catches due to colder waters pushing the lobsters further out to sea. This in turn has pushed UK lobster prices up.

A BRIEF HISTORY

LOBSTER DID NOT BEGIN to become widely popular until the mid-nineteenth century when New Yorkers and Bostonians developed a taste for it. Previously, lobster was a mark of poverty or used as a food for indentured servants. Ironically, some servants specified in their contracts they would not eat lobster any more than twice per week. Lobster was also served to inmates in prisons, much to their apparent displeasure.

Commercial lobster fisheries began to thrive after the development of the lobster smack, a custom-made boat with open holding wells on deck, which served to keep the catch live during transportation.

Today, there are two types of commercially important lobster; the American and European lobster. There is much debate about which is best.

Often called the 'King of Seafood', lobster is the pride of Atlantic Canada. This crustacean has a long body and five sets of legs, including two large front claws, one of which is flat and heavy, while the other is smaller and thinner. The body, tail and claws are hard-shelled.

Live lobsters range in colour from brownish-rust to greenish-brown; all lobster shells turn bright orangey-red when cooked. The white flesh is firm and dense with a rich, savoury flavour.

GEOGRAPHY

LOBSTERS ARE FOUND in many areas of the world's oceans. The species found off Canada's east coast, *Homarus americanus*, commonly known as the American lobster or Atlantic lobster, is unique to the north-west Atlantic Ocean. The Atlantic lobster is found from Long Island Sound to the southern part of the Labrador Sea, from the waterline out to the edge of the continental shelf. Adult lobsters prefer rocky substrates, but can also live on sandy and muddy bottoms.

Lobsters migrate seasonally, and this is primarily in response to changes in water temperature. In spring, lobsters move towards shallow waters to moult, reproduce or hatch eggs, returning to deeper water in the autumn. Lobster moulting is influenced by the size (or age) and gender of the lobster and also by temperature and food conditions. Mature females grow more slowly than mature male lobsters. In the Gulf of St Lawrence, it typically takes 15–20 moults over a period of 6–9 years for lobsters to reach minimum legal size to catch.

HOW LOBSTER IS PRODUCED

IN **CANADA,** lobsters are harvested and processed throughout the Atlantic Provinces (Newfoundland, New Brunswick, Nova Scotia, Prince Edward Island and Quebec). Landings peak twice a year, once in the period from April to June, when the spring season opens, and then again in December, after the winter fishery opens in south-western Nova Scotia.

Most lobster fishing takes place relatively close to shore, inside the Gulf of St Lawrence or around Nova Scotia and Newfoundland, but there are some vessels that fish the deep basins and outer banks off south-western Nova Scotia.

The main fisheries in the UK are around west Scotland, south and west England and all of Wales. Despite British waters producing fabulous lobsters, we export about 70 per cent to Europe, while half of the lobsters we actually eat in the UK come from Canada. The majority of lobsters in British supermarkets are Canadian crustaceans.

Licensed lobster fishers use small boats to fish with wooden-frame or plastic-coated steel-mesh traps, which are weighted and lowered to the sea bottom. Traps are hauled by ropes attached to brightly painted buoys that mark their location. They are baited, usually with dead fish (mackerel, herring or flounder), and the lobster is attracted by the fish odour and enters the trap. The trap is designed so that lobsters legally large enough to catch cannot get out. Traps are attached one to the other and are placed on the bottom of the sea for a minimum of 24 hours before being hauled up. Live lobsters are removed and their claws are kept closed using rubber bands. Biodegradable panels in the traps enable trapped lobsters to escape in the event that the trap is lost at sea.

Lobsters grow by moulting, or shedding their shell. After a moult (typically in summer), the lobster is soft-shelled and filled with seawater it has absorbed in the process. Up to two months pass before the absorbed seawater is replaced by new lobster meat. As the shell hardens in the cold waters of the North Atlantic, the meat's texture and taste improve and the lobster acquires a denser, fuller feel.

Atlantic Canada's staggered fishing seasons are designed to protect summer moults, which allows the industry to deliver the hard-shelled, full-meated lobster. The waters of Atlantic Canada are divided into 41 Lobster Fishing Areas (LFAs), each with its own season, varying in length from eight weeks to eight months. Although the seasons vary along the coast of Canada and from one region to another, there are essentially three seasons: spring (May–June), fall (August) and winter (December). The spring season starts on 1 May and finishes at the end June. Lobsters from the fall fishery are often soft-shell with poor meat yields. Lobsters from the winter fishery are better than fall, but not as good as the spring. The spring season yields the best lobster because it is the first catch after the lobsters come out of hibernation from winter ice; meat is therefore at its fullest just prior to moulting (which starts to occur from end June onwards).

It is widely agreed in Europe that the native lobster has a superior flavour to the Canadian one (but across the pond in the US and Canada, they will say the opposite). The shell of a native lobster is dark blue, with cream or yellow freckles and, when cooked, the freckles are white and the red is deeper in colour than an imported one. The membrane on the meat is also a deeper colour, almost maroon when compared with the more orange colouration of the Canadian lobster. The claws of a native lobster are hefty and proportionally bigger than the claws of a Canadian lobster. Native lobsters are caught seasonally during the summer and are more expensive than the Canadian lobster, which can be purchased all year round by working through the seasons of the different fisheries.

WHY THE PRICE VARIES

ABUNDANCE

Around 3,000 tonnes of European lobster are landed in the UK each year. Annual Canadian landings are around 75,000 tonnes! It is not difficult to see why Canadian lobster is cheaper.

Rules differ between countries on the size of lobsters it is legal to land. Enforcing Minimum Landing Size (MLS) is a very effective conservation measure for lobsters. It allows animals smaller than a certain size to be returned alive to the sea. Minimum landing size in the UK is 87mm carapace length (but 90mm in Devon, Cornwall and the Isles of Scilly). In Canada, the legal sizes range between 72 and 84mm according to the area. In Maine the legal limit is 90mm. The small lobsters at the bottom end of the MLS in Canada are typically known as canners and can be 250–375g in cooked weight, depending on the catch season. In other words, a 350g cooked lobster caught in the spring when at its fullest is arguably bordering the MLS.

LOBSTER QUALITY

What to look out for:

- **Tail** A floppy or weak tail that isn't curled or pulled underneath the body indicates that the lobster may have died before it was processed and the meat will have an 'older' taste.

- **Soft-shell** A lobster with a soft shell indicates that the animal has recently moulted. This means that the lobster will be full of water and consequently the fullness and quality of its meat will be greatly reduced.

- **Claw fill** The ideal claws are the ones that are full of meat tight up against the inside of the shell. 'Empty' claws have a large gap between meat and shell.

They are typically full of water with shrivelled meat. Good claw meat will have a succulent, fibrous bite to it.

- **Roe colouration** If there is roe present, then this should be a deep-red colour (and sometimes almost verging on black).

- **Meat extraction** Tail meat that can be removed easily from the shell, leaving the red membrane intact, will be a far superior meat to any other, and is a good indicator that the lobster was not dead before it was cooked/processed. Tail meat should have a rich red membrane that contrasts well against the deep white colour of the meat below.

- **Stomach** An empty stomach indicates that the lobster has been purged before cooking. This means the digestive system has been emptied by putting the lobster in an initial container of water before moving it to the container of water in which it is stored before processing. This reduces the build-up of oily fish taints from the fish the lobster has recently eaten. If this process is done wrongly (i.e. too quickly) it can lead to a build-up of ammonia, which kills the lobster.

- **Overall appearance** Legs and claws should be intact and there should be little damage to the shell, plus a good overall red/orange colour that isn't too blotchy is a good sign.

PROCESSING METHOD

Processing factories near or on the dock are best for freshness. It is also important that lobsters are not landed in excess of the factory's capacity to process them, so that the lobsters do not die before they are processed.

After cooking, if lobsters are left to stand, they will lose natural juices (weight) and moisture. It is therefore imperative that lobsters are frozen as quickly as possible to lock in their freshness and sweetness. Rapid freezing is best, and my preferred method is submerging the lobster in brine at -18°C, followed by dip glazing, which prevents dehydration.

Some people believe that lobsters that have been high-pressure processed have a sweeter meat, and the meat is easier to extract from the shell.

SIZE

When shopping, look for a good-sized lobster of around 450g. This will yield more meat and has a better meat-to-cost ratio. Do not be fooled into buying a smaller and cheaper lobster. In terms of meat yield it is a false economy.

MEAT FILL

Squeeze the carapace (head). If it squeezes easily or deforms, this is a strong indicator of soft-shell lobster and it's therefore likely that the meat fill inside the shell will be poor.

If possible, try to buy spring lobsters, which will have the best meat fill and sweetest taste. And, where possible, buy a lobster that states its exact provenance. This will provide reassurance that the lobster has been bought from a known source and process, and is therefore less likely to have been 'traded' between factories.

ENVIRONMENTAL CONDITIONS

If it's a bad year for lobsters, the price will be high. In 2013, colder Scottish waters meant lobsters went further out to sea and the price per kilo went up from £15 to £25. Many restaurants had to take it off the menu.

TRY BEFORE YOU DIE!

–

450–500G LOBSTERS
££££

Lobsters that are bigger than 560g start to lose meat succulence and fresh flavour. Although the unit price of a 450–500g lobster may be at its proportional highest, it will produce the best value for money meat yield at best quality.

For me, the very best lobster is a European one, caught off the north Norfolk coast. The crabs and lobsters there have a unique habitat that makes them particularly tasty. There is a mixed limestone, clay and chalk seabed, which adds natural minerals to the water. The sea is unaffected by the Gulf Stream, so the waters remain cold, but protected from extreme cold coming from the North Sea. The seabed is rocky, with perfect nooks and crannies for crustaceans. Plus, freshwater from the Fens and Broads adds nutrients and the shallow water (no more than 100 metres deep all the way to the Netherlands) allows plenty of sunlight to penetrate, supporting marine plants.

European lobsters are in season from March/April to December, but the best time of year to enjoy them is from July to September. Earlier, they are still hardening their shells after moulting and from September the prices shoot up as lobsters are caught and kept alive in tanks for the Christmas market.

· ·

How to prepare live lobster

To boil

- Place the lobster in the freezer for 1–2 hours. This is the humane way to put the lobster to 'sleep' or subdue it before cooking.

- Bring a large pan of salted water to the boil.

- Add the lobster, bring the water back up to a simmer, and cook for 8 mins per 450g. Once the lobster is cooked the shell will be a deep terracotta colour.

- Next, cut the lobster in half.

- Lay the lobster flat. Insert a large cook's knife through the 'cross' on the lobster's head. Continue to cut through the lobster's head, then reverse the knife to cut down through the tail. Remove the stomach sac from the head end and remove the threadlike intestine from the tail.

- The lobster is now ready to eat. Try it simply with homemade mayonnaise and good bread and butter.

To grill (based on a 450g lobster)

- Put the lobster to 'sleep' as described above.

- Cut in half as described above, removing the intestine and stomach sac. Brush the lobster with melted butter and season with salt and a little cayenne pepper.

- Cook under a hot grill for 5–10 minutes on each side or until the lobster shell is bright red and the flesh hot and juicy. Serve hot with extra melted butter, a squeeze of lemon and claw crackers.

· ·

Oysters

I love oysters. As a family we've been going on holiday to Brittany for a long time. We stay in Dinard, which is close to the lovely coastal fishing village of Cancale. In Cancale there are a handful of tiny, ramshackle stalls on the slipway down to the water, selling oysters that have literally just been harvested, and the proprietors will even shuck them for you. There's something very special about eating them, looking out over the estuary towards the island of Mont Saint-Michel with its beautiful hilltop monastery.

There are many myths around this succulent bivalve. Casanova thought they boosted the libido and claimed to eat 50 for breakfast. In more modern times, tabloid newspapers delight in the 'dodgy' oyster story, but in reality they are responsible for considerably fewer cases of illness than chicken or even salads.

So, let's put the story straight.

A BRIEF HISTORY

OYSTERS HAVE BEEN PART of our diet certainly since Roman times, but any prehistoric population map of Europe would be drawn alongside oyster beds. There are mounds of discarded shells that predate the pyramids. In the United States, some of the great cities, such as New York, Boston and New Orleans, are all on old beds. Settlers realised that where there were oysters, there would be clean water and fish.

In England in the nineteenth century oysters were the staple diet of the poor. Vast quantities were consumed and some 50 million were sent to London. As Charles Dickens had Sam Weller remark in *The Pickwick Papers*, 'oysters and poverty always seem to go together'.

From early in the twentieth century, the beds started to decline, due mainly to overfishing, but assisted by toxic marine anti-fouling paints, run off from weed killer, fertiliser and general pollution from industry. This was aggravated by the First and Second World Wars and some bitter frosts. As production declined, prices rose and consumption gradually drifted to newer and more fashionable seafood. In the 1960s, the British government tried to revive the industry by introducing Pacific rock oysters to our waters to augment the declining native varieties.

The rock oyster is now the standard British oyster; around 30,000 tonnes of them were produced in 2014 compared to just 500 tonnes of native oysters. Unlike natives, which spawn in the summer months, rock oysters can be eaten all the year round, rather than only in months that have the letter 'r' in their name.

GEOGRAPHY

ENGLAND, SCOTLAND, IRELAND, France, Australia and the United States all have oysters that are named after the bay, cove or stretch of coast where they are grown. Each bay provides the natural environment – the *'terroir'* – that influences the unique flavour.

Since Roman times Colchester has been famed for its native oysters. They take at least four years to grow and are plumper than the introduced rock oysters that grow next to them in the shallow waters off Mersea Island. It's rare to find the native original so, if you do, try them.

HOW OYSTERS ARE PRODUCED

OYSTERS CAN GROW on any shore where there is a constant supply of nutrients for them to filter. Oysters thrive on most protected shores but their wants are modest:

continuous seawater with plenty of nutrients and minerals, which define their flavour, texture and colour.

The larva that initially attaches to a rock to become an oyster is called a 'spat'. Sometimes breeding is encouraged by putting oyster or mussel shells on the seabed.

Spats mature into 'seed' oysters. Sometimes seed oysters will be moved to a more suitable 'fattening' area to mature. Native oysters breed naturally in the UK but rock oysters are normally bred in hatcheries as the sea temperature is too cold for them to breed naturally.

They can be left alone to mature naturally and when ready will be harvested by dredging, or they can be cultivated by a more intensive and expensive approach, which reduces loss to predators. They are put in bags and kept together, or on racks that are positioned so they are above water level at low tide, or even glued to ropes and suspended clear of the seabed. At an oyster farm in the south of France that uses the latter method, ropes powered by solar energy are lifted clear of the water once a day to simulate the tidal system. No feeding is necessary as they get everything they need from the nutrients and minerals in the seawater. Oysters filter around 50 litres a day each.

The French discovered centuries ago that in disused salt-mining areas, shallow pools of water formed, where algae flourished abundantly, and oysters thrived in this nutritious soup. The oystermen levelled and partitioned the flooded salt flats into a series of parcels, called *claires*, which are connected to a network of canals that can flood or be drained as required. The longer the oysters remain in the *claires* the more special they become. These oysters are among the most expensive available due to the massive amount of extra labour involved.

Rock-oyster spats take around three years to grow into a mature adult, while the native varieties can take six or so years to achieve the same weight.

Oysters are graded 1–5 by size (weight) with the highest number indicating the smallest oyster. The associated weights per grade vary according to the quality of the growing season but can range from 40–50g for grade 5 to over 140g for grade 1 in a good year.

WHY THE PRICE VARIES

PRODUCTION METHOD
Naturally grown oysters are produced less intensively than those that are cultivated, and so are more expensive. More intensive farming methods can reduce the price as the collection of the oysters requires far less labour.

VARIETY

In the UK, native oysters grow much more slowly than rock oysters. They are therefore more expensive.

SIZE

Larger oysters command a higher price, although the time of year/season has an impact on the quantity of meat inside a shell.

ABUNDANCE

The abundance or scarcity of a particular type of oyster, and how sought after it is, will affect its price considerably due to the simple principles of supply and demand. In the UK, fewer native oysters are produced than rock oysters; therefore they tend to be more expensive.

TRY BEFORE YOU DIE!

–

HIX'S OYSTER AND FISH HOUSE
£££

I recommend visiting Hix's Oyster and Fish House in Lyme Regis and trying the three local oysters: Portland Pearl (my favourite), Porthilly and Brownsea Island. The range is constantly changing with the season and you will always find a mix of rock and native varieties on sale.

And don't forget the native Colchester oyster, famed since Roman times, if you are lucky enough to come across some.

Caviar

Traditionally, caviar, which is essentially the salted roe of a sturgeon, has been called the food of the gods but it has been relished by lesser mortals, too. Ancient Phoenicians used caviar to sustain themselves in times of war and famine, Pliny and Ovid sang its praises and tsars and emperors reserved it purely for themselves. To this day, caviar remains the most sought-after delicacy in the world, and certainly the most exclusive.

I have tried it on a number of occasions over the years, it would be fair to say I was underwhelmed and wondered what all the fuss was about. Two experiences changed my mind. The first was a business trip to St Petersburg and the second was a friend's wedding when a Russian guest brought a tin of the uber-expensive stuff for everyone to try in celebration. I realised then that not all caviar is equal. The differences between varieties are considerable and are reflected in their price.

A BRIEF HISTORY

STURGEON HAVE BEEN AROUND for over 250 million years and are found only in the northern hemisphere. In the wild, some live most of their lives in brackish water or saltwater but, like salmon, return to freshwater for spawning, which can occur many times throughout their fairly long life – 120 years is not uncommon. They can also grow extremely large; 7.2m is the longest on record.

Originally, there were several species of sturgeon. Vast quantities were to be found in Western Europe, which supplied local markets, and large quantities in the Caspian Sea. However, thanks to increasing demand and a lack of fishing controls, European sturgeon became extinct. At the end of the 1800s, sturgeon were found on the east and west coasts of North America with a comparable quality roe to that of the Russian sturgeons, but again overfishing took its toll and by the 1920s the fisheries were closed to sport and commercial use. This left the Caspian Sea to supply 95 per cent of world demand for caviar. In the 1950s, the Russians started building dams on the major rivers, which meant that fish couldn't access their spawning runs. Russian scientists therefore worked out how to spawn sturgeon artificially and then began to build hatcheries below the dams. With the break-up of the Soviet Union, strict controls relating to production of caviar were relaxed. Poaching increased and a handful of large companies took control of the Russian product. Iran, which is at the southern tip of the Caspian Sea, still maintains tight controls and produces a high-class caviar but in very small quantities.

The British royal family has had a long affinity with sturgeon. In 1324, Edward II decreed sturgeon to be a royal fish, so all sturgeon found within the foreshore are the property of the monarch. When a sturgeon farm was started in Devon, the farmer had to request permission, and received official notice from Buckingham Palace that the Queen would not extend her royal prerogative over their caviar!

HOW CAVIAR IS PRODUCED

SADLY, AS A RESULT of almost unregulated overfishing, stocks of sturgeon were depleted to the extent that they have been protected under the Convention on International Trade in Endangered Species of Flora and Fauna (CITES) since 1998. This state of affairs had become apparent to some of the more enlightened suppliers, and the first farm in France was started in 1975 to overcome the decline of the wild sturgeon. Farming has since proliferated. In the United States, France, Italy and China these farms have developed on a large scale and produce practically all the caviar available today.

Most roe to make caviar is extracted from the female sturgeon by stunning and killing the fish, then opening it up to extract the ovaries, but some farms are increasingly surgically removing the eggs so the fish can carry on producing. Once the eggs are extracted they are washed and graded.

There are three traditional types of caviar, which depend on the particular species of sturgeon; in descending order, according to those considered best quality, these are: Beluga, Osetra and Sevruga (although there are 26 species of sturgeon).

To start the creation of caviar, the caviar master grades the eggs by size and colour and determines the maturity of the roe. The female can produce eggs and not spawn for 24 months if she doesn't find the appropriate conditions, so the roe can vary considerably in maturity. This maturity will have an influence on the finished taste and texture of the caviar. The eggs, once graded, are put in small batches weighing 5–15kg; pure salt is added and very gently mixed in to create the unique flavour of caviar. The amount of salt is judged on the eggs' maturity and according to the particular processor's skill in assessment. The caviar is then packed in tins, firmly sealed with a press to expel any surplus oil and salt, and a wide rubber band is placed round the tins. Inside the tin, the eggs swell up until they are perfectly round. The whole process should take no more than 20 minutes to ensure maximum freshness and so that exposure to the air is kept to the minimum.

WHY THE PRICE VARIES

ABUNDANCE
The cost of caviar is simply relative to the amounts produced. At Christmas 2014 a discount food chain announced it would be selling caviar at £10.00 for 20g, but closer inspection revealed that while it was indeed eggs from a sturgeon, the fish was a hybrid cross that is extremely prolific compared to the pure-bred fish, which is very slow growing. This fish produces caviar with a much less intense taste and softer texture.

SIZE AND COLOUR
The reality is that the most desirable and expensive caviar is the one with the lightest, almost golden colour and the largest eggs, which will also be the rarest. For example, a tin of Prunier Heritage, which is an exceptional caviar that is prepared according to traditional Persian traditions, will cost £345 for a 50g tin. For the ultimate indulgence there is Almas. This golden caviar from an albino sturgeon is sold in gold-plated tins for £3,500 for 250g.

SHELF LIFE
Caviar can be pasteurised to extend the shelf life, making it much cheaper. However, experts say this process spoils the delicate flavour and completely changes the texture of the egg so the end product is much less desirable.

TRY BEFORE YOU DIE!

–

PRUNIER CAVIAR
££

While you can spend a fortune on caviar, it is still possible to enjoy real caviar for a more modest price. You can buy Prunier Caviar made from eggs harvested from young *Acipenser baerii* Siberian sturgeon with a gorgeous delicate texture and small dark grains, currently £50 for a 50g tin. The structure is lightly salted, yet complex, and is a perfect introduction to the delights and mysteries of caviar. There is, of course, a range of differing tastes and textures in different caviars; like wines, so much is in the hand of the master who controls the infinite subtleties from the outset.

Apart from Prunier, which is in partnership with Caviar House, there are other companies specialising in farmed caviar, such as Petrossian, Mottra, Caspian Caviar and, of course, the Exmoor Caviar Farm for something more local!

Fruit and Vegetables:
A General Note

During the Second World War, the Dig For Victory campaign encouraged people to grow their own vegetables. I think that at that time people had a better understanding of the seasonality of food, where it came from and how it was produced. We are no longer close to the land and as a consequence we often don't have the knowledge to make informed choices about what we are putting into our baskets.

I often hear people boast how cheaply they can buy fruit and vegetables, with the clear inference that they are all the same. After all, they grow in the ground or on trees and bushes, the producer picks them and they end up on the supermarket shelf. What could be simpler? Or so the train of thought goes.

Well, it's not that clear cut at all. Variety, season, growing conditions, growing region, production method, storage, transportation and business ethics all have a bearing on the price you will pay.

With so many varieties to cover, I have tackled produce alphabetically. First though, let me list some general reasons why prices vary, which are common to each of the fruit and veg listed. Then I will go through each one individually to show the unique issues that cause price fluctuations.

WHY THE PRICE VARIES
CONSISTENT AVAILABILITY
Every day in the Netherlands, a series of wholesale auctions takes place for flowers and fresh produce. It happens at the world-famous Aalsmeer site where, for instance, boxes of tomatoes can sell for £12.50 or for as little as £2.50. Buying like this is cheap, but offers no relationship with the grower. Usually if it is sunny, or at the shoulders of the season, tomatoes are a high price but volatility is legendary. British supermarkets can and do use the auction, but some buy direct from the grower. That means the grower knows they have a customer for their produce and can plan for their business in the long term, and

the retailer knows exactly how and by whom the produce they sell is grown. It is possible by working with growers directly to plan supply through the year to ensure produce is consistently on the shelves (where seasonality permits). Buying at auction makes this much harder.

FARMING AND PRODUCT-QUALITY STANDARDS

The standards set by retailers for factors such as the environmental impact of farming practices (pesticide use, and water and soil management, for example), treatment of workers and quality specifications vary considerably. Those with higher standards have expert teams who work with growers to ensure the very best standards of production, and they will invest in innovation of process and products to bring the customer new varieties in the longer term.

Organic standards are the very highest environmentally but in most cases lead to much reduced yields for growers so they are often more expensive.

Without a strong supplier relationship all of this quality control becomes impossible.

SHELF LIFE

Keeping products chilled from the field to your shopping basket is very expensive! The cooler products are kept at all stages, the longer the shelf life. There is some debate, however, as to whether this has a negative impact on flavour.

Asparagus

A BRIEF HISTORY

THE WORD *ASPHARAGOS* is found in ancient Greek literature, including Homer's *Iliad*. It originates from the Persian *asparag*, meaning 'sprout' or 'shoot', and there is evidence of this wild shoot all over the ancient world. It is pictured as an offering on an Egyptian frieze dating back to 3000 BC and can still be found growing on the slopes and river banks in many ancient areas, including Syria and Spain.

Asparagus first appeared in England around AD 1000 and by the sixteenth century it was commonly referred to as *sperach* or *sperage*, but later reverted to its classical root. It has been called asparagus ever since, although the 'a' has been dropped and reappeared at various points in history, and it has been referred to as 'sparagus', and 'sparagrass'.

It was the Romans who probably first started cultivating asparagus, which they did more than 2,000 years ago. Back then, asparagus was eaten only in season. Preservation, through drying, was commonplace but some very forward-thinking Romans are said to have frozen it in the Alps for the feast of Epicurus, transporting it to the feast using fast chariots. Emperor Augustus created the 'Asparagus Fleet' for hauling the vegetable around the Roman Empire. The oldest surviving book of recipes, Apicius's third-century *De re coquinaria*, features asparagus recipes.

The Chinese also have a very long history with asparagus, dating back over 4,000 years, and are the world's biggest consumer of asparagus today. The New World didn't take up asparagus until 1850, when it was first grown in the United States.

GEOGRAPHY

ASPARAGUS IS NOW GROWN all over the world. Peru is one of the largest growers as its coastal fringe provides the perfect climate for fast-growing asparagus giving a yield range of 15–22 tonnes per hectare per annum.

The UK, on the other hand, yields a meagre 1–2.5 tonnes per hectare. Traditionally, it was available from St George's Day (23 April) to Midsummer's Day (21 June) but advances in growing methods have extended the UK season to start from early April. Asparagus in the UK grows very slowly (in comparison to Peru) and therefore develops a much greater depth of flavour, due to the accumulation of naturally occurring plant chemicals, such as anthocyanin, which also give the slower growing asparagus a slight purple tinge.

Asparagus contains a number of different compounds that are metabolised in the human body to produce sulphur-containing products that give urine its characteristic 'asparagus' odour. The smell is reported to be more pronounced after eating young asparagus as opposed to the older woody spears.

In the UK and much of the world, asparagus is eaten green. In Germany and some other northern European countries, as well as in Spain, white asparagus is favoured. It is exactly the same species of asparagus as the green, but soil is ridged up around the plant, preventing chlorophyll (the green colour) from forming in the shoot. A large machine is used to cut the white shoot below the soil surface. White asparagus is traditionally more fibrous than green and has, in the opinion of some, less flavour. About 90,000 tonnes of white asparagus are eaten worldwide, 60 per cent of it grown in Germany.

There is also a variety of red asparagus. This has been selected and bred over a number of years for its colour. It has a slightly more bitter taste than the green and loses some colour when cooked.

HOW ASPARAGUS IS PRODUCED

ASPARAGUS IS UNIQUE in the way that it is cultivated. A year after a seed is planted, the young plant produces a tangle of swollen roots called a crown. These crowns are carefully lifted and gently replanted into rows or beds with even spacing. The crop is then watered and fed to enable it to establish fully. It takes up to three years before any asparagus can be harvested. The yield of the crop is usually dependent on how good the summer was the previous year.

Once the soil temperature has reached 12°C, shoots start to push up from the crowns and slowly poke through the soil. Only young asparagus shoots are eaten. Once the buds start to open (a process known as ferning out) the shoots quickly turn woody and fibrous.

A field of asparagus in harvest in spring is probably the most underwhelming sight in farming, as from a distance it looks like bare soil. It is only when you look closer that you see the asparagus spears emerging from their winter slumber. In the UK, from 21 June (the longest day) the crop is no longer harvested and the remaining shoots are allowed to go to fern.

Fern growth is very important and a grower will go to great lengths to ensure that it is looked after. The fern grows 1.5–2m high and is an incredible sight compared to the point of harvest. In late autumn the fern turns yellow along with the trees, and the crop starts to die back. This is an important time as all the carbohydrates produced in the leaves during summer are sucked back down the plant and stored in the crown, ready for the big push of new shoots in the spring. The more energy taken into the fern through the leaves in the summer, the more energy can be stored in the crown during the winter, and the more energy there is to go into producing asparagus spears come the spring.

In hot countries, such as Peru, things are a little different since there isn't a winter. Instead, Peruvians use water to control the crop. By stopping the water and drying the crop, they trigger senescence exactly when they want. This can be done in sequence, allowing asparagus spears to be produced all year round from the same site. It also allows the crop to complete two cycles a year, meaning two harvests from the same crop.

When the asparagus shoot (or spear) has reached the desired length, it is harvested by hand with a knife, cut at the surface of the soil. In good growing conditions a spear can grow at up to 5cm per day, so harvest can take place every day or two. In Peru, the crop can grow even faster with growth of over 7cm per day. This requires a harvest first thing in the morning and in the evening as well! Spears of all shapes, lengths and widths are harvested at the same time and are sorted in a factory.

Chilling is key to keeping asparagus as fresh as possible. As soon as an asparagus spear is cut, it starts to die and therefore it must be chilled quickly. The first stage is to cool it to about 8°C in a chiller. If asparagus is cooled too much at this stage, it will bruise when handled in the grading process. Grading is traditionally done by eye and hand, but more recently purpose-designed grading machines costing over £250,000 do this task. Asparagus is graded so that every spear in a bunch looks the same.

In the UK, asparagus is cooled further and transported straight to supermarket distribution centres. In Peru it will be cooled and often placed on a flight bound for either the United States, Japan or Europe. Technology has enabled sea containers to be controlled not only in temperature, but also atmosphere. By reducing oxygen and controlling carbon dioxide, it is possible to ship asparagus from Peru to the UK at a fraction of the carbon footprint of a plane.

Traditionally, asparagus has been sold in bunches, but is now increasingly sold in protective film wrappers. This method uses less plastic than the old label and rubber band and stops dehydration, keeping asparagus fresher.

WHY THE PRICE VARIES

GROWER RISK

Asparagus is an expensive item because it takes three years for the first harvest. A grower has to invest significantly before seeing a return. The land is then tied up for ten years producing asparagus, and as most landowners don't want this length of commitment, land for growing asparagus comes at a premium. The crop is also susceptible to poor weather, which increases the risk.

YIELD

Slower growing and season-limited British asparagus usually costs more than the faster growing Peruvian variety due to the amount of crop that can be produced from the same area of land.

LABOUR

Every asparagus spear has to be harvested by hand and meticulously graded so it is labour intensive. No harvesting machine has yet been developed that can harvest asparagus to the same degree of accuracy or the level of quality of a well-trained human.

SUPPLY AND DEMAND

The price of asparagus can vary wildly throughout the year. Most of the world's trade is based on a supply-and-demand model, where high prices naturally follow a tightening in the market and lower prices follow a glut. In fact, the UK eats 40 per cent of total consumption during the short UK season.

The price of asparagus could well be much higher in the future as a lot of the land used in Peru to grow asparagus is reaching the ten-year limit at which it needs to be used for another crop. It is important to rotate the land after this length of time. If you continue with the same crop, disease resistance builds up and the soil becomes less productive. Therefore farmers are planting other crops, such as avocados, grapes and citrus, on these prime asparagus sites.

TRY BEFORE YOU DIE!

—

UK SEASON FRESH ASPARAGUS
£££

As enjoyed by Julius Caesar 2,000 years ago, early season, fresh British asparagus with melted butter, salt and pepper cannot be beaten by any other asparagus. In my view it's even better with a few shavings of parmesan cheese and a soft-boiled egg. Early season asparagus has a purple tinge to the spear and a more intense flavour. By keeping the asparagus slightly *al dente*, you maintain the texture and flavour that are lost if it turns soft.

· ·

Cooking and keeping asparagus

Asparagus should be steamed for 3–6 minutes (depending on thickness) and served straightaway. Alternatively, you can bake asparagus in the oven (200°C) for about 10 minutes, brushed with a little olive oil, then top with gently fried chorizo and a poached egg. It is also great on the barbecue.

If you want to keep your asparagus fresher for longer, put it in the fridge, in a jug, with water covering the bases to stop it from drying out.

· ·

Brassicas

A BRIEF HISTORY

BRASSICAS HAVE BEEN GROWN for several thousand years. Unearthed pots containing cabbage have been discovered in Asia dating back to 4000 BC. There is considerably more evidence relating to the importance of brassicas during Greek and Roman times. Greeks were using kale, while Romans also used a loose-hearted leafy cabbage and an early type of broccoli.

When pickling was introduced into Europe by the Tartars in the eighteenth century, it allowed brassicas, and particularly cabbage, to be stored for longer periods of time. This pickled cabbage, now known as sauerkraut, was an excellent health food, high in vitamin C. It was taken on long voyages by Dutch and British colonists, such as Captain Cook, to keep their crews healthy and as a defence against scurvy.

The green leafy vegetables we have in supermarkets today, such as cauliflower, cabbage, broccoli, kale, spring greens and Brussels sprouts, are all members of the brassica family. Wild uncultivated brassicas can still be found today. They are native to several European countries and regions of Asia. Wild broccoli grows in Italy, and wild kale and cabbage in Britain and France. They are often found in coastal locations due to their salt tolerance and on limestone soil due to their ability to survive high-alkaline conditions.

Brassicas are now regarded as health foods, high in fibre and vitamins and playing an important role in reducing the risk of cancer and heart disease. As a result, world brassica production has continued to rise and there are now over 75 million tonnes of cabbage and 25 million tonnes of cauliflower and broccoli produced annually. China and India are by far the largest producers of brassicas. These two countries combined account for 74 per cent of world production of cauliflower and broccoli.

GEOGRAPHY

HISTORICALLY, BRASSICA PRODUCTION in the UK took place on many thousands of small market-garden farms spread across most areas of the country. Today, production is in the hands of a few large specialised and efficient growers. Advances in mechanisation and commercial price pressure for cheaper food have resulted in larger farming units, which take advantage of economies of scale to cut food-production costs.

Lincolnshire, Cornwall and the east of Scotland are the only three areas of the UK now producing any significant volume of brassica vegetables, although smaller volumes are still grown in Yorkshire, Norfolk, Suffolk, Kent and Lancashire. The largest area of brassica vegetables is on the flat Lincolnshire fens. The deep, highly fertile, silty soils are moisture retentive and have a naturally high alkaline pH, which is ideally suited to brassica farming. Many years ago these fertile soils were once under the North Sea but they now form some of the best-quality agricultural land in the country. You can still see the remains of seashells in the soil today, making it rich in calcium.

Cornwall and areas along the south coast, such as the Isle of Wight, enjoy the warming effect of the Gulf Stream, which helps winter production of cauliflower and spring greens.

In Scotland, the cooler wetter summers lend themselves to broccoli production, and the relatively winter-hardy Brussels sprout crop does well during the colder winter months.

HOW BRASSICAS ARE PRODUCED

BRASSICAS ARE GROWN FROM seed in greenhouses and transplanted into the fields from early March to the end of September.

Most brassicas can be stored for a few days or weeks only. Thanks to this short shelf-life, a constant supply of fresh vegetables is essential to ensure continuous availability. This is achieved by manipulating planting dates in the fields and by growing many different varieties, which mature at different times of the year.

The majority of brassicas are still hand-harvested due to the delicate, tender nature of the crop. Each vegetable is inspected to ensure it meets quality specifications before being cut. The brassicas are transported to cold stores as soon as possible after harvest, in order to remove the field heat from the product. The quicker the temperature of the vegetable is reduced, the longer its shelf-life will be.

WHY THE PRICE VARIES

SUPPLY AND DEMAND

When the temperature increases, we eat more salads and fruits, and fewer brassicas. However, as the crops grow faster in warmer growing conditions, there is an excess of vegetables in summer months, which are difficult to sell or store and so prices fall. Similarly, as temperatures drop during cold blasts of winter weather, demand for brassica vegetables rises considerably. This is just the time when supply of brassicas tightens, as the colder weather slows the vegetables' growth. Any brassicas imported cost more because of the transport.

VARIETY

Historically, brassica breeding has focused on achieving the highest yields possible. However, over the past 30 years, much more focus has been placed on improving the flavour and increasing the nutritional value of brassicas. For instance, varieties of broccoli such as Tenderstem and Bellaverde cost more due to their superior, sweeter flavour and because they have a lower yield than standard broccoli. Beneforté broccoli sells for more, as it has three times the amount of beneficial glucosinolates (which help to prevent cancer and heart disease) than traditional broccoli, and also has a lower yield.

Redarling Brussels sprouts, available over the Christmas period, are mild tasting, a vivid red/purple and high in anthocyanin, a beneficial antioxidant found in other superfoods, such as red berries and red beet.

· ·

One more thing...

Never overcook brassicas. The more you cook brassicas, the more vitamins and antioxidants are lost. Always steam instead of boiling.

· ·

TRY BEFORE YOU DIE!

–

FLOWER SPROUT
££££££

This is a real superfood! It is a cross between a kale and a Brussels sprout. It looks like a baby kale with tiny green and purple frilly leaves, but has a more delicate, sweeter flavour than traditional kale. Flower sprout is a good source of vitamins B, C and E, and is packed full of beneficial antioxidants, which help to boost the immune system. It is also high in glucosinolates, which can help to prevent cancer and heart disease. Flower sprout is a versatile vegetable, great stir-fried, roasted, steamed or microwaved. It is a UK winter gem, starting in October and finishing in March.

ROMANESCO
££

Romanesco is one of the most visually beautiful vegetables with a taste to match its stunning looks. Originating from Italy, Romanesco is a cauliflower made up of tightly packed, lime-green spiral florets. It has a crunchy, solid texture with a slightly sweeter, nuttier flavour than traditional white cauliflower.

As with all brassicas, Romanesco is super rich in antioxidants, high in vitamins C and K and dietary fibre. Romanesco is great simply lightly steamed or roasted with a little olive oil. Alternatively, it is a fantastic addition to a salad: simply thinly slice the raw florets to maintain their stunning appearance and add to a salad for a delicious nutty crunch. The UK Romanesco season is from mid-June to November.

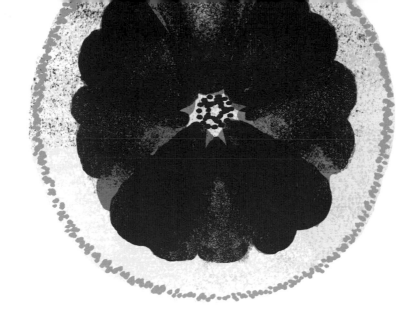

Citrus Fruit

A BRIEF HISTORY

CITRUS IS A COMMON term for flowering plants in the rue family, Rutaceae. The best-known citrus fruits include oranges, grapefruit, lemons, limes and smaller varieties, such as tangerines.

The origins of citrus fruits can be traced back to the subtropical and tropical regions of Asia and the Malay Archipelago. Before the fruit was eaten it was variously described as a medicine, poison, perfume and repellent to moths. By the end of the Roman Empire, citrus had arrived in southern Europe, where it flourished through the Middle Ages. The first citrus fruit to be known by Europeans was the citron. Later, the Spanish and Portuguese were responsible for introducing citrus to the Americas during their explorations of the New World.

Kings and queens cultivated gardens of citrus trees, and the blossoms and fruit were used to make cosmetics, while various essences were used to colour grey hair. By the sixteenth century, sweet or sour oranges were used as condiments for fish and meat, but were only eaten as fresh fruit later that century.

World citrus production and consumption have grown strongly since the mid-1980s, boosted by continuing improvements in transportation to provide year-round supplies of high-quality fresh citrus fruit.

GEOGRAPHY

CITRUS TREES ARE PLANTED in every tropical and subtropical region around the world in a total of 140 countries. There are two main markets for citrus; the fresh fruit market and the processed market. About a third of citrus-fruit production goes for processing and more than 80 per cent of that is for orange-juice production.

The largest citrus-producing countries are China, Brazil and the United States. Oranges make up over half of all citrus production, with Brazil being the biggest producer. In Europe, Spain and Italy are the top producing countries, and both come in the top-ten producing countries in the world.

Citrus trees need sunny, humid conditions with fertile soil and adequate rainfall or irrigation. The plants cannot withstand frost or temperatures below -2°C, except for some hybrid species but these do not currently produce great quality fruit. Water quality is an important factor for the health of citrus trees; high salt content can cause leaves to burn and low salt content can cause poor tree growth and reduced fruit bearing.

Environmental factors play an integral role in quality. Consistency of humidity levels and the variation of day-to-night temperature (diurnal range) have a critical effect on the sugar-to-acid ratios and colour of citrus fruits. This means that since citrus is naturally high in acid, it will become more acidic in a dry-heat environment, creating an unpleasant-tasting fruit with thick peel. But in a favourable environment, the same species will develop more sweetness and a superior taste.

HOW CITRUS FRUITS ARE PRODUCED

CITRUS TREES THAT ARE grown naturally from a cutting produce fruit that varies in sweetness and size. To get consistent crops, with high-quality fruit, many growers graft a different preferred top (the scion) to good rootstock (the healthy root of an already established plant).

Trees bear fruit after 3–5 years, but are not fully mature until 10–14 years of age. They reach peak production around 25 years of age after which the amount of fruit they yield declines.

After flowering, most citrus trees are pollinated by insects. However, some citrus fruits can develop without pollination through a natural process called parthenocarpy. If parthenocarpic flowers are not naturally pollinated by insects, the fruits they produce do not contain seeds.

When fully grown, citrus fruits are left to ripen on the tree. Starches convert to sugars, acids decrease and the colour of the fruit softens. Citrus fruits do not ripen after they are picked, unlike other fruits, such as pears.

Oranges were not named for their colour. In tropical regions, fruits remain green until maturity and, in warmer countries, the skin of ripe oranges is green. The word 'orange' did not emerge until 300 years after the fruit appeared in Europe. It is possible that oranges get their name from the Sanskrit word for fragrant, 'naranja'.

WHY THE PRICE VARIES

VARIETY

Premium varieties achieve higher prices because the volumes are regulated under licence to control the amount of trees planted. The licence holders set quality parameters to which the variety has to comply to give the best eating experience and protect the characteristics of the variety.

SUPPLY AND DEMAND

Weather conditions are a driving factor for quality and availability within the fruit industry. Volumes available during a particular season are determined by the growing conditions leading up to harvest. If the conditions are favourable for citrus growing, availability may exceed demand and have an influence on the price.

BUYING TIPS

The heavier the fruit the larger the juice content. Unlike other fruits, scarring does not generally adversely affect the eating quality.

And it's worth remembering that the maturity of the rind and maturity of the flesh of the fruit are not always synchronised. The fruit can be edible even when the rind still remains green.

ORANGE JUICE

We consume a lot of our citrus fruit as orange juice so it makes sense to explain why the price varies so dramatically between fresh juice and that from concentrate. This is mainly down to transport. A standard lorry tank carries around 30 tonnes of orange concentrate, which makes about 170,000 litres of juice. To transport the same amount of fresh orange juice would require six lorries. It is therefore much more economical to transport the concentrate and then add water nearer the point of consumption. This is true for many other types of juices and drinks, such as cider.

TRY BEFORE YOU DIE!

–

BLOOD ORANGE
££

The best blood oranges come from Sicily; 60 per cent of Sicilian orange production is pigmented. They need a temperate climate in which to grow with a hot season and cooler weather to bring out the true colour. The season usually runs from the end of November to the beginning of May.

ORRI MANDARIN
£££

The Orri is a mutation of Orah mandarin from Israel. The Israeli Orri is by far the best as it has a beautifully balanced sweet flavour with high sugars and low acidity.

NADORCOTT
£££££

The Nadorcott is easy to peel and its distinguishing feature is the deep red-orange rind. The Nadorcott has a very rich flavour with high sugars and high acid giving it a beautiful flavour.

MANDARED
£££££

The Mandared is a triploid hybrid created from crossing a Nules clementine with a Tarocco orange, and has no seeds. The fruit has an oblate shape with a thin, deep-orange skin and distinctly red flesh when ripe. The fruit is unique and incomparable.

The Nadorcott and Orri are both licensed and protected varieties produced in small volumes, making them more expensive and sought after.

SORRENTO LEMON
££££

According to some sources, the lemon was brought to southern Italy in the first century BC by the Jews, for whom it had a ritual value. The portrayal of the lemon in mosaics and paintings that came to light during excavations of Pompeii shows their common use in the Neapolitan area since ancient times. Citrus fruit has certainly acclimatised incredibly well to the land in Campania and has prospered marvellously. It would be impossible to imagine the Amalfi and Sorrento coasts without their charming, beautiful and extremely fragrant lemon gardens. Local people are much attached to the lemon to the extent that there is hardly a family in the area that does not have a plot of lemon trees.

This lemon is medium-large and elliptical, with an attractive skin colour. It is very fragrant and has particularly juicy and acidic flesh. Today, it is grown in all the communes of the Sorrento peninsula and all over the island of Capri, both in the province of Naples. It is a tardy fruit, so that, although it is produced on the tree all year round, the best fruit is obtained from spring to the end of autumn.

Most of the produce is reserved for the domestic market; 40 per cent is destined for fresh consumption and the remaining 60 per cent is used to make the famous Limoncello liqueur from the Sorrento and Amalfi area.

Demand for the Sorrento Lemon is constant and, consequently, the prices are always decidedly higher than (and sometimes double) that of ordinary lemons on the market. Sorrento lemons and Amalfi Coast lemons have had PGI status for over ten years.

Remember to roll your lemon or lime on a hard surface before squeezing to get the most juice.

Strawberries

A BRIEF HISTORY

STRAWBERRIES GREW WILD in Italy as early as 234 BC and were mentioned in ancient Roman literature for their medicinal use. The French began taking wild strawberries from the forests to their gardens and cutting the shoots, or runners, from the plant, to produce new plants from the1300s.

Strawberries became more interesting to botanists in Europe, and three distinct species were identified by the end of the 1500s. These were *Fragaria vesca*, *Fragaria moschata* and *Fragaria virdis*.

Today's strawberries are a result of a cross of *Fragaria virginiana* (a strawberry found in eastern North America) and the Chilean strawberry *Fragaria chiloensis*. The first *Fragaria chiloensis* was brought to Europe in 1714.

GEOGRAPHY

WITH THE EXCEPTION of deserts and polar regions, varieties of strawberries grow in most parts of the world, easily adjusting to the climatic conditions. British

Tomatoes

A BRIEF HISTORY

TOMATOES ORIGINATE FROM the Andes in South America, where they grow wild in what is now Peru, Bolivia, Chile and Ecuador. They were first cultivated by the Aztecs and Incas as early as AD 700.

It is no surprise then that the English word tomato comes from the Aztec word *tomatl*. Tomatoes first arrived in Europe in the sixteenth century, although how they got there is unclear. Some say that they were brought back by Spanish conquistadors, while another legend suggests that two Jesuit priests brought them to Italy from Mexico. The first cultivated tomatoes were yellow and cherry-sized, originally earning them the name

- **Classic tomatoes** These are the familiar, round variety and are the most popular type of tomato. They are good for salads, grilling, baking or frying.

- **Cherry and cocktail tomatoes** These are both smaller than the traditional classic tomato; cherry tomatoes are the smallest and cocktail tomatoes slightly larger. Both are very sweet and have a concentrated flavour. Most cherry tomatoes are red, but golden, orange and yellow varieties are also available. Cherry tomatoes are delicious eaten whole and raw or cooked.

- **Plum and baby plum tomatoes** These have a distinctive oval shape. Their flesh is firm and they have less juice. They are the natural choice for pizzas and pasta dishes and their fleshy texture makes them ideal for the barbecue. The production of baby plum tomatoes has increased dramatically in recent years as new varieties are delivering much improved sweetness and flavour.

- **Beef tomatoes** These are larger than the traditional round tomato. Their size (above 82mm in diameter) and shape make them excellent for stuffing and baking whole.

- **Vine or truss tomatoes** These may be of any of the types mentioned above, but are marketed still attached to the fruiting stem.

If your tomatoes have 'vine-ripened' written on the pack, it means the tomatoes were picked when ripe, i.e. they ripened on the plant. This gives optimum flavour, but makes the fruit more delicate. All British tomatoes are vine-ripened as they have only a short distance to travel to market. Imported tomatoes are usually picked less ripe so they can withstand the lengthy journey here by road or sea, and firmer, long-life varieties are commonly used.

The vine provides a very good indication of the freshness of the fruit since the calyx, the green spiky bit to which the fruit is attached, deteriorates quickly after harvesting.

WHY THE PRICE VARIES

PRODUCTION METHOD

UK-grown tomatoes need significant investment to produce the perfect fruit: land, greenhouses, heat, CO_2, water, feed, labour, bees, insects, transport and refrigeration. Tomatoes are sold and managed by weight. It is possible to select varieties that tend to be large, reduce their nutrient feed to lower costs and water them more to increase the weight. So you may end up with a beautiful large tomato but full of water!

To get a flavoursome tomato, growers carefully manage the feeding and watering regime of their plants. They prune them meticulously when the flowers have appeared to ensure that only the right amount of fruit is on the plant for it to be able to deliver the best possible fruit. If all the flowers were pollinated, there would be masses of fruit on the plant but it would get weak, the flavour would less intense or more acidic, and the fruit would be very sensitive and not last. For full flavour, fruit needs to be left to mature on the plant and that requires heat, which is very expensive. Light, time and careful tending ensure the nutrients are correctly balanced to enable sugars and acids to develop.

Varieties

Many varieties look very similar to one another, but it's their genetic make-up that makes the difference. Some growers favour high-yielding cheaper varieties, while others prioritise flavour over volume and so prices are higher. The lower yielding crops tend to have higher seed prices and often an additional licence fee together with higher production costs.

Tinned tomatoes

There is a big price variation in tinned tomatoes, too. Here's why:

- **Specification** Specifications for economy products allow greater tolerances for skin, seeds, green pieces and so on. The economy specification does not require so many workers on the line to inspect the product.

- **Brix levels** Brix level is a measurement of the thickness and sweetness of the juice that tomatoes are packed in. This is made by crushing the tomatoes and sieving them to remove skins and seeds. The higher the brix, the sweeter the product. Economy products generally have a brix level of 4.5, whereas the level for a standard product is 5.4–6.5. Higher brix means higher costs.

- **Packaging** Economy products are often not packed in lacquered cans (which are treated to stop any corrosion of the can by the acidic tomatoes) and may not have a ring pull as that adds cost.

TRY BEFORE YOU DIE!

—

ENGLISH PICCOLO CHERRY VINE TOMATOES
££££

This variety produces the pinnacle of tomato flavour to my mind. They remind me of the tomatoes my grandfather grew in his greenhouse in my youth. It's the vine management and slow maturity that delivers these characteristics. Magnificent fresh, but also fabulous roasted.

. . . .

How to keep tomatoes

To really savour the flavour that your grower has created, don't keep tomatoes in the fridge. Keep them at room temperature and enjoy them as intended. You might also like to pop them in boiling water for a few seconds before you prepare them to bring out some extra flavour.

Tomatoes create plenty of the natural gas ethylene, which can be used to ripen other fruits but if you keep bananas and tomatoes together, they will go off very quickly!

. . . .

Apples

A BRIEF HISTORY

YOU MAY BE SURPRISED to read that the apple is a member of the rose family, along with pears and quince, and it includes hundreds of cultivated varieties. It probably developed its own biological path around 50 million years ago.

Archaeologists have found evidence that humans have been enjoying apples since 6,500 BC. The origin of the sweet apple we enjoy today can be traced back to the fruit forests of the Tien Shan (mountains) between western China and Kazakhstan.

The Silk Road from China to Europe passed through the Tien Shan, taking apples from east to west. It seems to have taken around 6,000 years for apples to reach Western Europe, though, and it wasn't until more recent centuries that they began to occupy the rest of the temperate world, through colonisation, with apple-tree cultivation beginning in North America in the early seventeenth century.

The apple is today the fourth most economically important fruit crop in the world, (just behind bananas, citrus fruit and grapes) which is good news as an apple a day probably does keep the doctor away. Apples are high in fibre and vitamin C, are fat and cholesterol free and have just a trace of sodium. A medium-sized apple contains about 80 calories.

GEOGRAPHY

THERE ARE **96** COUNTRIES registered as producing apples commercially. China produces nearly half of the world's crop, mostly for the juice concentrate market. The United States is the next largest producer with Turkey and Poland next on the list. The UK is about 40th in the producer league table.

HOW APPLES ARE PRODUCED

THERE ARE EFFECTIVELY two apple harvests a year. The northern-hemisphere harvest starts in August and finishes in November. The southern-hemisphere harvest starts in February and finishes in May. Fruit is monitored and when the crop reaches the right level of maturity for its intended marketing period, it is harvested. Typically, due to the use of cold storage in apple production, the first fruit picked is usually the last fruit sold in the season.

New varieties start as a seed, but to reproduce a variety it is necessary to bud, or graft, the chosen variety onto a rootstock (root of an already established plant). This is because, when propagated, each seed of an apple produces a new variety, which may or may not have strong similarities to its parents.

Commercial production systems have changed over the last 100 years, from standard trees reaching in excess of 7.5m tall, via bush trees, which became popular after the Second World War. The 'Spindlebush' tree, with a height controlled at 2–2.5m, became the favoured format in the 1970s because it was most suited to tree management and picking ease. Today, the Spindlebush is still favoured by many growers, but progressive growers are adopting the hedgerow system. This is where trees are planted 1–1.5m apart in the row and allowed to grow to 2.5–3m tall; they are supported by large wooden stakes with wires running the length of the row. Irrigation systems are now becoming standard, as is fertigation where feeding nutrients are added to the water.

Crops are harvested by handpicking fruit from the tree and placing the apples into bucket-style bags. These are emptied into large wooden or plastic bins that can hold around 350kg of fruit.

The apple bin is then removed from the orchard by a tractor and placed into cold storage, normally within six hours of the apples being picked.

Apples are either kept in chilled storage conditions, between 0.5°C and 3°C, for short-term marketing, which is usually less than three months, or placed into controlled atmosphere and chilled conditions. A controlled atmosphere is a large refrigerated room where the atmosphere is manipulated to remove almost all the oxygen, while carbon dioxide levels are lightly increased. Removing the oxygen reduces the rate of respiration in the fruit and practically puts the fruit to sleep. This means fruit can be stored for extended periods of up to 12 months for some varieties.

Apples are removed from storage conditions when they are needed for sale. The large bins of apples are emptied into a grading system that separates fruit into different size ranges and quality standards. Fruit is transferred through the grading system via water as this is the most effective way to move the fruit while not bruising it.

After being graded, fruit is packed into its final customer packaging.

WHY THE PRICE VARIES

SUPPLY AND DEMAND
The price of apples is inevitably influenced by global competition; yields vary from year to year and that fluctuation is a barometer for seasonal retail prices.

GROWER INVESTMENT/RISK
Growing top fruit is a very capital-hungry industry and growers usually see their investment breaking even a minimum of five years after planting. Typically, growers aim to replant 5–15 per cent of their orchard per annum, so the generation of good returns is critical to fund the regeneration of the farm. The investment required in storage to extend product life has also increased in recent years.

SIZE
The quality of the fruit on retail shelves is constantly reviewed; eye-catching appearance and optimum texture, flavour and fruit size are important factors. The format for selling apples is increasingly by count, rather than weight. The grower must not only seek to achieve the best eating attributes of the variety, but grow apples of the optimum size. This dramatically influences the grower's financial return as apples above the optimum size for each pack size will result in 'give away'.

LABOUR
Approximately 30 per cent of the annual cost to the grower comes from growing the apple to the point of harvest. The remainder is accrued through harvesting, storage, packing and distribution. Apples are handpicked and this is very labour intensive; with the prospect of higher minimum wages, growers' costs can only rise further.

TRY BEFORE YOU DIE!

–

DELBARD ESTIVALE
££££

This variety represents the perfect way to start the UK season. The apples are crisp, juicy and have a sweet flavour.

JAZZ
££££

A perfect combination of juicy texture and sweet flavour.

SMITTEN
££££

Once bitten forever Smitten. But you'll have to judge for yourself!

Mangoes

A BRIEF HISTORY

THE MANGO HAS BEEN CALLED the 'King of Fruits' and for good reason, as its sweet, aromatic flavour and juicy, silky texture make it without doubt one of the most popular and widely appreciated tropical fruits. It belongs to a large group of species and is in the same family as the pistachio and the cashew.

The mango evolved in the tropical rainforests of south and south-east Asia and is endemic to the Malay Peninsula, the Indonesian archipelago, Thailand, Vietnam, Cambodia and the Philippines. The common mango we know today was probably domesticated independently in several different regions, including Bangladesh, north-eastern India and Myanmar. It is believed that the mango has been cultivated in India for more than 4,000 years and it is said that Buddha meditated in the shade of a mango tree.

The mango spread from India throughout south-east Asia along with Buddhism. A Chinese traveller, Huen T'sang, took the mango to China from India in the early seventh century, and it was known in Baghdad from around the same time. The Persians took mangoes to East Africa in the tenth century where it was reintroduced in the sixteenth century by the Portuguese, who also took it to West Africa and Brazil. From there the mango arrived in the West Indies, in Barbados in about 1742 and then in the Dominican Republic and Jamaica about 40 years later. The Spanish introduced the mango to Mexico in the early nineteenth century.

As the mango moved throughout the tropics, new varieties developed as they adapted to local conditions. Nowhere has this been more important than in Florida where the first successful introductions in 1861 were followed by hundreds more from India, south-east Asia and other mango-growing regions around the world. Within half a century a large number of varieties had been produced through breeding programmes and from natural cross-pollination. These became known as the Floridian mangoes and since then have been widely distributed around the world. Varieties include Haden, Tommy Atkins, Kent and Keitt.

GEOGRAPHY

THE **MANGO IS BEST SUITED** to a warm, tropical monsoon climate, with a pronounced dry season followed by rains. However, one of the reasons why the mango is so widespread is its tolerance, which has enabled it to adapt to so many different environments. It can thrive on different soil types and in a wide temperature range as well as survive both drought and short periods of flooding. Although most mangoes are produced in the tropics and subtropics, it is also possible to grow them in warm, temperate Mediterranean areas, such as Israel, southern Spain, the Canary Islands, California and Florida.

The main mango-producing countries are India, China, Thailand, Indonesia and Pakistan, although India produces more than the other four combined. The main exporting countries are Mexico, India, Thailand, Brazil and Peru. Most mangoes sold in the UK come from South and Central America, West Africa and Israel with smaller quantities from India, Pakistan and Spain.

HOW MANGOES ARE PRODUCED

MANGOES ARE PRODUCED in orchards or plantations. Old orchards tend to have large, tall, widely spaced trees, but the tendency in recent years is to plant at much higher density and prune them to 2–3m in both height and spread. This makes crop husbandry and harvesting the fruit much easier, less dangerous and more economical.

In most commercial plantations, a Floridian variety, such as Kent, will be grafted onto a locally adapted rootstock. The young trees are then pruned to encourage an open canopy so that sunlight can ripen the fruits. The young trees do not bear fruit until they are about four years old.

About a week after harvest, the trees are pruned. This usually coincides with rains and produces a flush of new growth. As the flush grows and ages during the rainy season it enters a resting phase. Then, as the rains stop and the dry season begins, the trees start to flower. This can often happen in an irregular manner, making accurate crop forecasting quite difficult. Once the tree has been pollinated and fruit has begun to grow it takes about four months until harvest, which is done entirely by hand.

WHY THE PRICE VARIES

Ripening

Most mangoes are shipped to the UK by sea, but some are held on the tree a little while longer to produce a more mature, fuller tasting fruit and then air freighted. These mangoes will be sold as ready-to-eat or premium-flavour fruit at a higher price than the others, reflecting the additional costs of production, transporting, handling and packaging that a riper, more delicate fruit requires.

Variety

In recent years a wider preference within Europe for fibreless varieties, such as Kent and Keitt, compared to the more colourful, higher yielding but fibrous Tommy Atkins, has also pushed up the price of better-eating varieties. Some varieties are grown in just a few places and in small volumes, such as Maya from Israel and the Gambia. Such varieties, although premium tasting, are often more difficult to handle and ship, and their price will reflect this and their relative scarcity in the market.

Harvest conditions

Harvest seasons can sometimes last a few weeks only and yields are unpredictable. Due to market demand, an importer may convince a grower to harvest later to extend the season. This can be done for some varieties, such as Keitt, which can be held on the tree. However, a later harvest means that the trees have less time to flush and so they will produce a smaller crop the following year. The grower will argue that he is sacrificing the following year's crop for the current year and he will expect this to be reflected in the price paid for his fruit.

GEOGRAPHY

POTATOES ARE GROWN in many different countries since they are a very accommodating crop, making better use of water and nutrients than most others. Some countries produce particularly celebrated varieties. Cyprus exports a lot from its lush red soils and the French have developed connoisseur varieties, such as the blue-fleshed Vitelotte and La Ratte from the rich, flavoursome soils of Brittany. Yet the medal must surely go to the island of Jersey, which even has a PDO (Protected Designation of Origin) for its appropriately named Jersey Royals.

In the UK, potatoes used to be grown extensively but, since 1960, the number of farmers has shrunk from 20,000 to under 3,000. This is due to the demand for efficiency in order to produce cheaper potatoes. The best yields and quality can come from the Eastern countries, partly due to the soil types and partly the climatic conditions. The potato plant does not like long periods of rain (blight risk) or wetness at harvest, which makes harvesting difficult.

HOW POTATOES ARE PRODUCED

IN THE UK the crop is usually planted between February and May. Early maturing varieties are planted first and ready to be sold as 'new potatoes' in June. The bulk of the planting is in April, when the weather is drier and soil temperatures higher. Most potatoes are 'ridged up', which means the soil is pulled into tall rows into which the potato plants are planted, allowing the tubers to grow underneath. All commercial crops (even organic ones) are sprayed with a fungicide to prevent blight attack. Only a very few varieties are truly blight-resistant. The crop is machine-harvested from June through to October and held in large cold stores for winter use.

WHY THE PRICE VARIES

SIZE OF THE CROP

The economics of supply and demand mean the better a crop, the more potatoes are on the market and the cheaper they are. Conversely, in a poor year, the price is higher.

VARIETY

Sadly, many consumers know very few varieties other than the generic description 'reds and whites'. Variety descriptions are often in small print or not given at all. This has encouraged us to think of the potato as a boring staple, for which poor culinary performance is tolerated. Some varieties blacken when cooked, fall apart, explode in the oven or taste like soap. The only way to avoid this is to know your varieties. There are more details and tips about key varieties at the end of this chapter. A useful guide, if you want to know your spuds, is Alan Wilson's *The People's Potatoes*.

PRODUCTION METHOD

Some producers grow to higher standards of environmental care and sustainability than others, which is reflected in the way they manage their soil and use irrigation, fungicides, pesticides and fertilisers. These all have cost implications.

GRADE

Once harvested, potatoes are graded to remove any that are rotten or inferior. They are then sorted by size and quality, which determines the market into which they will be sold. As with all fresh produce, buyers will have particular specifications the potatoes must meet. For example, customers in a supermarket buying a baking potato will want a large potato. However, as with any crop there will be variation and they can't all be grown to the optimum size. A company making chips won't be worried about needing large potatoes so can take the smaller ones.

TRY BEFORE YOU DIE!

—

There are flesh colours of white, red, blue and black. There are skin colours of white, cream, russet, blue, black, red, pink and stripy, and shapes to match the most imaginative mind. I would recommend you try the dry-textured Red Duke of York, which has a striking, deep-red skin. For a French variety I lean towards the slightly bent La Ratte, which has a hint of chestnut. This variety is cream-fleshed as is the Pink Fir Apple, which is even waxier and can be very knobbly.

JERSEY ROYAL
£££

The Jersey Royal is the favourite of many, but do watch out as it has to be harvested at the optimal time, when the flavour is at its best. Leave it in the ground too long and even the Jersey Royal can disappoint.

. . . .

Different potatoes for different uses

Potatoes are generally divided into two categories; waxy or floury. When it comes to seasonal availability, that varies. Different varieties may be bought at different times of the year.

Charlotte

These long oval potatoes have a firm, waxy texture and a subtle, nutty flavour. They have a light yellow skin and yellow flesh.

Uses: Suitable for boiling, baking or salads.

Preparation: Scrub thoroughly under cold running water or peel.

Desiree

One of the most popular red-skinned potatoes, Desirees have a smooth skin and creamy yellow flesh. They have a firm texture.

Uses: Especially good cooked as wedges or roasted because they hold their shape. Also suitable for boiling, mashing and chipping.

Preparation: Scrub thoroughly under cold running water or peel.

Estima

A light, yellow-skinned potato with a firm, moist texture and a mild flavour. They are usually oval-shaped with yellowy flesh.

Uses: Boiling, mashing and especially good for baking.

Preparation: Peel and chop for boiling and chipping or scrub thoroughly for baking.

King Edward

King Edwards have pinky-red skins and distinctively flavoured creamy-white flesh that's packed with carbohydrates, fibre, iron and vitamins, including foliate. Cooking them in their skins provides the most nutritional value.

Uses: Good for baking, chipping or roasting.

Preparation: Rinse in cold water and peel for chipping and roasting. If necessary, cut out any bruises or green parts.

Baby potatoes

These are available all year round and the different varieties encompass a range of skin and flesh colours. They are small, waxy, oval-shaped potatoes. Buy little and often for the best flavour as they don't store very well.

Uses: Best boiled whole in their skins and delicious served warm or cold, with spring lamb, salmon and salads.

Preparation: Rinse in cold water and cook whole or sliced. To obtain the most nutritional value, leave their skins on. If preferred, remove the skin by gently rubbing it away with your fingers.

Red Duke of York

These potatoes have light yellow flesh, distinctive red skin, and a firm texture.

Uses: Best for boiling.

Preparation: Peel and rinse thoroughly in cold water before boiling.

How to keep potatoes

It is essential that potatoes are stored in a cool, dark area away from sunlight and in a frost-free, airy place preferably in a brown paper sack. If potatoes are exposed to light, they may turn green (which can be poisonous) or start sprouting. Small amounts of green can be removed but very green potatoes should be discarded. Do take potatoes out of the plastic bag that they are usually sold in; potatoes are likely to go mouldy if kept in plastic for a long period. Potatoes should not be stored in the fridge. New potatoes should be eaten within 2–3 days of purchase, while old potatoes can, if stored correctly, be kept for several months.

· ·

Store Cupboard Essentials:
A General Note

It is very easy to look into a jam-packed store cupboard and take for granted the stories behind the products inside. With basic groceries it is hard to imagine there can be any significant variations in quality. The natural assumption is all that matters is low prices. When one discount shop or another is promising amazing value, it's easy to be seduced by what seem like 'incredible offers'.

This chapter will help you understand where true value lies in the most basic of store-cupboard staples: salt, pepper, herbs and spices, plus balsamic vinegar.

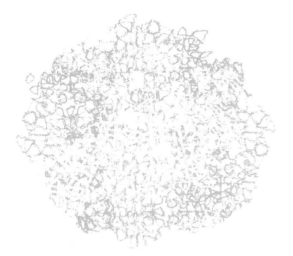

Salt

A BRIEF HISTORY

IN THE ANCIENT WORLD salt was precious. It preserved food, added flavour and had numerous other uses. It was essential to the ancient Egyptians, who used it in the mummification process, and to the Greeks, who bought slaves with it (which perhaps gave us the phrase 'not worth his salt'), while Roman soldiers were sometimes paid with it. The word 'salary' derives from the Latin word *salarium*, possibly referring to money given to soldiers so they could buy salt.

HOW SALT IS PRODUCED

ALL SALT COMES FROM SEAWATER, either by evaporating the water from today's seas (sea salt) or mining salt deposits left from ancient seas underground (rock salt). Rock salt is simply mined out of the ground, either solid or as brine. Salt from today's seas is obtained in a number of ways.

SOLAR EVAPORATION: SEL DE MER

Seawater floods salt flats when the tide comes in. Once the tide goes out, the sun and wind evaporate water left behind in special pools. The resulting salt is raked and transported for drying. Of course, this is only possible in the right climates with enough heat and sunshine to evaporate the water naturally. The fine salt that is scraped off the top is called *fleur de sel* and considered to be one of the finest salts.

OPEN-PAN PRODUCTION: FLAKED SEA SALT

Seawater is pumped through natural filters, such as mussel beds, and then further filtered before entering open tanks where overhead heaters replicate the sun's heat. Salt crystals form on the water, and are scooped off and placed on drying racks. The crystals that are formed using this method are often called pyramid salts. This was the traditional method of production in cooler climates, including Britain, and is how artisanal brands, such as Maldon and Halen Môn, are made.

CLOSED-PAN PRODUCTION UNDER VACUUM: TABLE SALT

About 100 years ago, companies began to produce table salt. This is created when seawater (or brine solution from rock salt) is pumped into evaporation tanks where a partial vacuum speeds up the evaporation process. This process gives the greatest amount of salt most quickly so is the cheapest production method. Its invention led to the decline of open-pan production in the traditional salt-producing areas of the UK, such as Essex and Cheshire, although these traditional methods have been reintroduced by artisanal sea-salt makers in recent years.

Table salt is refined to strip it of the 80 or so naturally occurring trace elements, which are sold to the food-processing and chemical industries as supplements. The problem is that salt naturally absorbs water causing it to form clumps, so anti-clumping agents need to be added. Iodine is also often added following concerns of the World Health Assembly in 1995 about iodine deficiency. Advocates of unrefined rock and sea salts emphasise the fact that they still include all their trace elements in comparison to table salt, as well as having a superior flavour and texture.

WHY THE PRICE VARIES

PRODUCTION METHOD

The main reason for variations in the price of salt is the production method. Table salt is cheap to produce on an industrial scale. Open-pan salt production is more labour intensive and it takes longer for the salt crystals to form. *Fleur de sel*, harvested by hand from the top of the salt pools, is the most expensive because of the time and skill required.

When it comes to rock salt, the way it is extracted impacts on price. For instance, some varieties of Himalayan Pink Salt are mined by hand, compared to industrial mining of rock salt or extraction of brine.

TRY BEFORE YOU DIE!

—

The quality of salt is very subjective but I would suggest rock salt is used in mills. Flaked sea salt and *fleur de sel* are best at the table and *sel de mer* is a good cooking salt as it is slightly damp and can be used for mixing with herbs and spices to create a rounded seasoning.

F̲LEUR DE SEL
£££££

Expensive due to the labour-intensive methods required for its extraction and the small amounts produced in each cycle.

K̲ALA N̲AMAK
£££

This rock salt is from the Himalayan mountain ranges. It has a pungent smell due to the levels of hydrogen sulphide. The salt is used in Indian cooking and gives a savoury note to dishes.

Pepper

A BRIEF HISTORY

PEPPER WAS AN IMPORTANT PART of the spice trade between India and Europe as early as Greek and Roman times. It remained largely unknown in Western Europe until the Middle Ages when great explorers, including Vasco de Gama and Columbus, discovered new sources and spice plants.

Much has been written about the history of pepper; if you want to know more, read *Pepper* by Christine McFadden.

HOW PEPPER IS PRODUCED

THE **PEPPER PLANT** (*Piper nigrum*) is a perennial spreading-vine, growing up to 4m in height on supporting trees, poles or trellises. It produces small white or yellow flowers on spikes, which then develop into the small green berries that become peppercorns. The spikes grow up to 15cm long as the fruit matures. Plants bear fruit from about four years of age and can go on producing for up to 30 years.

When harvested, the fruit-covered spikes are collected and spread out to dry in the sun and the peppercorns are then stripped off.

Pepper needs a very warm, humid climate with moist, well-drained soils, so it is suited to tropical areas, such as the Malabar Coast of India, which is considered one of the best places to grow pepper and is where it was first commercially cultivated, as well as Vietnam, Brazil, Indonesia and Malaysia. Pepper exhibits *terroir* just like wine, coffee or olive oil and connoisseurs will seek out specific varieties from particular plantations all across the world for their special flavour and aroma.

As they ripen, berries turn from green to black to red, and the point at which the berries are harvested, and how they are then processed, is what determines the type of pepper produced.

Green peppercorns are picked when unripe. They deteriorate very quickly when fresh so are often pickled, freeze-dried or canned to preserve them. These are the kind of peppercorns used in classic peppercorn sauce and in Thai cooking.

Black pepper, the most commonly used, is harvested once the berries have ripened further and just as they reach the red phase. They are boiled briefly to clean and rupture them to facilitate the drying process. They are then left to dry in the sun or in a mechanical dryer until they shrivel up and darken.

White pepper is produced by removing the hull of a nearly ripe berry to extract the inner seed. This can be done by soaking the berry in water so the hull decomposes or can be rubbed off, or by a mechanical or chemical process. The seed is then dried to produce white pepper, which is milder than other forms of pepper.

Red peppercorns (not to be confused with pink peppercorns) come from the fully ripened berries. Like green peppercorns, they deteriorate quickly from fresh so are dried or pickled to preserve them.

Pink peppercorns are, in fact, not from the *Piper nigrum* plant at all but an entirely different South American plant. Similarly, Szechuan pepper comes from a different plant; it looks quite different from a normal peppercorn.

WHY THE PRICE VARIES

TYPE OF PEPPER

Green, red and white pepper, all tend to be more expensive than black pepper because of the additional processing required to preserve them, in the case of green and red peppercorns, and to extract the seed for white pepper.

SIZE

Larger, denser peppercorns are considered better quality and cost more than smaller peppercorns.

PRODUCTION METHOD

White pepper is traditionally produced by removing the outer hull through soaking but it is cheaper to do this by mechanical, chemical or biological methods. This reduces white pepper's signature smell.

The way pepper is graded has an impact. Good-quality pepper should have a regular size throughout the product (smaller sizes within pepper are used to reduce the cost), be free from stalks, pests and mould to show it has been stored correctly, and ensure the highest possible amount of volatile oils that deliver flavour are maintained.

GEOGRAPHY

Some plantations can command a premium price for the specific flavour of their peppercorns. Mount Tellicherry, on the Malabar Coast in India, is widely known for producing the highest quality peppercorns in the world. It has a series of quality designations similar to PDOs. Other parts of the world produce larger volumes of lower quality pepper and therefore charge a lower price.

ABUNDANCE

According to the rules of supply and demand, quality peppercorns from plantations that produce smaller amounts will often be more expensive.

ETHICS

Ethical production and processing of pepper whereby workers are treated fairly and producers are paid a fair price (e.g. Fairtrade) costs more, as do sustainable farming methods, such as organic.

TRY BEFORE YOU DIE!

–

BOURBON PEPPER
£££££

Bourbon pepper, also known as Voatsiperifery pepper, is the rarest (the crop produces just 1,500kg per year) and most extraordinary pepper. It grows in the hot and humid south-eastern Madagascan rainforests, where the pepper vines can reach 20m tall, and it grows in the wild, making picking very difficult. The unripe berries, which are only on the young sprouts on top of the tree, are all hand-harvested by local village communities and left to dry in the sun, which turns the berries black. It has a strong, pine-forest nose and medium heat and is distinguished by light, zesty flavours and a gingery aroma with a hint of cloves. Particularly long tasting, it goes well with lamb and pork as well as fruits and chocolate.

TELLICHERRY PEPPER
££££

Commonly regarded as the best-quality pepper, Tellicherry comes from the Malabar Coast in India and is grown on Mount Tellicherry. The peppercorns are much larger than normal black peppercorns as they are allowed to ripen on the vines for longer, leading to complex aromas. Tellicherry Garbled Special Extra Bold is the largest grade of pepper from the Malabar Coast pepper-growing region. The Tellicherry name is protected by quality designations, and a great deal of skill goes into knowing when to harvest the pepper at just the right point – the maximum size but before turning red.

Herbs and Spices

I'm prepared to wager a small amount that your food cupboard is stuffed full of half-used old packets, jars and boxes of herbs and spices. My ambition in this section is to get you to embrace these little-appreciated seasonings for the extraordinary effort that goes into their production.

A BRIEF HISTORY

AROUND **400** BC, Hippocrates listed 400 medicines made with herbs and spices, half of which we still use today, including saffron, cinnamon, thyme, coriander, mint and marjoram. From 3000 BC to 300 BC a spice trade route was developed across the deserts of southern Asia and the Middle East. Arabs controlled the route and made fortunes trading locally produced goods and spices.

Later the Romans started sailing from Egypt to India to trade spices. The trip would take up to two years, which is why spices were available to the upper class only and were as valued as gold. So valuable were they, in fact, that in AD 65 the Romans burned a year's supply of cinnamon as a show of honour at the funeral of Nero's wife.

When the Goths overran Rome in AD 410, their leader, Alaric, demanded 30,000lb of peppercorns, along with gold and jewels, for sparing the lives of the population.

Spice use and trade in Europe collapsed after the fall of the Roman Empire, only to be revived in the Middle Ages. Venice became the most important trade port until the

Portuguese and Spanish found prices too high and began searching for their own routes to the spice-producing lands. Vasco de Gama, a Portuguese explorer, sailed around Africa's Cape of Good Hope to reach Calcutta to trade pepper, cinnamon and ginger.

In 1492, Christopher Columbus arrived in America while searching for a direct western route to the Spice Islands. He did not find the Spice Islands but he did bring back allspice, vanilla and red pepper from the West Indies.

As the middle class grew, so did the popularity of spice. War broke out between European nations over the Indonesian Spice Islands and continued for 200 years. Spain, Portugal, England and Holland all fought for control until Holland finally gained control of most of the Asian spice trade.

In 1672, America entered the world spice race. Elihu Yale, a former clerk of the British East India Company in Madras, began his own spice business. After making a fortune, Elihu later helped the nascent Yale University by donating a valuable parcel of goods to the founder.

In 1797, ships sailed from Indonesia to Massachusetts with large loads of pepper. The huge profits recorded led to nearly 1,000 American ships sailing the route over the next 90 years.

As their influence grew, Americans made many new contributions to the spice world. Texans developed chilli powder, while in 1889 food researchers in California developed techniques for drying onion and garlic, and in 1906 Eugene Durkee wrote the first standards for purity of spice.

The Second World War encouraged interest in international foods as soldiers brought home new taste experiences. This trend has gown with internationalisation and increased travel.

GEOGRAPHY

HERBS AND SPICES COME from all over the globe and those we typically use in the UK come from over 50 countries. For example, pepper is often from India, parsley from the UK, cinnamon from Sri Lanka, paprika from Spain and allspice from South America.

HOW HERBS AND SPICES ARE PRODUCED AND WHY THE PRICE VARIES

AN ENORMOUS ARRAY of products comes under the herbs and spice category, and trying to tell you about each and every one would need a whole book all to itself, so I have picked a few examples that demonstrate different reasons why the price can vary. In general, though, how the crops are grown and the amount of labour involved, the investment required in machinery, grading for quality or ethical standards, where and how the product is packed and simple supply and demand are the key factors that have a bearing on the price you pay.

VANILLA

The vanilla plant is a creeper that grows on a support and is part of the orchid family. In its natural habitat it usually grows on small trees that offer support and shade to the creepers.

In Madagascar, which is the largest vanilla producer, pollination is done by hand. Once pollination is complete the flower will become a vanilla pod. Following harvest, green pods are sorted according to their type (split and non split) and quality (immature, mature and too ripe). After sorting, vanilla pods are put together in different lots for blanching, and the green pods are placed in hot water for a few minutes. Once blanched, pods are left to drip dry and placed in boxes where they are kept warm to start their ageing process. After a few hours in the boxes, the vanilla pods are put out to dry in the sun for a few hours every day with strict temperature control. From there, they are wrapped in a type of blanket to carry on the ageing process. After the drying and ageing process is complete, the pods are sorted and massaged to make them straight. In the final stage of the process vanilla pods are placed on screens in the shade. At this stage the pods are massaged every day to develop their aromas and shiny texture.

Clearly, the process is highly labour intensive and time consuming, which makes vanilla very expensive and means that the much cheaper artificial vanilla flavouring is more commonly used as a flavouring than real vanilla pods. See the chapter on Ice Cream (page 89) to find out more.

PAPRIKA

Paprika comes from the dried and ground fruits of peppers of the species *Capsicum annuum*. These plants are native to the Americas, from where they were introduced to Europe by the Spanish in the 1500s. Paprika, known in Spain as *pimentón*, is added to recipes to give colour and flavour and can also be smoked for extra flavour. It can range from mild to hot and flavours vary subtly between the many different countries in which the peppers are grown.

The general process of paprika manufacture is to harvest ripe peppers, dry them (typically, naturally by air) and then send them for processing. The smoking process is carried out in Spain. Oak logs are burnt and the smoke generated is filtered through water before being blown into a product smoking chamber. The process lasts for between a day and a week.

There is an internationally recognised system, known as American Spice Trade

Association (ASTA) colour units, for defining paprika quality and therefore price. This measures its extractable colour. A high ASTA value represents a high-quality, deep-red coloured paprika, and a lighter coloured product has a lower ASTA colour rating and consequently a lower price.

STAR ANISE

Star anise is one of the central spices of Chinese cooking. It is obtained from the star-shaped pericarp of a medium-sized native evergreen tree of the magnolia family. It grows in mountainous woodlands of south-west China and north-east Vietnam. Trees grow up to 15m tall and picking the fruit is typically done by hand. The flavour, which is contained in both the seeds and the seed pod (star) itself, is very sweet and liquorice-like, similar to aniseed, although the plants are not related.

For cooking purposes, star-anise fruits are harvested just before ripening, when the essential oil content is high, and are then sun-dried. Star anise is sold either whole or as broken pieces, or in ground format. Whole is more expensive as the fruits have a distinctive eight-pointed star-shape and must be carefully handled to avoid breaking them. While the broken pieces of star anise lose none of their flavour, the visual appearance is less appealing and therefore the cost of broken star anise is lower. Ground star anise is cheaper still as visual quality has no restriction and packing density is at its greatest.

This spice is not only prized in cooking but is also used in perfumery, soaps, toothpastes, mouthwashes, skin creams and, most recently, in the pharmaceutical industry. Up to 90 per cent of the world's star anise crop has been sent for extraction of its shikimic acid, which is used to make the anti-influenza drug oseltamivir, more commonly known as Tamiflu. In 2005 and 2009, increased demand for Tamiflu after flu outbreaks led to shortages of star anise and sent prices soaring.

LEMONGRASS

Lemongrass is a very widely used herb in Thai cooking and is one of the most aromatic and flavoursome ingredients. It can be eaten as a chopped stem, as a pulped stem or boiled to give an infusion. It can be used fresh or can be dried whole, chopped or powdered.

Lemongrass is, as the name suggests, a type of grass from the same family of plants as citronella (the natural scent used as an insect repellent). It is grown in Thailand on raised mats of soil that are separated by irrigation canals. The farms are divided into 2.5 acre plots to allow for controlled and scheduled planting, growing and harvesting of the crop. Plants take approximately six months between planting and harvesting, so two crops per year can be grown in the same plot.

Harvesting is done by hand and the stems are dressed on site and tied into bundles. Once at a processing plant, cut stems are steam-cleaned, using wet steam at 100°C for three to five minutes. When drying lemongrass, the general method used is freeze-drying. It is then packed into foil, nitrogen-flushed bags for transportation, which helps reduce the potential for moisture uptake that could lead to product spoilage.

CINNAMON

Cinnamon is the inner bark of a tree in the genus *Cinnamomum*. There are, however, many species in the genus and it is the *Cinnamomum verum* species that is believed to be the best, or 'true', Ceylon cinnamon. Cinnamon taken from four other commercially produced species is referred to as cassia cinnamon. Although the trees are easier to grow and therefore the spice is much cheaper, it is considered to be inferior in flavour. Cassia cinnamon is much darker and harder than Ceylon cinnamon.

Ceylon cinnamon is native to Sri Lanka, as the name suggests, and 80–90 per cent of the world's current crop is still grown there. Indonesia is the largest producer of other types of cinnamon.

Cinnamon trees are grown for a couple of years before being cut back to the base. The following year new stems shoot up from the roots. These are cut and the outer bark is scraped off. The inner bark, the cinnamon, is then carefully prised off the stem in long rolls. These are then dried and curl up into the 'quills' we know as cinnamon sticks. Cinnamon is graded according to the diameter of the quills, and smaller quills or fragments can be ground into powdered cinnamon, which, like broken star anise, can be sold more cheaply.

SAFFRON

Saffron is the most expensive spice in the world. It originates from West Asia and Arabs had brought it to Spain by the year 960, but it is thought that returning Crusaders brought crocus corms back to the rest of Europe in the thirteenth century. Believe it or not, the Essex town Saffron Walden got its name from growing and trading saffron in the sixteenth century.

Saffron is produced from the dried stigma of purple crocus flowers. The crocuses need hot dry weather in summer and cold winters. Spain and Iran are the countries most famous for producing it. The extreme cost is due to the very small amount of saffron that can be got from the crop and because growing it is so labour intensive. Each flower has just three stigma, which means that 85,000 flowers are needed for just one kilo of saffron. What's more, the stigma are roasted to remove the moisture, which reduces their weight by 80 per cent. Therefore, from 1kg of harvested stigma, you get just 200g of saffron! The bulbs are sown and the flowers harvested by hand.

Beware of cheap substitutes. There is a thistle-like plant called safflower, which is often dried and sold as saffron abroad. While this can be used as a substitute for saffron, providing a yellow colour, it has none of the flavour, or aroma, of real saffron.

TRY BEFORE YOU DIE!

–

TARRAGON VINEGAR
£££

The leaves of the tarragon plant are used as a distinctive herb that has a delicate aromatic, sweet, liquorice-like taste, which especially complements fish and chicken. This herb can also be used to infuse vinegar to add the magnificent sweet herby flavours to an otherwise everyday condiment. In addition to the taste enhancement, the visual impact of tarragon vinegar makes this a product to try before you die. Make it at home by simply combining tarragon and a good-quality vinegar.

TONKA BEANS
£££££

Deep in the forests of South America, the Cumaru, a gigantic tree, produces orange fruit that resemble mangoes. When ripe, this fruit produces red oblong seeds the size of an almond. The seeds are dried for around one year and then submerged in a strong alcohol (usually rum) for a 24-hour period. After this lengthy process, they are dried again and become black and wrinkled.

The tonka bean has an aroma of almond, vanilla, caramel and clove. The taste is a warming and sensual bitterness not too dissimilar from cocoa.

Try grating over creamy desserts, such as a panna cotta or a crème brûlée, or savoury soufflés. They also work very well infused into spirits, sugar syrups or the sugar itself. Tonka beans can be purchased from specialist suppliers online.

Balsamic Vinegar

Many wonderful foods have arrived on our shores from Italy and few can be as versatile as balsamic vinegar; what seems to be a simple ingredient can transform a meal from good to superb.

In the UK, we regard it as a traditional salad dressing, either combined with olive oil or on its own. But it's worth noting that the higher the quality, the greater the number of uses. Thicker, sweeter products can be used in salads, but also go very well with cold meats, cheeses, soups, fruits and even ice cream. These are traditional Italian uses for balsamic vinegar and, hopefully, one day will be fully embraced by the UK shopper.

A BRIEF HISTORY

BALSAMIC VINEGAR HAS BEEN USED for centuries but, like many high-quality products, it was originally available to royalty and the highest nobility only. In this case, it was regarded as a tonic. The Italian word *balsamico* is a derivative of balsam, meaning balm, which is a far cry from its current use as a food-cupboard staple.

Traditional production centres on the Italian region of Reggio Emilia where Trebbiano and Lambrusco grapes are grown. These sweet grape varieties are perfect for the production of balsamic vinegar.

Due to its value, many families who started making balsamic vinegar used to hide barrels of it in their attics to keep it out of reach of thieves. Even today, this attic style is the preferred ageing location for the traditional Balsamic Vinegar of Modena. It just so happens that an attic space has the perfect atmosphere for the ageing process.

GEOGRAPHY

BALSAMIC VINEGAR has been awarded official DOP or IGP status (in translation, Protected Designation of Origin and Protected Geographical Indication). This means that balsamic vinegar that is traded under the name 'Balsamic Vinegar of Modena' may be made in the Modena region of Italy only, although the process of making balsamic vinegar is not exclusive to the Modena region, and it is made in other parts of the world. However, Balsamic Vinegar of Modena DOP or IGP is protected by law and may also bear the official logo of the 'Consortium for the Protection of Balsamic Vinegar of Modena'. The consortium monitors the market and will come down hard on any products that contravene this protection.

HOW BALSAMIC VINEGAR IS PRODUCED

TRADITIONAL BALSAMIC VINEGAR FROM Modena DOP is made from cooked grape juice and matured in wooden barrels for over 12 or 25 years. The grape juice must be made of pressed grapes from Trebbiano and Lambrusco and undergoes natural fermentation, which gradually concentrates the must. It is transferred into smaller wooden barrels as the volume decreases over time and the concentration intensifies.

After ageing for over 12 years, the liquid taken from the smallest barrels may be labelled Traditional Balsamic Vinegar of Modena (at this age known as *Affinato*), whereas the extra-old grade must be aged for at least 25 years (known as *Extra Vecchio*). Both products must be bottled in the signature Giugiaro-designed bottle, with its unmistakable round belly and rectangular base.

The result of this natural process is a rich, shiny dark-brown liquid, with a well-balanced bittersweet taste and a smooth syrupy texture. This is the top-of-the-range balsamic vinegar that commands a price of around £50 for the 12-year-old product and double that for the 25-year-old, and that is for 100ml.

Clearly, at this price, it is out of reach of the vast majority of shoppers, which is why the better-known Balsamic Vinegar of Modena IGP (rather than the DOP) features heavily on supermarket shelves. These are made using either cooked grape must or concentrated grape must, which is blended with wine vinegar and aged in barrels for either a minimum of two months or for over three years for an aged product.

The skill of creating this IGP product is in the blending of the grape must with the wine vinegar. A wide spectrum of blends can be produced, with differing flavour balances between sweetness and acidity. Undertones can be generated by the grape must varieties and the type of wooden barrels used in the ageing. The basic rule of thumb is that an acidic profile and less dense product is cheaper, while using more wine vinegar and a sweeter, higher density profile makes for a more expensive product that uses a higher proportion of grape must.

A relatively new innovation is balsamic glaze or cream. It is made with a base of balsamic vinegar and grape must, blended with a thickening agent. The result is a very thick, viscous liquid that can be used as a glaze for meats to be cooked on the barbecue, as a marinade, in soups and on cheese. It can also be used as a drizzle on a finished plate of food to make the dish look pretty, which is the modern way. This product is also the perfect medium through which to introduce other flavours, such as chilli, fig and lemon. It is not able to call itself a Balsamic Vinegar of Modena IGP, but it carries the basic profile of the original recipe.

The flavour and profile of the finished product is determined by a number of things including:

- the grape varieties used (such as Lambrusco, Ancellotta, Trebbiano, Sauvignon, Sgavetta and Berzemino)

- the type of wood in which the vinegar is stored and aged (such as oak, chestnut, mulberry, cherry, ash or juniper)

- and the quality of the cooked grape must

One element that must not be underestimated is the skill of the producer and the blending of the vinegar. The best producers have a passion and knowledge that has been handed down through generations. They understand the delicate balance that needs to be struck between the sweetness and the acidity and can react to the inevitable annual crop differences of the raw materials to ensure that they continue to produce the balsamic vinegar to the flavour profile that consumers know and love.

WHY THE PRICE VARIES

THE MOST IMPORTANT FACTOR influencing price is the proportion of grape must used. Traditional balsamic vinegar uses 100 per cent grape must, whereas the IGP version will use a varying proportion of grape must and white-wine vinegar.

INGREDIENTS

Based on the facts mentioned in the previous section regarding the production of balsamic vinegar and the overarching governance of the consortium, you might believe that all is clear and easy to understand for the shopper. However, this is not the case for a number of reasons.

Firstly, the quality of the product is in general determined by the sweetness/acidity balance combined with the density. To create a balanced, thick vinegar takes time and involves quality ingredients, which obviously increases the overall production cost of the end product.

Producers determined to find a shortcut to this balance introduced caramel into the mix. Immediately, this allowed less grape must and more wine vinegar to be used, and required less ageing. This, in turn, meant a cheaper production cost, but a vinegar that tasted similar to the more expensive brands. This point presents a crossroads for the producer; do they pass on the cost saving to the shopper and sell at a real price or do they continue to sell as if the product was of a higher quality?

The reality is that the market has become confusing for shoppers. They see some balsamic at 67p for 250ml and what appears to be the same product at more than £10.

A second reason for confusion is that, although the consortium approves production to ensure it is made within Modena, there is no official benchmark level of quality to which the entire market adheres. If you see a one-star hotel at £20 a night you know what you are getting and similarly if you see a five-star hotel at £300 a night, you naturally expect more. If there is no standardised star-rating system, how do you know what is good value and what is not?

Therefore, the responsibility for offering the correct product at the correct price falls to the producer and the retailer. The blending process employed in the production of balsamic vinegar allows producers to make a vinegar that can fit the commercial requirements, but every time there is a reduction in price, quality and the costly elements are reduced in favour of the cheaper ingredients. To mask the extraction of the quality ingredient, a colouring is added. There is nothing wrong with these products made with caramel provided they are made to a high standard, but the caveat is always: are they being sold at the correct price?

TIME

The time over which vinegars are matured makes a difference. Obviously the longer a vinegar is kept, the greater the cost.

QUALITY RATING

As has been noted above, there are two distinct balsamic vinegar products. The ultimate experience is the Traditional Balsamic Vinegar of Modena. This is the most expensive, but also the best. It is sold in 100ml special bottles and not much is needed to enhance your meal. Although an investment of possibly more than £50 for a bottle means it is pricey, when tried it will not be easily forgotten.

With regards to the most widely available product, my general advice is always to ensure that you buy a brand that you trust. Make sure the bottle clearly shows that it is the authentic DOP/IGP consortium-approved product from Modena. Some labelling shows a 'Grape' rating, which starts at 1 Grape and goes up to 5 Grapes. If you trust the brand, then this is a good indication of the quality of the balsamic vinegar.

Bear in mind what you are using the balsamic vinegar for; if it is for a salad dressing, it will require a different balance of sweetness and acidity from that required for meats and cheeses. It may be that you have to try a few levels before you find exactly what you prefer.

TRY BEFORE YOU DIE!

–

ACETAIA GIUSEPPE CREMONINI TRADITIONAL BALSAMIC VINEGAR OF MODENA PDO – REFINED, 12 YEARS OLD AFFINATO
££££

This Traditional Balsamic Vinegar PDO is aged in small high-quality wood barrels for at least 12 years and develops an intense aroma. Not particularly sweet, it is ideal on raw meat and fish dishes; also great on risotto and eggs and for preparing vegetable-based sauces.

ACETAIA GIUSEPPE CREMONINI TRADITIONAL BALSAMIC VINEGAR OF MODENA PDO – AGED, 25 YEARS OLD INVECCHIATO
£££££

This Traditional Balsamic Vinegar PDO is aged in small high-quality wood barrels for no less than 25 years. Its full, mature balsamic flavour makes it a perfect complement for aged cheese, meat fillets, dried figs, ice cream and strawberries.

For the less expensive IGP product try:

JAMIE OLIVER BALSAMIC VINEGAR OF MODENA
£££

This is made the traditional way by maturing cooked grape must and wine vinegar in wooden barrels. Try drizzling it over Italian cheeses, and it's also delicious drizzled on salads, roasted vegetables and even fruits, including strawberries for a tangy treat.

Further Reading

Abbott, Elizabeth, *Sugar: A Bittersweet History* (Duckworth, 2010)

Agard, John, 'English Girl Eats Her First Mango', *New England Review and Bread Loaf Quarterly*, 7:4 (1985): 518–20

Ayto, John (ed.), *An A–Z of Food and Drink* (Oxford University Press, 2002)

Barber, Joseph (ed.), *The Chicken: A Natural History* (Ivy Press, 2012)

Bennion, Edmund B., *Breadmaking* (Oxford University Press, 1967)

Bray, Francesca *et al.*, *Rice: Global Networks and New Histories* (Cambridge University Press, 2015)

Bruner, Greg, 'Brassica oleracea', *Botanical Bytes*, http://botanicalbytes.blogspot.co.uk/2012/04/brassica-oleracea-ornamental-kale-and.html (23 April 2012)

Clarke, Chris, 'The physics of ice cream', *Physics Education*, 38:3 (2003): 248–53

Coe, Sophie D. and Coe, Michael D., *The True History of Chocolate* (Thames & Hudson, 2013)

Darton, Mike and Buckland, Jim, *A Potted History of Fruit* (Ivy Press, 2011)

Fielding, Henry, *The Grub-Street Opera* (Gale ECCO, 2010)

Griffiths, John C., *Tea: A History of the Drink that Changed the World* (André Deutsch, 2011)

Harrison, Lorraine and Wheeler, David, *A Potted History of Vegetables* (Ivy Press, 2011)

Hemphill, Ian and Hemphill, Kate, *The Spice and Herb Bible* (Robert Rose, 2014)

Kurlansky, Mark, *Salt: A World History* (Vintage, 2003)

Lamb, Steven, *Curing and Smoking: River Cottage Handbook No. 13* (Bloomsbury, 2014)

McFadden, Christine, *Pepper* (Absolute Press, 2014)

McKenzie, Liz, 'Cautionary tales: why the past matters' ['Salmon: History of Salmon' section], *Encounters Wild Explorers*, http://www.encountersnorth.org/wildexplorer/salmon/history-of-salmon.html (accessed 26 October 2015)

Millon, Marc, *Wine: A Global History* (Reaktion, 2013)

Mueller, Tom, *Extra Virginity: The Sublime and Scandalous World of Olive Oil* (Atlantic Books, 2012)

Rimas, Andrew and Fraser, Evan D. G., *Beef: The Untold Story of How Milk, Meat and Muscle Shaped the World* (Harper, 2009)

Robinson, Jancis and Harding, Julia, *The Oxford Companion to Wine* (Oxford University Press, 2015)

Tierney-Jones, Adrian, *1001 Beers You Must Try Before You Die* (Cassell, 2013)

Velton, Hannah, *Cow* (Reaktion, 2007)

Whitley, Andrew, *Bread Matters: Why and How to Make Your Own* (Fourth Estate, 2009)

Williams, A. (ed.), *Breadmaking: The Modern Revolution* (Century Benham, 1989)

Wilson, Alan, *The People's Potatoes* (Alan Wilson, 2011)

Young, Allen M., *The Chocolate Tree: A Natural History of Cacao* (University Press of Florida, 2007)

Acknowledgements

I would like to acknowledge the invaluable and unwavering support of Tor Harris, Christine Watts and Zoe Marson, and the encyclopaedic knowledge of the amazing Waitrose buying team and wonderful suppliers.

WAITROSE SUPPLIERS

Arla Foods UK: Graham Nichol, Bethan Parsley, Brenda Davies
Barfoots of Botley Ltd: Keston Williams
The Barts Ingredients Company Ltd: Lara Light McKelvaney, Kelly Field
BerryWorld Ltd
The Big Prawn Company Ltd: William Rash
BQP
Cropwell Bishop Creamery Ltd: Ian Skailes, Robin Skailes, Julian Hurford
Dairy Crest Group: Bill Gray, Mark Pitts-Tucker, Debbie Williams
Dalehead Foods: Liz Rees and the Lamb Procurement Team
De Cecco: Nathan Baker
Délifrance UK: Stéphanie Brillouet
Dovecote Park Ltd: Kate Sutton, Jack Gunner
The English Apple Man: John Guest
Eurilait Ltd: Laura Newmarch, Sally Ryves
Fayrefield Foods
Fiona Cairns Ltd: Fiona Cairns, Matthew Cook
Guernsey Dairy: Andrew Table
Isigny Ste Mère: Caroline Scarato
Keith Graham Ltd: Angela King
Kerry Foods: Sophie Davies
Kettle Foods
LDH (La Doria) Ltd: Russell Brooke
Mackie's of Scotland: Karin Hayhow, Kirstin McNutt, Ivan Jefford
Macrae Edinburgh Ltd: Kelly Wright
Moy Park Ltd: Justin Coleman, Joe Lawson
New England Seafood International Ltd: Dan Aherne, Max Ropner, Steven Reeves, Fionn Somers Eve, James Robinson, Cesar Basalo
Nicholas and Harris Ltd: Simon Staddon
The Oil Merchant: Charles Carey
Primafruit Ltd
R&R Ice Cream Ltd: Kiera Riordan, Bryony Anderson
Rare Tea Company: Henrietta Lovell
The Silver Spoon Company
Staples (Vegetables) Ltd: George Read
Stonegate Farmers Ltd: Richard Kempsey
Suncrop Produce Ltd: Veryan Bliss
Tims Dairy Ltd: Sally Dorling
Veetee Group: Steve Fisher
Viva Foods Ltd: John Broke-Smith

ACKNOWLEDGEMENTS

W. & H. Marriage & Sons Ltd: Philip Bunn, Hannah Marriage
Wealmoor Ltd: Paul Tilbury, Guy Self, Avnish Malde
Westcombe Dairy: Richard Calver, Tom Calver
Wilkin & Sons Ltd: Scott Goodfellow
Willie's Cacao Ltd: Willie Harcourt-Cooze
Winterbotham Darby & Co. Ltd
Worldwide Fruit Ltd: Tony Harding
Yeo Valley Farms (Production) Ltd: Rebecca Garland, Debbie Wills, Steve Wickham, Denise Quirke

WAITROSE TEAM
Polly Astbury
Jonathon Bayne
Graham Cassie
Kate Chapman
Louise Cooksley
Gen Cotter
Bryan Davies
Chris Dawson
Samantha Douglas
Giles Fisher
Adrian Gash
Philippa Godden
Chloe Graves
Stacey Green
John Gregson
Peter Heywood
Jane Hills
Nicki Hobbs
Rob Hues
Nikki Jutsum
Adam Kennedy
Jeremy Ryland Langley
Jan Maish
Richard McGinn
Chris Noel
Rachel Pearson
Pierpaolo Petrassi
Tim Shaw
Duncan Sinclair
Jo Skelton
Carla Smith
Alistair Stone
Lizzie Sutcliffe
Nicola Waller
Frances Westerman
Alan Wilson

Index

Mark Price

Mark joined the John Lewis Partnership in 1982 as a graduate trainee and had numerous roles during his 34 years with the organisation. He spent 17 years on the board of Waitrose, becoming Managing Director in April 2007 and held this post until March 2016; he was also Deputy Chairman of the John Lewis Partnership from 2013.

Mark was appointed Chairman of Business in the community in January 2011, a post he held for four years, and was also appointed Chairman of the Prince's Countryside Fund in 2010. Mark will publish a number of books during 2016 and beyond.